The Arabian Parts Decoded

Lind Weber

ISBN-10: 0-86690-471-9
ISBN-13: 978-0-86690-471-1

First Printing: 1997
Second Printing: 2007

Cover Design: Jack Cipolla

Published by:
American Federation of Astrologers, Inc.
PO Box 22040
6535 S. Rural Road
Tempe, AZ 85285-2040

Printed in the United States of America

Dedication

To Carole Arbour, who persevered with
the typing and my handwriting
through hurricanes,
hardship and home repairs.

Special Thanks

To Barbara Digamber for calculating all charts.

And to Sophia Mason for advice and encouragement over the last year and a half.

Contents

Preface

PLEASE READ THIS.

This book evolved from a speech through two stages to a book with examples and forecasting techniques. That is, not just what the Arabian Parts are but how they probably were used and may again be used.

That is part of the choppiness. More comes with the repetition of the formula as new matters are treated. The reader will learn why I decided to keep this repetition.

A couple of charts are reexamined, not repeated.

I finally whipped the dead horse with O. J. Simpson.

I find the house rulership midpoints effective—usually ruler of the Ascendant, ruler of a house. After doing it for some time I realized the obvious, A/B by sortilege.

Example Ascendant ruler/ruler ninth, Point of Luck, Ascendant ruler/ruler eighth, Point of Life and Death. The reader will come to understand their potential. The simplest technique would be a conjunction to the Ascendant. A reciprocal position to B would also come to the Ascendant.

I started reading some Charles Jayne. He understood A/B = C/D, but failed to grasp the rich potential of the Arabian Parts, calling them the predecessor of Witte's planetary pictures (*The Best of Charles Jayne*, AFA, 1995, p. 81). He does not note that the Parts count to four and Witte only to three.

The crash of TWA Flight 800 off Long Island, New York in July 1996 has brought at least two assertions that the cuspal Parts use Placidus houses. Placidus lived in the seventeenth century. Al Biruni collected cuspal Parts in the eleventh century. While they might have used Porphyry cusps (trisection of Midheaven to Ascendant, trisection of Ascendant to IC) (second to third century B.C.) an understanding of the Parts as Ascendant-based pleads for equal house. Equal house nine, the house of luck would be a trine; equal house eight would be a quincunx, both called lucky and death dealing to this day. The mysteries of the Parts have always been before us in plain sight.

Forecasts on Bill and Hillary and Charles are now dated. They were hits which only Carole Arbour saw.

Your forecasts using the Parts will be my vindication.

Enjoy your trip into the past and use its knowledge wisely.

Lind Weber

Creation
of A Mystery

T he Arabian Parts, also called Points, Lots and Fortunes, are more than 2,000 years old. Just who originated them or when they were first used is not known with historic accuracy. According to Robert Zoller, Manilius refers to some form of them in the first century.

Even then it would appear that they were old and not much understood. Long before Al-Biruni collected the Parts as used, they had acquired a mystique. At the same time the basic formula of the parts A + B - C = D enabled them to proliferate. Al-Biruni himself complained in his *Elements of Astrology* that "the number of these lots multiplies daily." Zoller also notes that Al-Biruni apparently used the parts in moderation.

In the eleventh century the Parts were widely used, but they were not understood. Using the engineering principle of practical success, two planetary energies with the Ascendant were worked to produce a point D which gave results—apparently and often enough to maintain usage.

Al-Biruni probably indirectly contributed to the growing confusion. He was primarily a collector of Parts, not necessarily a great user or scholar of them. His chart is in Robert Hurzt Granite's *Fortunes of Astrology* Sun/Pluto = ASC, Mars/Jupiter = ASC; definitely a man who would shoot from the lip to further his own ends. Other midpoints to his Ascendant and the eastern emphasis further corroborate his self-interest. He wrote, "All Fortunes involve the beginning of the matter, the end of the matter and the casting off point or catalyst." Quantum mystification occurred and 900 years late Robert Hurzt Granite writes regarding the Part of Fortune: "So, to the Ascendant we 'add' the Moon. To complete this triad we must cast off or cut out something. The one thing that stands in most people's way of receiving benefits is their own will which tries to force things to fall into a

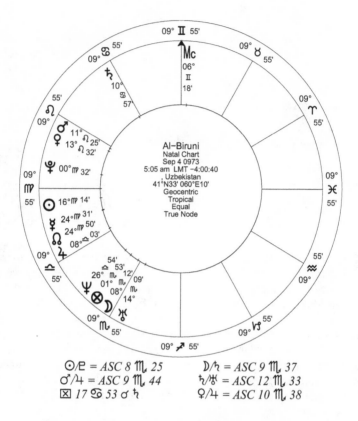

09° ♊ 55'

♋ 55'
09°

Mc
06°
♊
18'

09° ♉
55'

♄
10°
♋
57'

55'
♌
09°

09° ♈
55'

♂
♀
11°
13°
♌ 25'
♌ 32'

Al-Biruni
Natal Chart
Sep 4 0973
5:05 am LMT −4:00:40
, Uzbekistan
41°N33' 060°E10'
Geocentric
Tropical
Equal
True Node

09°
♓
55'

♔ 00°♍ 32'

09°
♍
55'

☉ 16°♍ 14'
☿ 24°♍ 31'
☊ 24°♍ 50'
♃ 08°♎ 03'

09°
♎
55'

54'
26° ♏ 53' 12'
01° ♏ 09'
08° ♏
14°

♆
⊗ ☽
♇ ♅

09° ♏
55'

55'
♒
09°

55'
09° ♑

09° ♐ 55'

☉/♇ = ASC 8 ♏ 25   ☽/♄ = ASC 9 ♏ 37
♂/♃ = ASC 9 ♏ 44   ♄/♅ = ASC 12 ♏ 33
⊠ 17 ♋ 53 ♂ ♄   ♀/♃ = ASC 10 ♏ 38

pattern that they can understand. So we subtract the Sun to get rid of that."

A hair's breadth from understanding the three Ascendants, Granite too fell in Al-Biruni's trap. Please reread that quote several times for I'll also define Fortuna to illustrate my concept of the Arabian Parts further on in the text.

In Nicholas De Vore's *Encyclopedia of Astrology* there is a section on the Parts where the text quotes Sepharial: "Ptolemy borrowed the symbol of Fortuna from the Arabs but applied to it his own reasoning while Placidus in an attempt to deal with it mathematically, improved it out of existence."

Confusion reigns. It is noteworthy that Sepharial thought the Parts were Arabic in origin, a conclusion I also came to for a disturbingly obvious reason.

Regarding Placidus, I believe the Parts were used originally in equal house charts. I view house systems as astrological public work projects mostly undertaken during the Renaissance period. In one of his texts Noel Tyl overlaps the house systems. I began using equal

2

houses the day I saw it. The point being that asymmetrical houses discouraged the visual working of the Parts, this in itself adding further mystification.

In July 1994 I attended the AFA Convention in Los Angeles. I gave a lecture on the Arabian Parts which was relatively well attended and, surprisingly to me, well received. Several who attended told me I'd clarified matters for them.

Here is what I said. Taken from the Ascendant (A) the energy of planet B is defined in terms of C and yields D, the Point. I had made a step forward for I'd defined C as the dynamic planet. It is this same Planet C that Al-Biruni and Granite "cast away"!

I left the lecture sad, for even as I scribbled at the blackboard I realized I had not really said anything about the resultant Point or D—"the underbelly of the chart," "no one knew exactly why it worked," and several other such statements were among my remarks that day. The audience was most satisfied. And I did get them to C.

In his *Encyclopedia of Astrology* De Vore notes the house correspondences of Fortuna and the Parts to the solar chart. Granite does this as well. Thus Ascendant chart Fortuna is in the same house position as the Moon is to the solar ascendant in a Sun chart. I've even heard it said based on this that it was all invented to save paper or papyrus or parchment. This is the geometric Line AD = Line BC.

The mystery deepens and the Parts, even more in use once again, are still not understood and very misunderstood.

One of the reasons that the Parts have remained a mystery is that Western astrologers can only count to two.

I suppose some will say that is a strange statement. Not so. We have aspects between two planets, planets in signs, and planets in houses. Most attempts to enhance these binary concepts are adjectival. The binary integrity is preserved. Modern midpoint practitioners can count to three.

According to the laws of semantics all actual astrological concepts have been profoundly influenced by this. Not knowing that they only count to two, western astrologers have not been able to figure out the Parts and instead have learnedly cloaked them in mystery.

Doldrums
and Discovery

J ust before the 1994 AFA Convention my first book, *The Astrology of Earthquakes and Volcanoes*, had been published by AFA. As many beginning writers have learned, editing can be more difficult than writing and by the time I saw the book in print, I was still tired.

I gave an impromptu lecture on the book when someone failed to show. As I opened it for the first time I realized some charts had been misplaced in the text. I got through the lecture and the convention but burnout that was waiting in the wings had been triggered.

Transiting Saturn was at 12 Pisces in wide conjunction to my Fortuna at 21 Pisces and transiting Jupiter at 4 Scorpio opposed my Sun/Moon midpoint at 3 Taurus.

Sometime in the spring of 1995 in an issue of the *The Mountain Astrologer* I read in passing that the signature of burnout is progressed Sun to Pluto. My progressed Sun was 3 Aries and my natal Pluto is 4 Leo, retrograde, progressed 3 Leo retrograde. I cannot go back and find the reference, but whoever you are, thank you for the insight. I was true for me and I corroborated it in other charts.

By the spring of 1995 the burnout was in full swing, and I was in the doldrums. I was scheduled to go to an Astro Rama Convention in Ohio in late April 1995. As the time approached I found myself without heart, mind, or money.

Transiting Saturn stood at 18-19 Pisces. I had not picked up on the significance yet.

On April 15, 1995, I sat at my kitchen table, unemployed, waiting for a phone call from a stonework customer. If he called and I got the money I'd go to the convention. If not I would cancel out. He didn't and I did, but as I sat there waiting for the phone call I was staring at a chart.

The Arabian Parts fell into place. There was no longer a mystery. It

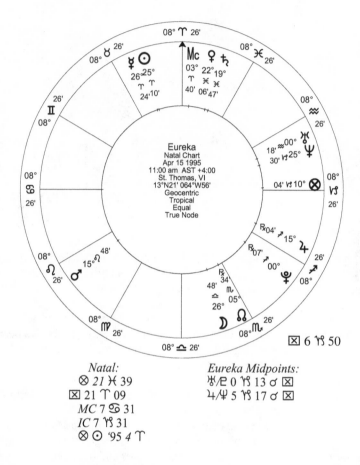

Natal:
⊗ 21 ♓ 39
⊠ 21 ♈ 09
MC 7 ♋ 31
IC 7 ♑ 31
⊗ ☉ '95 4 ♈

Eureka Midpoints:
♅/♇ 0 ♑ 13 ♂ ⊠
♃/♆ 5 ♑ 17 ♂ ⊠

fell into place as I sat there.

It was about 11:00 a.m. AST, St. Thomas, U.S. Virgin Islands, 64W56 18N21. I was so amazed that I did not jump up to check the time—a quiet stunned amazement: transiting Sun at 24 Aries, transiting Mercury at 25 Aries, Spirit at 21 Aries, transiting Venus at 21 Pisces, transiting Saturn at 19 Pisces, and Fortuna at 21 Pisces.

It took only moments from then to understand the astonishing simplicity of an entire system of astrology.

I should have been in a state of great enthusiasm. I wasn't. Burnout and depression were the day to day realities of Saturn even as he dealt me this great gift. Any planetary energy acts on many levels. Paradox is easy for such energies, not tied to concepts of consistency.

It would be idiotic for a man who barely passed high school algebra to believe that the basic algebraic formula A + B - C = D had not been decoded or known. Of course it had been. The simple algebra was probably understood by Arab practitioners up until the times prior to Al-Biruni when the system of the Parts was lost or obscured, probably through the secretiveness of competitive court astrologers as well as several other reasons.

The zodiacal rendering of the equation is the most commonly noted one in contemporary astrology. That is that the zodiacal distance A to D is the same as B to C. Usually this is noted in regard to an ascendant part, most usually Fortuna (ASC + Moon - Sun). The same house position from the ASC to Fortuna as from the Sun to the Moon are also commonly noted. Both are the same thing, the geometric rendering Line AD = Line BC of the algebraic formula. Nevertheless the formula was not understood.

To the many astrologers not familiar with midpoints or who reject their usage this like mud covered the ground. They could now move forward with a more or less irrelevant bit of information.

But many did connect this with midpoints. More or less a thousand years after Al-Biruni, the Uranian astrologers may have understood the midpoints inherent in the equation:

1. A+B-C=D
2. A/B=C/D

But to recognize a pattern does not necessarily mean you understand it's significance. Since the Uranians had also only been trained to count to two and were now making the leap to three the inner significance of A/B=C/D was not explored. Their hands were full delineating A/B=C, the planetary picture.

I read Granite's book several times before noting his early observation that the Uranians had created the Trans-Neptunian planets from Parts. I was not able to decode them and stand neutral on this hypothesis:

> "The Hamburg School chose the most relevant fortunes (according to them) and renamed them Trans-Neptunian planets producing an astounding ephemeris of their transiting position."

He gives as source for this statement Calvin Hanes in an informal discussion in the summer of 1972 at the First Temple of Astrology in Los Angeles.

If this is so, these were planetary Parts, not ascendant Parts and I'll deal with them in a later chapter with some examples where you will know how to make them too.

April 1995—I wanted to get my observations out, but I also didn't want to dash out and find I had reinvented the wheel. Common sense said the midpoint connection had to have been noticed—which I promptly figured out regarding the Arabs and had to research regarding the moderns.

I subscribe to *The Mountain Astrologer*. A bit pedantic, it's nevertheless filled with wondrous astrology and I recommend it to all.

In the December 1995 issue, Tom Bridges answers the question "What is the Part of Fortune" (p. 74) in his column, ``TMA Q&A.'' He comes very near but still misses the boat. He fully understands A/B = C/D and notes the significance of a conjunction as completing "symmetry." He does not go further with significance of a four part midpoint system, but moves to interpreting Fortuna in the humanistic mode.

> "If the Sun is the male principle, the Moon the female principle, and the Ascendant your relation to other people, then the Part of Fortune shows how the synthesis of male and female in each person as visible to other people."

As with other twentieth century scholars of the Parts he has wedded twentieth century thought to a B.C. system. It is like claiming that cave men had second thoughts or environmental neurosis when they made a kill.

Bridges quotes Hans Niggemann, pioneer of the Uranian system of astrology in the U.S: The Part of Fortune is "the native's (Sun) relation (Ascendant) to the public (Moon)."

Both of these definitions are merely expanded keywords. Neither one is the essence of Fortuna and all have missed in understanding the Parts. Like many, Bridges notes the rulership of Fortuna as promoting a personality type. Close and true, but not quite the whole matter.

It is now time to put forward my position.

Fortunes and Lots, Parts and Points

I try to avoid repetition in my writing but it seems that I always end up mentioning bottom line, paper bag semantics. If you understand what a word means you have power over it. If you don't it has power over you.

At present the words Fortune, Lot, Part and Point are used interchangeably by twentieth century astrologers. This has created a morass of confusion. Most of the mystery is semantic illiteracy.

First, I shall attempt to redefine the words—rather I would say give them back their original meanings. Second, I shall explain the significance and meaning of the midpoint system.

Third, why the Ascendant is the key to the true or most reliable use of the system. Fourth, I shall lay out a predictive system derived by an astrologer (Robert Hurzt Granite also believed in a single astrologer dealing with Fortuna, by context feeling Fortuna was the origin of the Parts; I tend to agree with him) gifted in algebra and intuition, not spiritual beings or men from Venus, a forecasting system which can lay out an entire life.

Finally I hope to debunk the spirituality of all the Parts, including the Part of Spirit (ASC + Sun - Moon), as bad astrology and worse spirituality.

The Word Point

In contemporary writing the words Point and Part are used interchangeably. I do it myself through force of habit and unless someone does some real fine editing I'm sure you'll find it in this text as well.

Point means one, a single non-linear position. Here this position would be a degree of the zodiac.

In the ancient Arabic system the word Point would have applied to D as in A + B - C = D. This point D is the degree that completes the midpoint sequence A/B = C/D. It is the degree that is as zodiacially far from A as B is from C. That is: Line AD = Line BC

Lines are geometric. The system is algebraic.

D is what we call the Point or the Part. The term Part here is only partially correct. It is the Point that must be contacted by a conjunction to complete the midpoint complex A/B + C/D. *Without a conjunct planet, A/B does not equal C/D.*

It must have a conjunction, any conjunction to complete the complex or *Part*. At this time remember that a point (degree) without a planet has no energy, a matter often forgotten. The misunderstanding of using other aspects in delineating Parts will be dealt with later as well as the reason that it apparently works and how it can be made to work.

The Arabian Point is D waiting for a conjunction, maybe even with one there already. D is what we name elaborately or give another glyph to as in Part of Fortuna.

Later on Al-Biruni's orbs will be given and examined.

The conjunction to the point, approaching or separating is wide by modern standards—until remembered that as a midpoint *the orb would be reduced by half.*

The Word Part

Historically the words Part and Point are used interchangeably, but the word part in its very essence means of more than one, say several. It also means that more than one is needed for the completion or totality of the matter at hand.

Here the term Part refers to A,B, or C. Parts to A + B - C.

Parts might also refer to the midpoint complexes A/B and or C/D, and is the general term for the equation as in the Part of Fortuna.

The Arabian Parts are a polarized pair of midpoints. A/B is always passive and in the original system generally referred to the blending of the Ascendant (A) with the properties of a planet (B). This is the passive or negative polarity.

The C Planet which I have described "in terms of" is one half of the active midpoint. Far from being "taken away" it determines the type of planetary energy being directed at the pair A/B. This planet C awaits a conjunction to D which will trigger the complex.

In a later chapter I will deal with what I call reciprocals, where B and C are interchanged but for now I will use two examples.

Fortuna: ASC + Moon - Sun = Fortuna. C or the Sun is the defining planet . This is a solar Part dealing with the energy of the Sun imposed on the Ascendant and Moon. With Mercury conjunct Fortuna it might have a mental twist to the will, with Venus self centered, Mars, aggressive etcetera. C is always the defining planet

Spirit: ASC + Sun - Moon = Spirit. Here C or the Moon is the defining planet. The energy would be lunar; needs emotions, habit, change, karma, imposing their energies on ASC/Sun or the ASC as related to the will and ego etcetera.

Take another simple example: ASC + Mars - Venus—the lady waits for a man to ask her to dance; ASC + Venus - Mars—the lady puts on a red dress and prowls.

The Arabian Parts are a polarized system of two pairs of midpoints; A/B passive-negative and C/D dynamic-positive.

In the classic Parts A is the Ascendant blended with the planetary energy of B. This is activated in terms of planet C in the positive pair when C is triggered by a conjunction to D, the point. The planet contacting D will influence the energy expression of C. It is also the trigger setting off the complex.

Any Arabian Part *when completed by conjunction* may now be understood using a midpoint book by referring to the pair C/D. For example Saturn conjunct Fortuna is Sun/Saturn to Moon, the Moon channeling this energy to the ASC (A/B or ASC/Moon).

The classic system used the Ascendant for reasons that will be noted throughout the book but the algebraic equation A+B-C=D will give the same results when say three planets are used. Asteroids are also fair game.

Finally, by personal use in charts a midpoint or several midpoints conjunct a point (D) has a telling effect. If a natal midpoint it would relate to character, if a transit midpoint it would relate to events and changes

The Word Fortunes

In Vedic astrology a concept exists called *Sudarshan*. It is the reading of a natal chart from the Ascendant by house and aspect, then turning to the Sun and Moon and using derivative house techniques assessing the Sun and Moon by house and aspect, treating the Sun and Moon as co-equal Ascendants.

This is called *Sudarshan* or the reading of the "three ascendants" Ascendant, Sun, Moon. What is sought is a concentration by house or aspect. If you glance at my chart you will see that the eighth house from Ascendant, Sun and Moon are all tenanted, I am an eighth house person.

Sudarshan is the Vedic answer to Fortuna and Spirit and proves that the Vedic system did not originate the Parts. *Sudarshan* is automatically used. By extension the Vedic system may read derivatively from other planets. The Parts except for several, probably sold by itin-

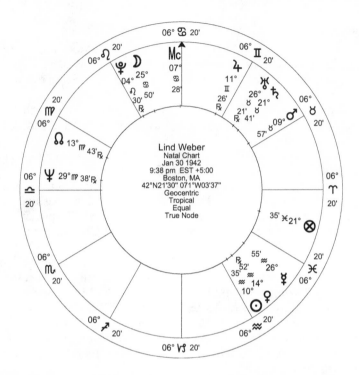

erant Arab astrologers to Indian court astrologers, are simply not used in the Vedic system. That the Moon's Nodes are not used in the Arabian Parts also indicates they did not come from the Vedics.

What are the Fortunes? First answer what the word fortune is. It is your luck or accumulated money and goods. Above all it is your luck.

Luck is always a very personal matter (Ascendant, Sun, Moon) No one's is the same.

The Fortunes of the Arabian system are the Jupiter conjunction and it's trines as related to Fortuna (ASC + Sun - Moon) and it's reciprocal Spirit (ASC + Sun - Moon) Fortuna is solar. Spirit is lunar. Since the Sun is the strongest planet, Fortuna is a bit greater than Spirit, the Sun here having the dynamic energy. Thus Fortuna is the most important degree of the chart; its *reciprocal*, Spirit, is the second most important degree. I would place the Ascendant itself as the third most important degree.

Why are these two degrees the most important? With the genius of algebra our astrologer picked the only two degrees in the zodiac that simultaneously stimulated the three Ascendants, Ascendant, Sun, Moon.

The secret of Fortuna and its reciprocal, Spirit, is simple. A planet stimulating their point by conjunction *must* produce a result.

12

Fortuna and Spirit are D or Points.

The implications of a must result degree with a sensitive immediate zodiacal area on either side become clear with the meaning of Lot. How the trines of Jupiter work is dealt with later.

The Word Lot

The word Lot is not used much anymore in English. The concept is clear. The irrevocable is mixed with luck as in to cast one's lot with, meaning risky commitment—or one's lot—the die is cast, your game-cock lost. You are sentenced—clear. Irrevocable, fated, hard—one's lot in life. Most uses are clearly Saturnian.

Such a condition would result with the conjunction squares and opposition of Saturn to Fortuna or Spirit. How the squares and opposition work is dealt with later. Two planets one representing good luck, one representing bad luck—forget spirituality, it doesn't enter the equation of simpler times, when Saturn was the siginficator of famine and Jupiter of plenty—meet the two points where it must come to pass. The entire life may projected from this *framework*: transiting Saturn conjunct Fortuna; transiting Jupiter conjunct Fortuna; transiting Saturn conjunct Spirit; transiting Jupiter conjunct Spirit. The great periods of luck, good or bad.

There would be one to three conjunctions of Saturn to Fortuna. With its approximate twenty-nine year cycle it might have struck Fortuna of a sixty-one-year-old native three times, or depending on its natal placement a forty-five-year-old native once.

The same would go for Spirit with the zodiacal distance between Fortuna and Spirit noting the time between two periods of good or bad luck.

In my chart presently (1995) with transiting Saturn conjunct Fortuna at 21 Pisces, I may expect another Saturn period in 2 $\frac{1}{2}$ years as transiting Saturn comes to Spirit at 21 Aries.

Conversely, with transiting Jupiter the luck would come within a one year plus period as transiting Jupiter moved from mid Pisces to late Aries. This would occur at the twelve-year intervals of a Jupiter cycle.

I have worked this through my chart. Work it through yours. Onto this simple framework you may add any amount or combination of astrological knowledge and enhancement.

Remember that not only are we dealing with a time factor, but each component. Fortuna Spirit, Saturn and Jupiter may be delineated by sign, house, rulership and aspect—for Saturn and Jupiter—or any other planet conjunct a point may now receive aspects, natal, progressed, transiting or synastric. Here too, midpoint squares and oppositions would come into play. Check the trines too even if Hamburg says no.

Everything in this chapter will be illustrated or elaborated on, but with the definitions you already understand the elegant simplicity and unerring accuracy of the ancient system.

In another chapter reciprocals will be examined. Inadvertently they show why the Ascendant is the third most important degree thus becoming the base (A) for the system.

The Arabian Midpoints

Most astrologers today are heavily influenced by Alfred Witte's monumental work *Rules for Planetary Pictures, the Astrology of Tomorrow.* This is the foundation of Uranian astrology.

I am not a Uranian astrologer, but use his midpoint delineations along with those of Ebertin and Munkasey. I also originate my own as many of us do.

Alfred Witte seems to have been the most equal of equals which included Herman Lefeldt, Friedrich Siegrunn and Ludwig Rudolph. Their names with the exception of Sieggrunn appear here and there from cover to page one in *Planetary Pictures*. Siegrunn is the fifth Beatle. Other than a picture, he is not mentioned because according to a Preface of the editor, Ludwig Rudolph.

> "So for instance, Friedrich Siegrunn has not contributed a single line in Witte's *Rules for Planetary Pictures.* The rules are originally Witte's combination work gained through his self created technical method of investigation—the working with the disc of 360 degrees."

This is a telling paragraph, the creation of the outcast and the deification of the master's system as noted by the disciple.

I will note here and there the nature of the times and the culture involved. Part of the mystery regarding the Arabian Parts has been the failure of scholars to view them in the context of their time and culture.

If you read the first sixteen pages of *Planetary Pictures*, you cannot help but be struck by it's ultra-German nature. I see the pupils in neat rows, all with their ties on, and Mr. Witte using a blackboard pointer like a general's swagger stick. Think German and later think Arabian.

Sometime after beginning this I spoke to a math teacher and asked if algebra simplifies. He answered in the affirmative and unasked noted that geometry complicates. The Uranian midpoints are geometric in nature and thus a product of their time. They came in the period of Bauhaus architecture and Cubist art—angles.

Uranian astrology took the circle and divided it decreeing that aspects, meaning midpoints be based on it's divisions. Later writers have noted the 8 phases of the Moon (forty-five degree angles) but I suspect this had little to do with Witte's system.

Thus Witte's midpoints demanded some division of the circle based on the division of diameter, $180°$, $90°$, $45°$, $22\frac{1}{2}°$. If not in such relationship it was not significant. I could go on but I'll cut to the chase. Working from this framework a native might be said to be more or less without certain *planetary pictures*. (A + B = C). This is true enough in a general sense but what I am getting to is that the Arabs dealt with this from a different perspective.

Our astrologer did not use geometry. Algebra was his weapon of choice. The question now became when (ephemeris) and where (zodiac) can I bring this [picture] to the native (Ascendant). Our astrologer was also pragmatic. He wanted it to work. Centuries later the Germans laid down a system. The system became the end not the means, as systems tend to do. I will use the Uranian term "picture" because it is good.

The Arabs knew by practice like the Vedics the importance of the Ascendant. What could be related to the Ascendant would be brought to pass. Having concluded this they realized that a four part complex was needed Ascendant, two planets, and the completion of the picture by the third planet.

At this point scholars turn to mystery and inspired beings. This probably was not so. Most great insights are the result of drudge work and finally the muse taps you on the shoulder. The process of intuition and creativity is well understood in the engineering sense. It often includes serendipity and a touch of the common or bizarre filtering through the creative psyche.

Once I knew a man, extremely intelligent and very cynical who noted that civilization grew up as man discovered that rivers could carry away his sewerage. He settled down and achieved his first leisure time from no longer having to scratch and cover like a cat. Which brings us back to the Arabs. The concept of the floating fourth part, the point was as nothing to these algebra wielding desert nomads.

I have hand calculated ten to twenty thousand Arabian Parts. They could be counted from my file charts. That would be a fool's errand. As someone noted to me regarding cockfights. You've probably learned most of it after the first seven or eight thousand.

They knew the answer all the days of their lives. Tent pegs.

<pre>
                         Peg 1   Peg 2
                              Peg 3
</pre>
And if we put Peg 4 just there, it won't be square but it will be symmetrical

<pre>
                              Peg 3   Peg 4
        Now we have
</pre>

<pre>
                    A1   B2
                         C3   D4
</pre>
Now we can prove it's symmetrical by midpoint and longitude (AD = BC)

The algebraic formula A + B - C = D was quick to follow. As they created their pictures, the significance of the Ascendant became ever more important as noted through the reciprocals.

Midpoints, ASC/planet or planet/planet were known long before by observation. Now our astrologer would notice that two pairs produced a polarity, passive—active and that they could seek specific energies this way. The basis for a system was now in place.

It may have taken a bit of time, a few minutes or so, for the lost founder of the Parts, our astrologer, to realize that in using the Ascendant, he had given each native a unique position for D or the *point*. Thus the same pictures could be uniquely timed for each native.

In closing this section I'll just add a few words on midpoints. They were never lost. Just judiciously used by the observant. My first knowledge of them was from the nineteenth century Italian astrologer Carelli and his book of degrees. He called midpoints "points of equidistance."

Today the most common form of midpoints is not Arabian or Uranian but computer. Again of it's time and culture. This is the listing in zodiacal sequence of all the midpoints including those generated by the Midheaven and North Node.

Bend this page. It takes only a second to convert the computer zodiacal sequence listing to the Arabic or Uranian pictures.

Arabian conversion: List the ASC/planet midpoints. Those conjunct or opposed are Arabian pictures.

Any Arabian picture completed by conjunction at D may be read out of any midpoint text in this fashion C/D = B, this related to Ascendant. As an example, I'll continue with the text example of my

Fortuna: ASC + MO - Sun = Fortuna (transited by Saturn conjunction).

This is the energy of transiting Saturn and the dynamic (C) Sun acting upon the passive Moon which forms the connection to the Ascendant.

Read Sun/Saturn = Moon in Witte, Ebertin or Munkasey and relate to Ascendant. The reciprocal or Part of Spirit, Ascendant + Sun-Moon is Moon/Saturn = Sun as related to Ascendant when conjunct Saturn.

Uranian Conversion

Any pictures 0°, 45°, 90°, or 180° from each other form Uranian pictures. Note them one below the other; especially note a *conjunction to the natal planet, the most powerful picture.* All are passive character modifiers in the natal chart (A/B).

When transited by planets and midpoints formed by transits of planets, which themselves function as transits, dynamic activity and change occur. (C/D).

In most cases forty-five midpoints are overkill; your choice for judicious use. Remember, none of us has the time we need.

Midpoint trine complexes work. Of course they are not super dynamic. They are trines, lucky, innate, or negatively a greased slide to trouble.

Trine complexes are readily seen in the computer zodiacal sequence midpoint listing or sort. They do not relate to the Uranian or Arabic systems. Trines effect the Arabian system when D is conjuncted.

Why the Ascendant Is the Key to the System

y both hands on practice and probably through contact with the Vedics, the Arabs had recognized the significance of the Ascendant. It's 360 degree daily rotation individualized the native in terms of his personality and immediate surroundings as well as creating the house sequence by degree and sign.

By examining the old Arabic Parts texts, it is evident that the Arabs did not to use the Moon's Nodes, themselves points. Doing the same to representative Vedic classics as well as modern texts, it is clear Parts and midpoints never got far in the Vedic system.

I offer the above as axioms. I doubt that there would be disagreement.

Elsewhere I wrote a small chapter on the classic Parts based on the Ascendant and seven planets then in use by both the Arabs and the Vedics. Sun, Moon, Mercury, Venus, Mars, Jupiter, Saturn. Of course the Vedics also used the Moon's Nodes which they called shadow planets, a poetic euphemism for nothing there which found favor with Parts. The points (D) where nothing was also received elaborate names. Nodes work, like parts by conjunctions. Furthermore they tap into solar and lunar energy. This is the secret of their power.

The unknown astrologer was busy at work. He had created a magnificent tool but he was not entirely sure how to use it. He worked the major Parts, for these related two Ascendants, either Ascendant and Sun (solar Part C) or Ascendant and Moon (lunar Part C).

He knew Fortuna and Spirit giving three Ascendants duplicated themselves. This is why there are twenty-two instead of twenty-four major Parts. When he punched them into his charts he noticed that they were equidistant above and below the Ascendant-Descendant axis and also the same side by east (Ascendant) or west (Descendant).

He moved to the next Part after Fortuna which he had not yet named the Point of Commerce and punched it in. Taking a cue from Spirit he transposed B and C, creating ASC + Sun - Mercury and punched it in. There it was. They were above and below the Ascendant axis, same side by East or West and equidistant.

He had discovered reciprocals

Reciprocals is my term. Since no one has dealt with the matter I needed a term. I think it's a good one.

With Parts the access to the Ascendant is indirect by midpoint. However if a planet transits each of the two reciprocal Points, here Fortuna and Spirit a direct jolt by midpoint transiting planets (the conjunctions to Fortuna and Spirit) would be given to the Ascendant, bringing together *both polarities of the picture*.

The wallflower (ASC + Mars - Venus) gets up and puts on her red dress and prowls A + Venus - Mars.

At the time of my breakthrough with the Parts, reciprocals were activated. I did not get the money for plane fare to the convention. Asc + Moon - Sun = Fortuna conjunct transit Saturn and transit Venus. I solved the Parts with ASC + Sun - Moon = Spirit conjunct transit Sun and transit Mercury. I would subsequently learn that in the main, Saturn dealt the whole hand.

Return to the wallflower. Let's call it the Part of Attracting for now. It is conjunct transit Saturn; the planetary picture is Venus/Saturn = Mars. Doesn't look so good.

In her red dress, let's call it the Part of Prowling for now. It is conjunct transit Jupiter. The planetary picture is Mars/Jupiter = Venus. The red dress is the way to go.

Now a contrary note must be added. There will be tension as transit Jupiter/transit Saturn directly hit the Ascendant. Transit Saturn brings the negative wallflower picture and transit Jupiter bring the potentially successful prowler.

A humanistic synthesis might be that she would not feel natural or at ease in the red dress even though it's a better move at this time.

Our Arab and this kitchen astrologer would tell her that the red dress will get her laid—which is what it's all about.

Thus with reciprocals, our astrologer saw that relating to the Ascendant was the way to go. *The reciprocals by switching polarities (B are C are interchanged) give a double perspective on the same issue.* ASC + Mars-Venus, ASC + Venus - Mars

Here to act in a Venus or Mars fashion to get sex. Remember that C is always the dynamic part when the Point is conjuncted. ASC + Mars - Venus is a Venusian Part (Wallflower) ASC + Venus - Mars is a Martian Part (Prowler).

Anyway I don't have to write a chapter on reciprocals now.

The Predictive System

hough I generally use "forecasting" in my personal work, this is not about me, and our astrologer probably used the term prediction. Make no mistake; this was not a time of subtlety. The client wanted results and the astrologer had better produce. The general historical consensus is that these were court astrologers, working mainly for the wealthy or royalty. Astrology was used to give an edge in a culture that did not view deceit and treachery as vices but strategies. Perhaps not coincidentally this viewpoint was also prevalent among Renaissance Italians where the Parts caught on strongest before our present period.

We've all seen western movies. They hung the rustler. For the Semitic peoples, both Jewish and Arabic, stealing sheep was a way of life as much interwoven into the culture as automobiles and computers are in our time.

Guns and bullets were not invented yet. Arrows took time to make. The archer, an elite warrior went into battle with only two or three dozen arrows. Decapitation was a sensible means of execution for felons, sheep thieves, traitors and dangerous or unwanted prisoners of war who would have seen slavery as salvation. Beheading does send a message.

Boredom could be alleviated by drawing and quartering. Horses or camels and a few lengths of rope were all that was required. Animals and rope would be little the worse for the wear.

I have often wondered how the Christian liturgy would have handled that one. Surely a goldsmith's nightmare, not to mention the theological implications. Fortunately the Romans chose to have their carpenters moonlight. To lose a job would be to starve. To poison a well and salt the earth was genocide.

These were poor times. Note how inexpensively they killed their fellow man. Warfare was in the main, not the expansion of empire, but small groups of men fighting for sheep, grain, and pasture land.

They also took woman prisoners, for which we can all be thankful today. This prevented inbreeding.

Not much spiritual here. They prayed to their gods for a successful harvest and to escape the next raid, or even that their raid would be successful, a tradition continued today in ball game locker rooms. This was their world. Make no mistake about it. Luck was needed. Luck was understood. They wanted their periods of luck and misfortune foretold.

Jupiter was good luck. Saturn was bad luck

Such was their world for millennia—until well after Al-Biruni's time. In this world, Parts of Captivity, Slavery, Year to be Feared for Death from Famine, Place of Murder and Sickness were planetary pictures suitable for their time and place.

By the way, Decapitation is 8th + Mars - Moon. Torture is MC + Saturn - Moon. The above courtesy of Granite.

In our time Marc Edmund Jones came along. We have Parts of Popularity, Loneliness, Misunderstanding, and Vanity. Perhaps we are moving toward a kinder gentler world, but I have my doubts.

The same planetary Parts will have varied meanings for different periods. I'll give one example. Mundane astrologers consider the interaction of Sun, Mars, and Jupiter as the signature of war. Thus planetary pictures involving the fire planets and waiting for the conjunction of another fire planet on the Point would have meant for the ancients sheep stealing time. For the Renaissance onward, national wars. For the 1990s, let's say corporate takeovers.

Our astrologer needed a certain system for this world of certain uncertainty. He came up with the midpoint system of the Parts.

The Framework: The Predictive System of the Parts

With Fortuna ASC + Moon - Sun and Spirit, Ascendant + Sun - Moon, our astrologer possessed the only two degrees in the zodiac where a planet conjunct them would integrate the energy of the three ascendants, Ascendant, Sun, Moon. The concept of the three ascendants as noted elsewhere is Vedic, and known as *Sudarshan.*

The approach used by the Vedic was to note the repetition of a theme with each ascendant by aspect or house tenancy—I have noted that by derivative house the eighth of my three ascendants is tenanted. I am an eight person.

Our astrologer chose to find a point, the fourth tent peg as it were, that would bring the specific planetary energy of a conjunct planet to the Ascendant, Sun, and Moon simultaneously.

The Vedic to this day reads the natal chart like an horary chart. Our astrologer probably dealt mainly in horary and event type charts, the point being both were familiar with the law of three. Three clear indicators should bring it to pass, whether character or event.

Coming from their respective positions the Vedic built his framework of prediction on character, than layered in his timing.

Our astrologer started with timing and a predisposition of this timing. Jupiter was good. Saturn was bad. These were the great chronactors.

With all three Ascendants simultaneously stimulated our astrologer could safely forecast something. He worked from the slow planets Jupiter and Saturn. The twelve year conjunctions of Jupiter to Fortuna and Spirit were times of unparalleled good luck, the twenty-nine year conjunctions of Saturn to Fortuna and Spirit would be viewed as times of terrible misfortune.

For the times, this was sound astrology. Since the system was Ascendant based the times of first, and then naturally, succeeding periods of good and bad luck would vary with each individual, as would the time between two periods of fortune or two periods of misfortune since the distance between Fortuna and Spirit varies with each native.

For example, in my chart, putting aside the question of orb which modifies considerably and will be treated separately, Fortuna 21 Pisces and Spirit 21 Aries would indicate two and a half years separation in Saturn periods and one year separations in Jupiter periods.

Here was the linchpin of the entire predictive system: Jupiter conjunct Fortuna, Jupiter conjunct Spirit, Saturn conjunct Fortuna Saturn conjunct Spirit. *The four components, two planets and two points were the framework of a life. Forecasts on them could extend far into the future.*

These super conjunctions creating super periods were delineated as we do today: house, sign, aspect, despositorship, rulership and planetary condition.

Alone this would seem to be a skimpy framework, but these four factors were never alone. For example, natal or transiting Mars might square the conjunct Jupiter or Saturn. The transits of the Sun were a given, easily assessed by eye. The Moon contacted by conjunction each month. An ephemeris was available for Mercury or Venus should they be needed by subject, such as business, sex, or money, or as sortilege meaning the rulers of a house.

Let's refer again to the war signature example, Sun-Mars-Jupiter. Transiting Jupiter is conjunct his Fortuna. He can steal many sheep, capture many women and return home safely. But he needs the time for the enterprise. Our astrologer now turns to Mars and gets an aspect to Jupiter. It is now a simple matter to find a solar transit to one or the other. Our astrologer lucks out and finds the Sun in aspect to both. *Remember the orbs.* Remember that in a midpoint system the orb reduces itself by half. Two days after the solar position our astrologer notes Moon trine Jupiter and says this should be the beginning of the enterprise. The ruler succeeded.

To get favorably married if with Jupiter conjunct Fortuna or Spirit, line up Venus and Mars as above and close with a good lunar aspect to Venus or Jupiter.

A life is not just infrequent periods of great success or terrible misfortune. More often good and bad times and events weave through one's life in some strange minuet. Can they be somewhat timed or sorted out?

According to this system the answer is yes. All aspect books note squares, trines, and oppositions to Fortuna—*which do not exist.* What exists is this planet square, trine, or opposing a planet conjunct Fortuna or Spirit. Thus, for example, natal Mars square Fortuna could have permutations of Mars square all seven planets. The Mars influenced planet, whichever of the seven, would bring its energy to the three ascendants in it's position conjunct Fortuna or Spirit.

Once this was understood our astrologer could use Jupiter or Saturn in other aspect to Fortuna and Spirit.

Let's use transiting Jupiter trine Fortuna. In this trine it turns out that Mars does not conjunct Fortuna, but transiting Sun does at a time that creates a close orb with Jupiter trine Fortuna.

Moon-Jupiter wins the lottery. Sun-Jupiter saves your hide. Our astrologer tells his patron to settle his diplomatic difficulties with the ruler to the east. A favorable Venus transit in three days time would be a good time to arrive at the gates. A favorable Moon is up at sundown. They should travel through the night.

For lack of a better term and since I'm forced to make one up I'll call these the intermittent times: square, trine, opposition of Jupiter; square, trine, opposition of Saturn to Fortuna and Spirit (and for that matter, of any planet in any aspect to any Part other than by conjunction). I will call these apects the *intermittencies*.

And this is the only way any planet square, trine, opposition ever works on a Part—when another planet conjuncts that Part. Without that you have an empty degree and an *incomplete and inactivated* midpoint complex A + B - C. Our astrologer went on to streamline the matter. He threw out the squares of Jupiter and trines of Saturn.

That was the system of the ancients, simple and elegant, as sweeping as the desert, as sharp as the headman's sword.

I may as well settle the matter of Spirit here. Our astrologer knew a couple things about it.

1. It is the reciprocal of Fortuna.

2. It is a lunar part (C) that is, in terms of the Moon, active and dynamic.

3. It delivers the goods when conjunct Jupiter: money, women, children, happiness. (The Sun deals with enterprise, survival, advancement.) Spirit's picture is Moon/Jupiter = Sun and this to the Ascendant.

4. Conversely Saturn conjunct Spirit was terrible—the worst of all aspects Moon/Saturn = Sun and this to the Ascendant. The misfortune of this aspect would be without mercy. Organization and discipline might mitigate Saturn conjunct Fortuna or Sun/Saturn = Moon and this to the Ascendant, but one did not expect this with Moon/Saturn.

5. Finally, he knew Spirit was the reciprocal of Fortuna so he always knew where it was. He just was not going to tell all the new guys on the block. Furthermore he probably sold the Part for a handsome price with a wondrous story of it's properties, that here was where the king's salvation lay. The abuse of Spirit had begun. It continues unabated today.

Spirit is nothing more or less than the second degree of only two where a planet conjunct it can integrate the energies of all three ascendants: Ascendant, Sun, Moon. As a lunar (C) Part, the Moon is of the active polarity and being Lunar is less important that the solar Fortuna. It is ASC + Sun - Moon.

Its planetary picture is Moon/transiting planet = Sun and this to the Ascendant.

In the predictive system of the framework Moon/Jupiter = Sun, Moon/Saturn = Sun would be the planetary pictures. Of course both to the Ascendant.

It is true the Moon rules karma and the lunar Parts are karmic. The lunar Parts also deal with habits and kitchen work. Karma is not spirituality. One is debt or lesson. The other is inner growth in some way related to God or a higher power. Simply the Moon is related to karma because the Moon also symbolizes the past lives.

This is a natural place to move to the next section after a couple observations.

Spirit is not the night form of Fortuna (change if by night). I believe that a misunderstanding arose regarding the reciprocal. Above the horizon was considered better in ancient systems. At night the Sun had to be below the horizon.

A later chapter will deal with the "change at night" in more detail. What is clear is that as reciprocals one will be day (above the Ascendant-Descendant axis) and one will be night (below same). We all have them both.

Of Astrology
and Spirituality

Astrology is not spiritual. People are spiritual. And most are not. Rather than pursue this in turgid prose I'll offer you a mental exercise. The transits of Jupiter and Saturn to Fortuna and Spirit in the chart of a saint and in the chart of a psychopath.

For that matter astrology is not inherently psychological or mythological, theosophical or pragmatic. It is a soul map that may be viewed from various perspectives, including spiritual and karmic—and these are not the same. Perspective is not that which is viewed, which here is astrology itself.

Like anything else astrology can be misused or abused. Again people do this. But there is nothing that says it must be used only in a spiritual, karmic, or humanistic way or that it can't be used pragmatically.

When clients come with a sexual matter in mind, I offer the suggestion that dealing with the matter on a sexual level is appropriate astrology. Remind them of AIDS, point out the benefits of forgiveness to old lovers and parents, and if no great harm results, help them get a partner.

Before I became aware of astrology I read some Buddhist texts which concluded with this dictum: If you practice the Golden Rule you do not need this book. The Golden Rule is "Do unto others as you would have them do unto you."

It is common to all the great religions. As they say in Alcoholics Anonymous, keep it simple. That is what I prefer to do.

The transit of Pluto through Scorpio and the Uranus-Neptune conjunction brought genuine spiritual progress to very few of us—as has always been the case. Rather, these placements influenced the nature of that spiritual progress that the few of us made. On a mundane level it brought about peace among some old enemies (advancement) even as it has sown tribalism and civil war elsewhere and for most of us brought general confusion.

Fortuna and Spirit

W̲ hat are Fortuna and Spirit? They are the two most important degrees in your chart. Fortuna because it is, in terms of the Sun, more important than Spirit, which is in terms of the Moon.

The formula for Fortuna is Ascendant + Moon - Sun = Fortuna.

The formula for Spirit is Ascendant + Sun - Moon = Spirit.

They are reciprocals; that is, in the formula A + B - C = D the positions of B and C have been switched.

Fortuna and Spirit are not exactly the same. When the astrologer is told to switch for a night birth, he is giving that person the Part of Spirit for his Fortuna.

Again, they are not the same. Obviously the concept or the deceit sprang up because if a person is born at night his Sun is below the horizon. He might then be considered to respond more readily to lunar energies. For all I know this may be true enough, but Fortuna is Fortuna and Spirit is Spirit and we all have them both.

Fortuna is a solar Part. Spirit is a lunar Part. They are the most important degrees in the chart because from a conjunction to them the Ascendant, Sun, and Moon are *simultaneously stimulated*. These are the three Ascendants of Vedic *Sudarshan*. When the three ascendants are simultaneously stimulated, matters must occur. The native will undergo activity and change. Here are two virtually fated degrees.

We have all read reams of description on Fortuna. Much by observation is correct, though an arrow in the dark. The best descriptions of Fortuna are generally by house. The reasons for this will be made clear as the nature of the Parts is illustrated. When Fortuna is considered the old rule that the ruler of the house be considered is apt. Fortuna activated is beneath the sway of this planet.

More precisely, I'll render the exact nature of that. When Fortuna or another Part is transited by conjunction, said planet and the ruler of the transited house influence each other, this reaching the Ascendant.

Fortuna has no properties when it is not aspected by conjunction. It

31

is an empty point in the chart. Other aspects to it work only when Fortuna receives a conjunction of the Moon—which it does every month or the yearly passages of the fast planets Sun Mercury Venus. At such times other aspects to Fortuna are activated. More precisely an aspect to the transiting conjunct planet is found. This alters its influence on Fortuna.

There is nothing inherently mystical about Fortuna. It is subject to all manner of conjunctions. It must affect the native since it involves the three Ascendants. Its effects will reflect the nature of the chart and the nature of the conjunct planet involved. Period.

The solar Parts (minus Sun in C positions), including Fortuna, appear to deal with the present and retain solar significance power, success, will, ego—the whole ball of wax among others.

The reciprocal of Fortuna is Spirit. B and C switch places in the equation: $A + B - C = D$. Spirit is Ascendant + Sun - Moon = Spirit.

Spirit is a lunar Part in terms of the Moon, which is the dynamic planet C. Lunar parts are clearly karmic. I have personally noted this in chart work. The Vedics emphasize the Moon in their system which is a very karmic astrology.

The Part of Spirit also dynamically affects day-to-day lunar matters in the life such as habit, function, women, change, ad infinitum. It too is activated by conjunction and the accompanying conditions noted with Fortuna apply to it as well.

The matter of how a Part is aspected by other than a conjunction, noted with Fortuna applies to all Parts.

The burnout flickered on. Its nature differs from depression in that you wish to act, but you cannot get the switch turned on—no wind in the sails and a sense of futility sets in. I finally understood how people leave good jobs. They can no longer face their inability to do that which they've known themselves capable of doing.

I did no work on the Parts, no writing. I confined myself to looking for example charts in the little bit of astrology that I did.

On September 15-16, 1995, Hurricane Marilyn hit the U.S. Virgin Islands, dealing a devastating blow to St. Thomas. It was full of small tornadoes or vortices spinning off the eye wall. These small storms within a storm generated winds of up to 240 miles per hour. Buildings died screaming as they were ripped apart. Whole roofs flew hundreds of feet.

At dawn my neighborhood, heavily hit, promenaded to view the destruction. We were all very careful not to show jubilation or self-pity. Though we did not know it then, we were all scarred as well.

I was extremely fortunate. We lost only a piece of our roof and in the end my wife, Kay, would save most of our books. We didn't lose any cats and I was paid in the coming months for rebuilding the family hotel. In short, most fortunate, but profoundly affected.

I have not recovered from the storm. Much seems futile and useless. I lost all interest in possessions. The drying books did not move me as possessions or knowledge. Nature had commanded my attention and I'll lay my foundations there for a while—scrap the entire social mental material spiritual gestalt for a while.

My Fortuna is at 21 Pisces 36. Transiting Saturn was at 16 Pisces. Transiting Mars at 6 Scorpio opposed my Sun/Moon at 3 Taurus and transiting Jupiter at 8 Sagittarius was conjunct my Ascendant/Sun at 8 Sagittarius.

Extremely lucky. Extremely vulnerable.

Eventually I began to read a little astrology by lantern light. However, by mid-December, I was still without electricity. I found I could read very clearly with no desire to go into detail.

Transiting Jupiter in Sagittarius in 1995 began a new Jupiter cycle if you choose to count from its rulership. I'll make a gratuitous forecast. We're in for a dozen years of excruciating astrological pedantry. Such was my conclusion as I read the magazines. Sometimes unbelievably good astrology, but too many words. Flesh will be flogged from the corpses of dead horses regarding scientific astrology and the Gauquelin effect. Regarding the first the correct term is "empirical." As for the second, the Uranus-Neptune conjunction of 700-plus years ago ended the dark ages. Station in life or the angles of the chart were no longer strict determinates. Motivation became the factor in determining one's destiny. Mars in the twelfth wants to be an athlete or surgeon.

My chart is here. I'm a natural born rebel. I resolved that I'd write this simply and briefly. The subject matter will stand or fall on its own merits. From my few examples you will be able to create your own proofs or not.

I also am deliberately choosing to write a spare text in honor of the inspired astrologer who several millennia ago created an astrological system of such elegant simplicity that it hid in plain view for millennia.

Cutting to the Chase

What are the Arabian Parts? Until now, this has not been answered. We use them but we don't know what they are.

The Arabian Parts are an Ascendant-based system of midpoints combining two pairs of midpoints, one static and negative—A/B—the other positive and dynamic—C/D. The formation of the Point D by conjunction allows three planets and the Ascendant to merge their energies at a midpoint of conjunction or opposition, pair to pair, A/B, C/D. Restated, a common midpoint is formed in the conjunction. An opposition midpoint is formed with the opposition. This midpoint or midpoints (opposition) is a secondary sensitive area and heretofore has not been examined.

Example: My Fortuna midpoint is 1 Virgo 06 and 1 Pisces 06 respectively, ASC/Moon and Sun/Fortuna. My progressed Sun at this period covered three to five degrees Aries. Transiting Uranus in 1995-96 in early Aquarius formed the same midpoint.Progressed Sun/transiting Uranus = early Pisces.

All true Arabian Parts are the results of the algebraic formula A + B - C = D. Because the formula is algebraic, which is mathematically a simplification, the Parts were probably a streamlined system created by an Arab astrologer.

The basic concept behind the Arabian Parts was to bypass the limits of the classic aspects by finding a degree that would unite *three* (completion) planetary energies through the creation of a four part aspect. These energies would flow to A, usually the Ascendant.

The original Arabian Parts would have been Ascendant-based, the Ascendant being the most personal of points, 360 degrees being available each day.

The Ascendant is also the person or event, a degree of activity and occurrence, of being and happening, doing and done to.

Taken from the Ascendant the energy of B in terms of C yields the Part D. D is actually the Point (see glossary and ongoing delineation).

Part refers specifically to A, B, C, or all of them, as well as being a generic name for the whole complex.

To use Fortuna as an example. The Ascendant (A) is combined with the nature of the Moon (B) for Ascendant/Moon. It will receive the energies in terms of planets (C); here it is the Sun when the circuit is closed by a conjunct planet to the awaiting degree, the Point (D) for Sun/Fortuna.

Thus ASC/Moon = Sun/Fortuna.

In this text I've used my chart because of the conjunction of Saturn to Fortuna as events unfolded.

When I resolved the Parts, this situation was in effect: ASC/Moon = Sun/Fortuna, transiting Saturn and Venus conjunct; ASC/Sun = Moon/Spirit, transiting Mercury and Sun conjunct.

Those of you who pursue the Parts will recognize the unusual nature of the above.

The A/B or ASC/planet B midpoint is passive. This is the planetary mix with your Ascendant and represents character in terms of the planet—Ascendant/Moon is the Ascendant blended with lunar influences. As Fortuna this will be stimulated by the Sun (C) when a planet contacts Fortuna, the Point or D by conjunction—again in my case Sun/Saturn. That is Sun/Saturn acted on my Ascendant/Moon.

All Parts function in this way. Theoretically any and all planets or planets, degrees, cusps may be used. Midpoints are being generated. Midpoints work, but unless judiciously chosen and efficiently understood, they also clutter.

Classic Parts followed the formula ASC + Planet B - Planet C = Part. Fortuna is such a part. Planets conjunct the Part close the circuit. This is D or the Point. Ascendant + Cusp B - Planet C = Part. The Part of Death, ASC + 8th - Moon is such a Part. Two planets are required to close the circuit, a conjunction to the eighth house cusp and a conjunction to Death.

The Parts of the Ascendant are also classic parts. ASC + ASC - C = D. Carl Payne Tobey was overjoyed to discover the solar Ascendant Part. ASC + ASC - Sun = Solar ASC Part, but apparently carried the matter no further.

I interpolated from him and began to use the lunar Ascendant Part; ASC + ASC - Moon = Lunar ASC Part. Like all lunar parts, it ranges from the petty to the karmic.

The Parts of the Ascendant got lost precisely because they were a known midpoint. The Ascendant Part of a planet is always exactly equidistant on the opposite side of the Ascendant or Descendant axis—that is, north or south and always on the same side as the planet east or west.

In my chart the Ascendant Part of Pluto falls at 8 Sagittarius conjunct my ASC/Sun midpoint at 8 Sagittarius. The conjunction of a planet to this degree yields a direct midpoint contact to the Ascendant. For example, in 1995 transiting Jupiter at 8 Sagittarius yielded Pluto/Transit Jupiter = ASC.

Simply stated, Parts of the Ascendant are the degree that if conjuncted would bring the C planet in question; for example, Pluto to the Ascendant in combination with the transiting planet.

The original parts probably were just solar and lunar. After all, both of these yielded at least two Ascendants and included the miraculous Fortuna and Spirit triple Ascendant combinations. I am calling the Parts of the seven planets classic, the solar and lunar Parts major with their two Ascendants, and the Parts for the other five planets minor.

Solar Parts

ASC + Moon - Sun (Fortuna)
ASC + Mercury - Sun
ASC + Venus - Sun
ASC + Mars - Sun
ASC + Jupiter - Sun
ASC + Saturn - Sun

Reciprocals

ASC + Sun - Moon (Spirit)
ASC + Sun - Mercury
ASC + Sun - Venus
ASC + Sun - Mars
ASC + Sun - Jupiter
ASC + Sun - Saturn

Lunar Parts

ASC + Sun - Moon (Spirit)
ASC + Mercury - Moon
ASC + Venus - Moon
ASC + Mars - Moon
ASC + Jupiter - Moon
ASC + Saturn - Moon

Reciprocals

ASC + Moon - Sun (Fortuna)
ASC + Moon - Mercury
ASC + Moon - Venus
ASC + Moon - Mars
ASC + Moon - Jupiter
ASC + Moon - Saturn

Taking out the duplication of Fortuna and Spirit, there were twenty-two major Parts. Reciprocals switch polar energies between B + C and a reciprocal is always exactly the same distance above or below on the Ascendant-Descendant axis as the Part, but on the opposite side of the Ascendant or the Descendent. Both are always east or west. Reciprocals form a midpoint to the Ascendant or Descendent when both are activated by conjunctions.

What was the basic system of astrology using the Parts? The key is in the words Lots and Fortunes. Any given chart pivoted on two points, Fortuna and Spirit, both the unique carriers of three Ascendants and two planets transiting Jupiter of good luck and transiting Saturn of bad luck. The Fortunes of Jupiter and the Lots of Saturn. I call the two points and two planets the framework.

With just these four components, an astrologer could forecast far into the future. He would start with transiting Saturn and outline one or two periods of misfortune. For example, I experienced my first conjunction of Saturn to Fortuna at twenty-three and twenty-four years of age. There was a bad marriage, made and broken in that time, and my fall into alcoholism. My second Saturn conjunction transiting to Fortuna occurred at fifty-two to fifty-four years of age and this is why some of its significance has been narrated.

Next the astrologer would examine Saturn conjunct Spirit. This occurred for me in May 1968. I had the largest stone job I've ever had, and as I reached my first bottom with alcoholism in November 1968, I was broke and the relationship I was in ended. I can look forward to a second dose of this from May 1997 to May 1998.

On this simple framework our astrologer could now hang his craft. He would look for modifying influences by Jupiter—I noted these in my narration. He would move Saturn forward to square and oppose Fortuna and Spirit. These would be *intermittent* periods of difficulty as the transiting fast planets, in particular the monthly Moon conjuncting Fortuna or Spirit would pick up the Saturn energy of the square or opposition.

The astrologer then performed the same activity with transiting Jupiter. About every twelve years it would contact Fortuna and sometime later Spirit. These were the basically fortunate periods of life. There was no questioning this, since all three Ascendants would be involved. A similar situation would occur as Jupiter made squares and oppositions—and trines. The astrologer would note fast conjunctions to Fortuna and Spirit which would trigger the complex even as the fast conjuncting planet contracted Jupiter by square, trine or opposition. As has been noted he may have chosen not to pay much attention to squares of Jupiter or the trines of Saturn.

On Midpoints

Midpoints have been around for a long while. Arabian Parts are midpoints and by the time we have a first documented historical source for them in Marcus Manilius somewhere around the first century, the Parts were already well misunderstood.

Zoller, in *Arabic Parts: Lost Key to Prediction,* notes that Manilius referred to the thirty degree positions from Fortuna, assigning them primarily numerical functions through the house and signs, not derivative house positions. Numerology created from a probably empty degree? I reject the proposition as I think Zoller does, but he is oblique. It is in the nature of things that some ancient garbage should survive.

So the concept of midpoints as put forward in the Arabian Parts had been around long enough to become confused. In those slower moving times some hundreds of years would be a reasonable guess. A generation would cause the same confusion in our fast moving times.

Let's say 2,000-plus years and call it close enough for government work. Putting aside earlier traditions of astrology, today's astrology is the direct descendant of three traditions; Vedic, Arabic, and Greco Roman.

Whatever the elaborate claims to lineage and pedigree, all are mongrel systems. One of the matters that can be known about the systems from documentation of the last two millennia is that the Parts are probably Arabic in origin for several reasons.

1. They are called Arabian Parts and were extensively used by "Arabs".

2. They are little known or used in the Vedic Tradition.

3. They are algebraic in nature.

4. The absence of any reference to the Moon's Nodes in the tradition of the Parts would seem to eliminate Vedic origins.

There are apparently four basic traditions for midpoints:

1. The observational or random use of them covering the existence of astrology.

2. The Arabian Parts are more that 2,000 years old, were in use until the sixteenth century, and have been in decline during the last two or three hundred years. High points were Al-Biruni in the eleventh century and Bonattti in the thirteenth century, great astrologers who attempted in their own ways to both preserve and bring coherence to the Parts. A resurgence of interest in the Parts has occurred in the twentieth century and has been gathering energy in the last twenty years.

3. The Uranian School of the early twentieth century, doing well and gaining adherents.

4. The computer sort or zodiacal listing of single midpoints, including those involving the Ascendant, Midheaven, and the Moon's Nodes, a newcomer of the late 1980s.

I'll examine these systems briefly. My idea is to show that they came about through a certain perspective, usually involving time and place of origin, and that their format both limited and directed their usage.

Observational Midpoints

These must be as old as astrology and astrologers are still observing them. In the nineteenth century Carelli called them points of equidistance. Often enough these are noted through a transit to an empty space. I personally have found transiting Saturn on the Sun/Moon midpoint many times, working from Saturn and the client's description of depression and loss of energy. I then forecast an end to the matter, bringing relief if not great insight to the client who at this point is in no condition for any form of insight.

Sex is never out of fashion. It just moves through socially open or repressive cycles. Astrologers through the ages must have noted that transiting Jupiter between the native's Venus and Mars has aphrodisiac qualities.

This is the kitchen system of midpoints. It is highly effective since the conjunction is the aspect most dealt with.

Sophisticated midpoint practitioners also use it, the simple essence of Midpoints A + B = C. Ebertin's midpoints belong to this category. His correspondences also have house value.

The Arabian Parts as Midpoints

This entire text is on the Arabian Parts. The thesis of this paragraph is that they were a forecasting system. Timing is the essence of the Arabian Parts—the conjunction by transit to the point or D brings about the activation of the complex $A + B - C = D$, otherwise encodeable as $A/B = C/D$. The fact that planetary energies B, C, plus completing D are linked to the Ascendant or more than one Ascendant

insured two things:
1. The timing of the matter.
2. That personal matters (Ascendant) in terms of the house, sign and rulership planet of D would occur and that their nature would be of B + C with C the dynamic position.

The subtraction of C, an algebraic procedure, became misunderstood as the subtraction of a planetary energy (note my early quotes of Al-Biruni and Granite). Personally I think the early practitioners (in the main court astrologers who were about as spiritual as lawyers) did this deliberately. Wherever they came to rest in the hereafter they are still chuckling.

I noted that the inspiration of the Parts might well have been tent pegs. I'm a stonemason and you also start from the corners like the tent pegs. The base line, usually the back of a building is AB, the front CD. The squareness is checked by the hypotenuses AD and BC, here also the zodiacal equal distances of the Parts.

By working from midpoints the limitations of classic aspects could be bypassed. With Arabian Parts, somewhere everything was in aspect. It just needed setting off—the upcoming point in time as defined by a conjunction to D, a point or degree in the zodiac having its own individual place in an Ascendant (timed) chart.

Uranian Midpoints

The Uranian astrology as developed by the Hamburg School of Witte and others in the early twentieth century is a midpoint system based on geometry. As the math teacher noted, geometry complicates. With the ninety degree dial or disc, Witte could superimpose midpoints occurring at forty-five, ninety, and 180 degrees. These planetary trees could relate by conjunction or hard aspect to a natal or transiting planet.

To use the Sun-Mars-Jupiter war or warrior configuration again, the midpoints to a planet might show a predominate frequency of the fire planets.

The trees themselves can become clumsy and ultimately they refer to a natal planet with conjunct midpoints especially noted.

The Trans-Neptunian planets according to Granite may be based on certain Arabian Parts. I'm not qualified to comment on this, not being a Uranian astrologer. I balk at Witte's sixteen page introduction as I do at Tolstoi's *War and Peace*.

Uranian astrologers I've met swear by its timing, accuracy, and the effectiveness of the Trans-Neptunians, a part of their system which I won't go into, being unqualified.

One problem that arose with the disc was the houses. Witte de-emphasized them and ultimately this may put him at the back of the pack in terms of the system, since the observational and computer sort also pay homage to the planetary conjunction to a midpoint, while allowing full and easy use of the houses.

The Computer Sort

Just as the Arabian Parts are algebraic and the Uranian system paid homage to the geometry that was in the air during the early twentieth century, notably in art and architecture, the computer sort is a product of the computer age.

All midpoints are listed in zodiacal sequence with the natal planets there in sequence too.

Its simplicity offers several advantages.

1. It may be used observationally.

2. It may be used as a rough indicator of Arabic Parts or Uranian Trees.

3. It shows house and sign emphasis of midpoints.

4. It allows use of trine midpoints

5. It preserves the houses.

6. It is efficient.

ASC/Planet midpoints conjunct or opposition planet/planet midpoints are Arabian Parts pictures as shown on the midpoint axis A/B = C/D. In the natal chart this would show Arabic pictures in place. C or D could be deciphered by remembering that zodiacal distance A/D or ASC/Point is equal to zodiacal distance B/C. B, of course, is the planet of the Ascendant midpoint A/B and the zodiacal distance of lines A/D and lines B/C are equal.

The Proliferations

I never settled for or became terrified of the term proliferation as used by Al-Biruni and the scholars. There had to be some inherent form of limitation as well as some meaning, given that they were midpoints.

I have explained the significance of Fortuna and Spirit and the tent pegs of Fortuna, Spirit, Jupiter, and Saturn where the framework of an entire life might be laid out.

But those are only two Parts and two planets. Clearly more detail is in order.

I explained how the divisions of the Jupiter and Saturn cycles could be brought to Fortuna and Spirit *intermittently* when they were transited by fast conjunctions, the Moon once a month, the Sun once a year, etc.—orb or moiety as Al Biruni called it, extending this into reasonable periods of time. I termed these intermittencies.

How many parts are there naturally? Restated more precisely, how many and how were the Parts used by their originator.

Our astrologer worked with the Ascendant and seven planets, or five planets and two lights.

The solar and lunar Parts with reciprocals, subtracting the duplication of Fortuna and Spirit, equal twenty-two Parts.

These Parts would have done the job in most cases because the solar and lunar reciprocals involved two Ascendants, making them the most personally significant after Fortuna and Spirit, the only two Parts with three Ascendants. When the reciprocal's D received a conjunction, the midpoint energy of two planets was dynamically present in direct midpoint to the Ascendant.

It is in the nature of astrologers to want more, so the remaining planets were also placed at C. The originators worked with the Ascendant and seven planets. I copied out the rest of them.

1:15 PM AST, December 31, 1995

By Planet	Reciprocal
ASC + SU - ME	ASC + ME - SU
ASC + MO - ME	ASC + ME - MO
ASC + VE - ME	ASC + ME - VE
ASC + MA - ME	ASC + ME - MA
ASC + JU - ME	ASC + ME - JU
ASC + SA - ME	ASC + ME - SA
ASC + SU - VE	ASC + VE - SU
ASC + MO - VE	ASC + VE - MO
ASC + ME - VE	ASC + VE - ME
ASC + MA - VE	ASC + VE - MA
ASC + JU - VE	ASC + VE - JU
ASC + SA - VE	ASC + VE - SA
ASC + SU - MA	ASC + MA - SU
ASC + MO - MA	ASC + MA - MO
ASC + ME - MA	ASC + MA - ME
ASC + VE - MA	ASC + MA - VE
ASC + JU - MA	ASC + MA - JU
ASC + SA - MA	ASC + MA -SA
ASC + SU - JU	ASC + JU - SU
ASC + MO - JU	ASC + JU - MO
ASC + ME - JU	ASC + JU - ME
ASC + VE - JU	ASC + JU - VE
ASC + MA - JU	ASC + JU - MA
ASC + SA - JU	ASC + JU - SA
ASC + SU - SA	ASC + SA - SU
ASC + MO - SA	ASC + SA - MO
ASC + ME - SA	ASC + SA - ME
ASC + VE - SA	ASC + SA - VE
ASC + MA - SA	ASC + SA - MA
ASC + JU - SA	ASC + SA - JU
ASC + MO - SU	ASC + SU - MO
ASC + ME - SU	ASC + SU - ME
ASC + VE - SU	ASC + SU - VE
ASC + MA - SU	ASC + SU - MA
ASC + JU - SU	ASC + SU - JU
ASC + SA - SU	ASC + SU - SA

ASC + SU - MO	ASC + MO - SU
ASC + ME - MO	ASC + MO - ME
ASC + VE - MO	ASC + MO - VE
ASC + MA - MO	ASC + MO - MA
ASC + JU - MO	ASC + MO - JU
ASC + SA - MO	ASC + MO - SA

With reciprocals and eliminating duplications, the total, including solar and lunar Parts and their reciprocals, comes to sixty-three Parts. I have noted again the solar and lunar Parts, which I have emphasized with the term "major" since they involve two Ascendants. Surely this was enough. In many instances it was.

How did these Parts work? Simple—just like Fortuna and Spirit, transiting Jupiter and transiting Saturn set them off by conjunction. So we had good sex and marriage as transiting Jupiter came to a Venus-Mars picture, and bad sex and divorce as transiting Saturn came to it. There were intermittent and lesser results with the cyclic divisions as explained in the Fortuna example.

Still this was not enough. Our astrologer's patron, whoever he was, was demanding. The *proliferations* enabled the search for more detail and timing. The key to this is the Parts surviving as collected by Al-Biruni that use Fortuna in the Ascendant position. *Fortuna is nothing without a conjunction.* Such a Part was in fact the position of a planet, the awaited conjunct planet.

Jupiter has come to our king's Fortuna and he wishes to wage war. Jupiter is moving slowly so there is a large window of opportunity but our careful astrologer wishes to choose the time of the first arrow carefully.

Ascendant + Moon - Sun = Fortuna (conjunct transiting Jupiter fairly close, approaching and direct).

Fortuna (transiting Jupiter) + Natal Sun - Natal Mars = Part of time to wage war.

Fortuna (transiting Jupiter) + Natal Sun - Natal Mars = transiting Sun conjunct Moon three days hence.

This is not as complex as it looks at first glance. Remember the conjunction to Fortuna energizes and integrates the three Ascendants, Ascendant, Sun, Moon. We have now in turn energized the energizer, transiting Jupiter (conjunct Fortuna).

Transiting Jupiter/Natal Sun = Luck (transiting Jupiter) in leadership (natal Sun) in terms of war (natal Mars) brought to fruition transiting Sun-Moon conjunct Part of Time to wage war. Fortuna transiting Jupiter/Natal Sun (A'/B') = natal Mars/transiting Sun - Moon (C'/D').

Such was the system of the ancients. Like everything else about the Parts, proliferations became a misunderstanding *whether practiced or denounced.*

Used correctly in the uncorrupted system, a proliferation was analogous to a progression, enhancing planetary energies, prospects, and timing.

If a Part is listed with Fortuna as an Ascendant (A), a planet was there. This is the energizer D energized. The same applies to any other Part used as A in Arabic Parts equation A = B - C = D. It is a proliferation.

If the Ascendant (A) was a planet, it merely moved to the planetary picture.

The astrologer might write the example as Fortuna (A') or Jupiter (A'). The actual situation was transiting Jupiter conjunct Fortuna either way. Over the centuries confusion would result.

There are with planetary Parts and reciprocals twelve Sun, eleven Moon, ten Mercury, nine Venus, eight Mars, seven Jupiter, and six Saturn Parts for a total of sixty-three planetary parts. The reduction in number moving from Sun to Saturn occurs by duplication in the reciprocals.

It might be said that there are only sixty-two parts. However, I've chosen to leave the Sun alone. Yes, I did say there were twenty-two classic Parts solar and lunar. This is an illustrative matter.

When a Part (of sixty-three) is aspected by conjunction, there are 63 X 7 (transiting planets for example) possibilities for resolution. That is, 63 X 7 = 441. With the proliferations these 441 could also be multiplied by seven. That is 441 X 7 = 3087, or approximately the endless amount.

The matter is nothing more than possibilities, as in the natal chart, chess, or musical notes. In fact the number of possibilities for the Ascendant-based system with seven planets is actually quite small when looked at in this way.

Remember that only a handful of Parts would be used in a given chart and proliferations would be even fewer, projected only from those Parts that received a conjunction, or were most relevant, or with the most potential. This whole paragraph can be summarized. Use common sense.

This matter was of course extended by cuspal parts. Moderns might extend it further with new planets and asteroids. Make no mistake about it, our astrologer fully understood all the planetary pictures of his seven planets, even to refining them by their position as reciprocals (wallflower—red dress).

Since the completed picture or Part with a conjunction to the Point (D) related directly to the Ascendant, he quickly figured out that he could examine the picture present in terms of personal character A, B in signs and houses. Then refine the forecast by relating similarly to the point (D), that is to the planet conjunct D as a sort of secondary Ascendant from the position D, now A' in the proliferation.

In honor of Al-Biruni, I shall use the term *proliferation* for such pictures. Since three planets and any sequence of them could be used in the proliferations, they seemed endless.

Go to Ebertin's *Combination of Stellar Influences*, take only the midpoints of the seven planets A/B, and use only the seven planets as = C. Count them. These would be proliferations of the original system. The planet conjuncting D multiplied these by seven (possibilities).

That the algebraic formula A + B - C = D applies to the MC, Moon Nodes, or asteroids, etc. has nothing to do with the matter. The only proliferations of the ancients were A + B - C *involving sequence and combinations of only the seven planets.* (Being astrologers, someone would use cusps, degrees, fixed stars, etc.) They would have been used as noted with the planet of conjunction to the point as D-A' seeking detail at D'.

When would proliferations be of most value in a chart? Precisely when transiting Jupiter or Saturn made their conjunctions to Fortuna or Spirit. Here the nature of luck and available potential could be examined in detail, both in nature and timing.

Conversely, proliferations to transiting Saturn conjunct Fortuna or Spirit would warn of danger, indicate avenues of avoidance and discretion, as well as giving some indication of the time and nature of misfortune.

Modern writers often remark or criticize the dire nature of some Parts. They forget, or rather have probably failed to reflect on the nature of the times and its astrology.

I have dealt with the former. A few words on astrology. Much of it was horary in nature even if applied to the natal chart.

Just as today a client at the time of a Saturn return might come and pose a horary question regarding relationship, in those long ago times a soldier with his enlistment bonus might ask a horary question regarding his fate in battle.

The following is taken from Zoller, *Arabic Parts: The Key to Prediction* (used by Al-Biruni in horary questions).

Base Part, The Part of Conquest, Ascendant + Mars - Sun. More correctly this should be called the Part of War. It is the Solar Part of Mars. But flatterery and puffery were part of the court astrologers repertoire. Conquest would more precisely relate to Jupiter's influence at point (D) or defeat might result under predominately Saturn influences to the Point (D).

Our querent receives a Jupiter conjunction yielding Ascendant + Mars - Sun = Conquest conjunct transiting Jupiter. Our astrologer now does the proliferation Sultan's Lot Jupiter + MC - Sun (I believe there is some confusion in this Part which merely wishes to confirm his luck in war, and use it only by way of illustration. Note the misapplied term Lot. It is a fortunate continuation. It should read Sultan's Fortune.) and success in battle, Jupiter + Moon - Mars = Battle.

ASC + Mars - Sun = Conquest (conjunct transiting Jupiter)

(Transiting) Jupiter + MC - Sun = Sultan's Lot

ASC + Mars - Sun = Conquest or Degree of Victory (conjunct transiting Jupiter)

Degree of Victory: Jupiter + Moon - Mars = Battle (success in)

The concept of Proliferations flowed from pencil to paper December 31, 1995, St. Thomas, Virgin Islands. I did not get up to check the time, but know it was about sundown from looking out the window.

This chart is suitable in a strange way. It probably is like many drawn in a time when clocks were not invented, and the correct time was not always just a glance away.

I offer the suggestion that you work your own proliferations directly from Ebertin's concepts. Do not let the names of ancient Parts rattle you. Such names were the keyword and astrological mystique of their times and cultures.

I can see our astrologer or Al-Biruni with the young astrologer. I'll sell you the Part of the Peach and the Part of the Iron Staff, Your lord's happiness will be much increased.

Of course I am referring to ASC + Mars - Venus - wallflower, Venus Part ASC + Venus - Mars - red dress, Mars Part.

For those who want the Part of Pilgrimage to a Holy Spot: ASC + Sun - Mars = Pilgrimage (conjunct Jupiter) which is our Part of War base signature. Ultimately, Sun-Mars-Jupiter together only mean "will initiates a great undertaking." The reciprocal would also be examined.

This matter might also be approached with Jupiter Parts.

There is one final example to demystify the Part names and show a proliferation at work. Al-Biruni has the Part of Torture, 9th + Saturn - Moon = Torture.

First you had to go to war—condition.

Second you had to be taken prisoner. Ninth as tenth of twelfth with a transiting conjunction to ninth; here, luck.

Third, transiting Jupiter or a fortunate planet might conjunct Torture and the soldier would escape torture.

Fourth, transiting Saturn or unfortunate planets might conjunct Torture in which case the soldier might be tortured if captured (ninth as tenth of twelfth, prisoner). Ninth/Saturn (A/B) luck turned bad (ninth luck) equals C/D.

Moon/Torture conjunct transiting Saturn: You are tortured; or Moon/Torture conjunct transiting Jupiter: You get lucky again. Similar results would occur if the Part fell conjunct natal Jupiter or Saturn.

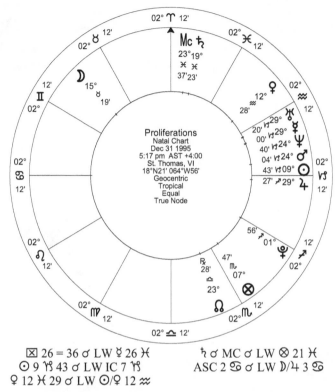

Proliferations
Natal Chart
Dec 31 1995
5:17 pm AST +4:00
St. Thomas, VI
18°N21' 064°W56'
Geocentric
Tropical
Equal
True Node

⊠ 26 = 36 ♂ LW ☿ 26 ♓   ♄ ♂ MC ♂ LW ⊗ 21 ♓
☉ 9 ♑ 43 ♂ LW IC 7 ♑   ASC 2 ♋ ♂ LW ☽/♃ 3 ♋
♀ 12 ♓ 29 ♂ LW ☉/♀ 12 ♒

Today this picture could be used for a major change or flip of luck.

In the earlier text I have used the Uranian term "picture" for the relating of three planetary energies. I'll use the term proliferation as originating from a Point (D).

Put another way, every proliferation is a picture. Not every picture is a proliferation. Both follow the algebraic formula A + B - C = D which is the formula for the midpoint complex A/B = C/D.

The picture would be a midpoint complex as related to it's A, just a Part using a planet as A.

The proliferation is analogous to a progression bringing potential matter, energy and timing to the Point (D) of the original Part:

ASC + Moon - Sun = Fortuna (conjunct transiting Jupiter)

Fortuna (conjunct transiting Jupiter) +Sun - Mars = War complex.

Common sense dictates that the proliferation is taken from the degree of the Point (D) of the original Part for simplifying reference to the chart. Here is the explanation for Fortuna + Sun - Mars versus Jupiter + Sun - Mars.

Again, the use of Fortuna as A may also indicate that transiting Jupiter has not yet arrived at D (Point).

Do We Change at Night?

W ith this overall view of the Parts came the realization of the combination of factors that created a mystery where none really existed. Another insight came. There was a set of ancient factors, cloaked in the mystique of age and history followed by the modern mystification creating its own mistaken mindset and techniques.

The work of Bonatti in the thirteenth century is a pivot point. Ancient and new confusions merge and the stage was set for seven hundred more years of confusion.

The failure to decipher the Parts rested initially on later astrologers missing the obvious as known by instructed astrologers. This would be natural, by studying notes, many times rewritten, describing an oral tradition.

In ancient times knowledge was guarded, not disseminated. Checks, partial explanations, and deceit were rampant.

However, human nature does not change. Several hundred years after our unknown astrologer developed the Parts, it would be natural to assume that they were extremely complicated.

The conversion of the algebraic "C" into the removal of planetary energy was probably deliberate with the Arabs. This would keep the uninitiated at a distance. It worked to this day as both Al-Biruni and Granite spoke of subtracting planetary energy C. I believe Al-Biruni did it deliberately.

Astrologers fell for it even as they described the Part in terms of C: ASC + Moon - Sun is a solar Part; ASC + Sun - Moon is a lunar Part.

C is with the influencing dynamic C = D which as C/D conjunct transiting planet influences passive A/B.

In the last generation, ignorance of, lack of belief in, or ambivalence towards them kept the Arabian Parts in the dark. This ambivalence is present in Tem Tarriktar's interview with Rob Hand in the January 1996 issue of *The Mountain Astrologer*, even as Project Hindsight progresses:

Tem Tarriktar: "Lots are the Arabic Parts, like the Part of Fortune, with specific formulas, right?"

Robert Hand: "Yes. They're all composed of an arc between two bodies added to a third, usually the Ascendant, but not always. There are a couple of lots that don't use the Ascendant at all. By the way, I think that the proliferation of lots was a methodological disaster comparable to the proliferation of asteroids today, except it had a much more deleterious effect - the abandonment of all lots. The Greek had less than a couple of dozen."

This is an interesting paragraph. The description of A + B - C is wrong. Second, the idea that the proliferation of Parts brought about their downfall is an assumption. It is more likely that loss of understanding as to how they worked eroded their overall use. If the Greeks had only a couple dozen, we might roughly date the time that shows true understanding of the Parts had been lost.

The Greeks had less than a couple dozen Parts. So what? We loped into the twentieth century like automatons, using only Fortuna. Most of the time we still just stick it in the chart, whether we use it or not, know what it means or not, or even care.

The failure to relate the Parts to their times, viewing them through the prism of modern perception and attitudes might be said to have covered them more with mud than mystique. I have mentioned the much abused Part of Spirit. In an age that has seen the development of Uranian astrology and Astro*Carto*Graphy why would the instruction of little green avatars be needed to develop the Parts?

Our astrologer, algebra, and the concept of the base line (A/B of the tent pegs) were all that was needed.

All of which leads up to our chapter, which may be shorter than its preface, the idea being that mystification and misunderstanding produced some errors in technique.

How do you progress or arc a Part? Can you? What are the real secrets of converse directions.

The key to all of this for me has been in front of some readers for years. Using the natal Ascendant and progressing the Sun, Fortuna moves conversely through the zodiac.

How can this be?

A + B - C = D

ASC + Moon - Sun = D

ASC + Moon - Sun increased by age (higher zodiac degree) = smaller D (converse zodiac direction)

Since Fortuna is the ultimate point, more equal among equals being

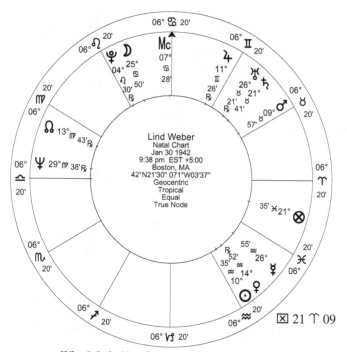

Chart details within wheel:

06° ♋ 20'

06° ♌ 20'

06° ♌ 20'

Mc 07° ♋ 28'

06° ♊ 20'

☿ ☽ 04° 25' ♋ 30' 50' ℞

♃ 11° ♊ 26' ℞

♅ 26° ♊ 21' ℞

20' ♍ 06°

21' 21' ♉ 41' ♄ 09° ♂ 57'

06° ♉ 20'

☊ 13° ♍ 43' ℞

Lind Weber
Natal Chart
Jan 30 1942
9:38 pm EST +5:00
Boston, MA
42°N21'30" 071°W03'37"
Geocentric
Tropical
Equal
True Node

06° ♎ 20'

♇ 29° ♍ 38' ℞

06° ♈ 20'

35' ♓ 21° ⊗

06° ♏ 20'

55' ℞ 52' ♒ 26° 35' ♒ ♒ 14° 10'

20' ♓ 06°

☉ ♀

06° ♐ 20'

06° ♒ 20'

⊠ 21 ♈ 09

06° ♑ 20'

Why I Only Use Converse Solar Arc Fortuna
1. Progressed or solar arc Fortuna 27 ♑ (1996)
1A. Reciprocal Spirit (solar) 15 ♊ (1996)
2. Progressed Spirit (done with Moon 16 ♋ [1996] 0 ♉ ASC + ☉ - P☽)
3. Solar arc or directed Spirit 27 ♒ (1996). ASC + ☉ - SA ☽
3A. Reciprocal solar arc lunar Fortuna 15 ♉ (1996).

the solar integration of the three Ascendants—Ascendant, Moon, Sun—progression could be held to this working with the increasing Sun yielding a decreasing ☽ or Fortuna.

As everyone knows who's read this far, Spirit is the reciprocal of Fortuna. That is, it will be equidistant above or below the Ascendant/Descendent from Fortuna. The reciprocals, any of them, when both are aspected by conjunction, form midpoints to the Ascendant/Descendant axis.

Using my Fortuna at 21 Pisces and Spirit at 21 Aries, 1996 progressed Fortuna is 27 Capricorn transiting in late 1995 at the time of this writing and the developments written of here. This makes it tightly conjunct transiting Uranus. It is also conjunct transiting Neptune according to Al-Biruni.

But notice that its reciprocal moves forward to 15 Gemini. (See Ivy Goldstein Jacobson comment later in the chapter.) This is the Fortuna and Spirit of the progressed Sun. Similarly my progressed Moon is 16

Cancer. Using progressed Moon to define progressed Spirit, I come up with progressed Spirit at 0 Taurus, and its reciprocal progressed Fortuna at 12 Pisces. This is the reciprocal of progressed Spirit. Here ephemeris progressions are used.

Something has happened here. There are two progressed Fortunas and two progressed Spirits. Both are correct, maintaining equidistance from the Ascendant-Descendant axis. I avoid overkill and generally just progress the Sun (solar Fortuna).

To backtrack a minute, note the natal position of Fortuna and Spirit. We know that Fortuna and Spirit are not the same. We know that they are reciprocals. There is no valid reason to use them interchangeably for day and night births.

That is just another mistake of the ages. Fortuna is a solar Part and Spirit is a lunar Part. They appear in each person's chart, period.

Back to the ancient times. The Sun would be signification of a personage or important person and the Moon of women, the public, and the common man.

In the ancient astrology, Sun below the horizon (night birth) would be in an inferior position. Such a person might be better judged through the Moon and the Moon might be emphasized in progression *or direction* (a degree for a year) giving the lunar generated Fortuna as a reciprocal.

I believe the "change at night" rule is an error. D is a trigger position, the Point awaiting conjunction. While one might handle a certain energy better in terms of the reciprocals (wallflower or red dress), the ancient surely recognized their intrinsic difference.

Furthermore, if in terms of the planetary picture C/D = B, this to the Ascendant, the three planetary energies are understood and the polarities change the equation and dynamics of the completed Part. A/B = C/D

ASC + Moon = Sun Fortuna conjunct transiting Saturn 21 Pisces (my chart).

This is: ASC/Moon = Sun/Saturn.

Spirit would be: ASC/Sun = Moon/Saturn were transiting Saturn at 21 Aries.

Somewhere here in the progressions may be the clue to the change at night scheme. Perhaps Spirit was progressed for some and Fortuna for others—for example, common man versus noble. It may also be a deliberate deceit that gained credence.

It is possible that the sophisticated progression and solar arc systems of today as well as the carefully progressed Moon were either unavailable, undeveloped, or unused when the Parts were developed and used properly. It is more likely that the biblical degree or day for a year was developed. I do not believe in the day/degree argument. Astrologers all knew the Sun moved about a degree per day. It is a matter of referring to the dog or his fleas.

For example let's use my directed degree for a year Moon, now called solar arc Moon. ASC + Sun - Moon + 54 (115 + 54 = 169) = Progressed Spirit = 27 Aquarius conjunct natal Mercury 26 Aquarius. Its reciprocal or directed lunar Fortuna, A + directed Moon - Sun is also shown at 15 Taurus. It is fifty-four degrees ahead of natal Fortuna for it is a reciprocal. When C is progressed or directed, converse movement in the zodiac results and the new Part is lower in zodiacal longitude.

Always direct the Part from C. It will move conversely while the reciprocal moves forward.

Now you've seen real converse directions. Moving backwards in the ephemeris, converse progressions are nonsense. Writing this, my directed Spirit is conjunct my natal Mercury—fitting for the matter at hand.

Any natal Part may be directed conversely. It is natural to direct the dynamic C. Allowing for the orb used in the Arabian system, a degree for a year was fine enough for government work. It still is. It would work by natal planetary conjunctions and also trigger proliferations.

To clarify some confusion: Progressions are a day for a year, ephemeris distance; directions are a degree for a year; solar arcs are directions based on the actual motion of the Sun as noted in the progressions—they are modern, accurate directions. I am much indebted to Ivy Goldstein Jacobson. I have all her books, which I studied and now sometimes just pick up and open by chance. There is always something good I had forgotten or didn't notice.

Nevertheless I must say you cannot direct a Part forward in the zodiac. I believe D was called the Point (degree) precisely because nothing was there —yet! You cannot progress nothing—a zodiac degree with nothing there. Second, the forward through the zodiac notion of a directed Point (D) destroys the entire complex or Part.

A + B - C = D

A/B = C/D

Line AD = Line BC

But the reciprocal will move forward (directed C in B's place).

Similarly you cannot aspect a Point that is D with nothing there. An aspect, say a trine to Fortuna, occurs only when Fortuna is transited by a conjunction.

I have not forgotten the Vedic concept of planets aspecting houses. It will not prove an exception. For example, Saturn is said to aspect its third house or sign, that is form a forward sextile. While a planet may aspect an area of the zodiac, it cannot reflect or cast rays from an empty point. This Saturn cannot reach A/B or C.

Let's use a hypothetical example which is common—natal Jupiter trine Fortuna. Our ancient astrologer would simply tell the native to initiate matters at the time of year covering a week before and after the Suns conjunction to Fortuna. This of course would be subject to yearly modifications considered by circumstance and the ephemeris.

The reader now knows our astrologer would see this native as extremely fortunate, especially when Jupiter was conjunct Fortuna and its intermittents, transiting Jupiter trine Fortuna and transiting Jupiter trine Fortuna—that is fifth and ninth positions, one of which would be transiting Jupiter conjunct natal Jupiter trine Fortuna. There would be a lucky Moon conjunction for a day each month. And a two-week transiting solar conjunction period each year.

Since this chapter is all about moving backwards, perhaps from nothing, it is an ideal place to look at something present in Vedic astrology—the aspect cast to a house without planets.

I'll use Jupiter as an illustration. All planets cast a 180 degree aspect according to the Vedics and Jupiter also casts the trine aspect, 120 degrees—that is, five and nine houses from its position.

It might be argued and I'm sure it has been that the degree 120 degrees from Jupiter is sensitized. The writing of a Vedic delineation clearing implies the empty house is sensitized. I suggest that these empty houses are like points. They await transits - the Moon each month, the Sun each year, etc. What is really being noted here is a planetary affinity for certain aspect angles. These affinities naturally fall in certain houses and we may regard them as enhanced houses. In practical Vedic delineation, usually only the heavies—Saturn, Jupiter, and Mars—are noted to empty houses. In Ancient Hindu Astrology for the Modern Western Astrologer, James T. Braha says:

> All planets aspect the seventh house from themselves. Mars aspects the fourth, seventh and eighth house from itself. Jupiter aspects the fifth, seventh and ninth house from itself. Saturn aspects the third, seventh and tenth house from itself.

On the same page he uses the example of how strong the empty seventh is from a stellium. True, of course, and I add it is transited every month by the Moon for two and a half days.

Even more important that any one or two conjuncted Parts is the overall intensification of the Sun and Moon. Remember only Fortuna and Spirit reach all three Ascendants, Sun, Moon, Ascendant. This reaffirms the higher state of the 20 additional major solar and lunar Parts (ASC + B - Sun, ASC + B - Moon) with their reciprocals, for these Parts can reach two Ascendants, ASC + Sun, or ASC + Moon.

Finally I'd like to close this chapter with an illustration. Thumbing through the files I came upon Lisa Steinberg's chart. She was the child abuse case of the year in 1987 when she died after a beating by her stepfather, Joel Steinberg, in Greenwich Village. He had battered both Lisa and her mother over a protracted period of time. He overdid it that time and she was pronounced brain dead on November 2, 1987 with the Moon in Pisces.

Again, synastry, midpoints, transits and progressions may all complete the conjunction to the Point (D).

Natal Fortuna at 14 Scorpio conversely progresses to 8 Scorpio, the transiting of the Sun on November 1, 1987. On November 2, 1987 transiting Sun at 9 Scorpio was conjunct transiting Pluto at 9 Scorpio (conjunct Lisa's progressed Fortuna).

Her Part of Death is at 2 Scorpio 17. Remember cusp Parts like Death (ASC + 8th - Moon = Death) need two conjunctions, one at B and the other at the Point (D).

Lisa's natal midpoint Saturn/Neptune, which I will read simply as Victim, is conjunct Death is at 0 Scorpio 50. This leaves an incomplete complex. We have ASC + 8th (nothing) - Moon = Death (conjunct Saturn/Neptune).

There is nothing in transits, progressions or natal to conjunct Lisa's eighth house 3 Aquarius cusp. I turned to Joel Steinberg's chart. His Pluto is at 2 Leo 22. Approximately three days earlier his rage was triggered as transiting Moon opposed his Pluto from early Aquarius, setting off his deadly rage. His daughter's eighth house cusp is 3 Aquarius.

Such is the simplicity and subtlety of conjunctions in the Arabian system.

That I called her the child abuse case of the year for 1987 was not a flippant remark nor was it a coincidence of any sort. Lisa's Ascendant was at 3 Cancer between U.S. Independence Venus and Jupiter. Check the most notorious U.S. crimes. Cancer is always present. It was strong in O.J.'s, Nicole's and Ron's chart.

I offer that the consistency of this observation upholds the validity of the U.S. July 4, 1776 chart as the prime U.S. chart. Hedda Nussbaum, Lisa's mother (born August 8, 1942), with her disfigured nose, was in the papers for weeks and then again at Joel's trial. Moon probably early Cancer. I felt 2 Cancer plus, Jupiter 13 Cancer conjunct U.S. Sun, afflicted by natal Sun/Saturn at 12 Cancer, Venus at 19 Cancer near U.S. Mercury, conjunct U.S. Sun/Mercury.

Returning to Lisa, that same deadly Moon transited her Spirit by conjunction some thirty-eight hours after conjuncting her Aquarius eighth house cusp. At 22 Aquarius her Spirit connected the unstable transiting Moon and natal Uranus to her Ascendants as it separated

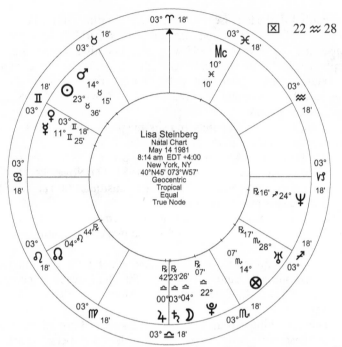

⊠ 22 ≈ 28

Lisa Steinberg
Natal Chart
May 14 1981
8:14 am EDT +4:00
New York, NY
40°N45' 073°W57'
Geocentric
Tropical
Equal
True Node

(Converse) solar arc Fortuna 8 ♏ ♂ transiting ☉ 9 ♏, transiting ♇ 9 ♏ on Novmeber 1, 1987. Death 2 ♏ 17 ♂ ♄/♆ 0 ♏ 50 (ASC + 8th - ☽ = Death). Rage in J. Steinberg triggered by transiting ☽ 2 ♓ ☍ his Pluto, conjunct her eighth—about three days prior to her death.

from Spirit (remember the orbs). Uranus at 28 Scorpio is the modern ruler of her eighth house.

Note that the exact conjunctions of the transiting Moon to her Spirit formed a partile trine with her natal Pluto, respectively 22 Aquarius and 22 Libra.

In negative situations trines should be read as greased paths to perdition. Here this transit enhanced Lisa's position as the object of Joel's rage.

Years ago I bought *Planetary Containment* by John Sandbach and Ron Ballard. It has 990 combinations of three-planet sequences (990 you say and scoff and run). Just remember you have sequences in your chart, about ten or eleven of them. The most important are those in one sign, that is a stellium.

The Moon in its monthly passage always transits your planets in the same order. This is your rut, your wagon wheel tracks in the dirt, your pattern of habit.

Joel Steinberg was born May 25, 1941. Speculatively I gave him a Leo Ascendant. It fit and I no longer have the case history to refer to. I didn't bother with minutes: Saturn, 20 Taurus; Uranus, 26 Taurus; Moon, 27 Taurus; Jupiter, 29 Taurus.

Saturn matters, e. g. frustration, led to volatility (Uranus) bringing on emotional reactions (Moon) leading to excess (Jupiter). Such was the bare bones dynamic of his rage. He was an absolute control freak. Saturn/Pluto at 26 Gemini conjunct Mercury at 23 Gemini—control by his mental perspective. Mars/Pluto at 19 Taurus conjunct Saturn at 20 Taurus—the ultimate control freak.

For those of you who may be interested in violent degrees, his Mars/Pluto, Saturn, Uranus, Moon, and Jupiter are all in violent degrees.

Could an astrologer have foreseen death here? If the astrologer were familiar with the situation (remember, the court astrologer was) the knowledge of this man beating this child would have been seen as extremely dangerous. The above is a glance at his solar chart. Now go back and tie it to the Arabian work on Lisa. The key is his Pluto opposition her equal house eighth cusp—always hit by the Moon.

In a balance chart of her Pluto (using it as an Ascendant at 22 Libra), his Saturn at 20 Taurus is conjunct its eighth at 22 Taurus.

Saturn was a deadly affliction as the Moon made its monthly conjunction to Spirit at 22 Aquarius. I have shown the example step by step. I have repeated the equation and the concepts until I'm tired of writing "conjunction." This is not a statistical study. Use the techniques. Watch them work. I have, and in your working of them you may validate my thesis for yourselves. The techniques are simple, but they will take practice and a certain mental self-discipline. The best place to start is your own chart. Then move to people you know well—family, files, or through fame. Another way that will give practice is to work from the events. Check ASC + Venus - Saturn and ASC + Saturn - Venus in Liz Taylor's separation (January 7, 1996).

The Trines of Jupiter and the Squares of Saturn

T he mind is stimulated by intense work. This resulted in an ongoing development in understanding the Parts and the nature of the probable forecasting system of the ancients.

Early this year I was driving home from work and the tarot card Triumph, or the Charioteer, popped into my mind. Its main connections are the fleeting nature of Triumph, which cannot last, and the tension involved in controlling the horses, where different natures make them turn away from each other.

The number of the Charioteer is VII in the Major Arcana. I had recently written of the Vedic concept of Jupiter casting a trine into an empty house and explained that every month the Moon transited these houses, five and nine to Jupiter. Moon-Jupiter is the aspect of luck.

In noting the transits of Jupiter and Saturn to the natal positions of Fortuna and Spirit I have used both square and trine for both Jupiter and Saturn.

I believe it should be the trines of Jupiter giving three periods of Fortune in its cycle and the squares of Saturn giving four periods of misfortune in its cycle. The term Fortunes would have applied to Jupiter and the term Lots to Saturn.

The Fortunes of Jupiter and the Lots of Saturn. "Lot" always has a fated unhappy edge to it. "My lot in life" is seldom a happy statement.

And of course three Fortunes and four Lots equal seven, the number of the Charioteer. The reader may take that to the extent he wants. The charioteer did clarify the concept in my mind.

Mohammed did not impose fatalism as theological dogma upon the Arabs. The sense of fate was deeply ingrained in the Semitic peoples long before the Parts, which preceded the Prophet by at least 1,000 years.

It is an error and assumption to state that the concept of fate robs one of his initiative. It does for some, but more important not for most, who note that if the bad times must come, then so must the good ones, and act according to the circumstances. If resignation is the general attitude for the Lots of Saturn, then initiative and daring would prevail during the Fortunes of Jupiter.

Fortuna and Spirit are the most important points of the chart, being the only two that can integrate the three Ascendants, Sun, Moon, Ascendant. This would indicate general periods of inescapable good or bad luck covering quite a few houses.

The positions of the Ascendants and Jupiter and Saturn would make each man's luck and its timing unique—all this the briefest of review.

Surely no man waits four years for a Jupiter trine nor reflects on the problems of the next Saturn square. Fortuna and Spirit are just that everyday breed, most equal of equals, of the solar and lunar Parts.

The solar and lunar Parts, twenty-two of them as previously listed, are the foundation Parts because each of them generate two Ascendants, Ascendant—Sun or Ascendant—Moon increasing the likelihood of an event occurring. Let's be clear: This was an event-oriented astrology in an event-oriented society. No king was ever told of inner transformation by getting in touch with his feminine side as he learned the lessons of Saturn. In a period too hardscabble for much introspection, the astrologer might have found himself the central figure in some more special occasion such as a drawing and quartering. "Let my next astrologer take a lesson from the fate of this fool" might well be the king's final muttering.

The laying out of twenty-two solar and lunar Parts created a rich tapestry of astrological potential. The astrologer now had no long waits of years, but could pretty much judge the natal chart on a horary basis, watching transits to the various Points. The Parts, when transited by Jupiter conjunctions, were the minor Fortunes and when transited by Saturn were the minor Lots.

ASC + Mars - Sun = solar Mars conjunct transiting Jupiter: time of war or great enterprises. Work some fire pictures and proliferations.

ASC + Venus - Sun = solar Venus conjunct transiting Mars: Our king is after a lady.

The astrologer of course has the reciprocal ASC + Sun - Venus. Now he may add the pictures: ASC + Venus - Mars (red dress). ASC + Mars - Venus (wallflower).

Should he not be on overload by now but perhaps wishing to increase favor with the king and build his purse, he could do the proliferations.

ASC + Venus - Sun = Solar Venus conjunct transiting Mars
Transiting Mars + Venus - Moon

Transit Mars + Venus - Jupiter
Since Western astrology only counts to two, a fundamental error in thought occurred. "There are so many Parts. Therefore they're useless. That has nothing to do with the fact that I don't understand them." It is not the number of Parts. Once they're recognized as midpoints, which are chosen by content, there is just the right amount.

Take the preceding example involving ASC + Venus - Sun = solar Venus conjunct transiting Mars. The reciprocal would be a general enhancement making the pictures more specific, indicating an attitude or house.

The proliferations are of extreme importance. They direct the planetary energy directly to the Point, (D).

It is the Point (D) when conjuncted that has directed the energy to the Ascendant.

To do your own research and verification, I suggest you start with your own chart. Work with the conjunction of Jupiter and Saturn to your Fortuna and Spirit. Branch out to the trines of Jupiter and the squares of Saturn. These are intermittent in energy, requiring other conjunctions to Fortuna and Spirit to activate them (for example, the transiting Moon each month).

Check some specific areas of your own chart. Use horary principles, whether in a natal or event chart. The failure of a Part to work or the absence of a conjunction to a Part which apparently would obviously be present does no damage to the system.

I make that assertion by experience because the Parts do not always punch in. The matter at hand came about through other chart potentials. My proof of this is the Vedic yoga or combination. The texts lay them out by subject and thus there may be several or dozens of combinations more or less dealing with an end result.

For example, here and there, I dealt with the Part of Death at length. Deciphered it is Ascendant/8th = Moon/Death conjunct transiting killing planet. The eighth also needs a conjunction of another killing planet or strongly enhancing planet for Death's conjuncting planet. For example, a good Jupiter can be a killing planet too—all planets can kill. A Part is only one yoga. Others for the same matter may be present or accomplish the same end without the presence of the Part. Such is the lesson of the Vedic listing of yogas.

This chapter should fine tune whatever you have learned from this text. It works and you'll confirm it for yourself.

This is as good a time as any to note in passing that whatever the relationship of the Vedic and Arabic system to each other, whoever came first, or whether they originated their systems independently, the single most important conclusion is their agreement on the Ascendant. With its daily wealth of 360 degrees, it individualizes the chart. The

Arabic system also strikes a strong blow for transits, its very nature indicating a need for a discriminating understanding of them.

One of the potentially rich areas for research would be the concept, implicit in the Arabian system, that it is not many transits that deal a blow, literally or figuratively, but one transit reaching a combination of the chart's natal planets and Ascendant. Furthermore, the enhanced power of this transit would come by direct influence on it. This is the lesson of the proliferations which activate the transiting conjunction to the Point (D) of the Part exactly as the conjunction activates the Ascendant.

$$A/B = C/D$$
$$(A') \ D/B' = C'/D'$$

Arabian Parts:
The Part of Death

The Part of Death (ASC + 8th - Moon = Death) was the first Arabic Part I ever heard of It was in Grant Lewi's *Astrology for the Millions*. He delineated the charts of Hitler and Mussolini, using the Part of Death. Taking some moral high ground of his times, he stated that his readers were not highly evolved enough to handle this Part.

No way to deal with an Aquarian. Needless to say I did eventually get to know the formula of Death and other Parts.

Properly speaking the Part of Death is the lunar Part of the eighth house cusp and in delineating it I'll show more of the nature of the Parts and how they work.

Death is an ancient Part, but just one of any number that can be formed by the algebraic equation A + B - C = D.

When a cusp or degree is used at B, two planets in two conjunctions to the two points or degrees B and D are necessary to close the circuit. One or both Points (B and D) with natal conjunctions would delineate but not activate the complex. This requires a transit or synastry contact. Progressions and solar arcs also might activate it, probably to a lesser degree. As in the modern concept of progression plus transit, a transit would be needed.

In my chart, Mars conjuncts the eighth or B and Moon is conjunct Death or D. Natally the circuits are closed, showing a character condition. When conjunctions hit those points the circuit is closed. With the involvement of the fast planets I suppose my circuits have been closed more than once, the point being that appropriate planets would be needed at appropriate times.

The appropriate planets might well be the natural significators of death when together; that is, Mars and Saturn or one of these in combination with my personal death dealing planets, the rulers of the seventh, eighth and third (eighth from the eithth). In my chart that would

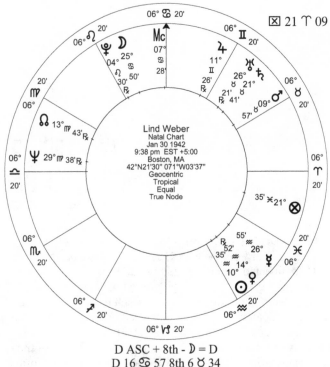

⊠ 21 ♈ 09

Lind Weber
Natal Chart
Jan 30 1942
9:38 pm EST +5:00
Boston, MA
42°N21'30" 071°W03'37"
Geocentric
Tropical
Equal
True Node

D ASC + 8th - ☽ = D
D 16 ♋ 57 8th 6 ♉ 34
Example: transiting ♂ 6 ♌ transiting ♄ 16 ♎
Later: transiting ☉ 6 ♉ transiting ☽ 16 ♋

be Jupiter of the natal third house. Mars duplicates as ruler of the seventh and Venus rules the eighth.

Here the matter is considerably narrowed. I need the double transit of some combination of Mars, Saturn, Venus, Jupiter. In these times I have little personal fear of being drawn and quartered, clearly a Mars-Jupiter-Saturn event.

This must also occur at an appropriate period, say when Fortuna or Spirit are under the influence of one of these. Suitable progressions and transits would be needed. It would need to be at an appropriate period in my life, or it might just be the onslaught of some lunar crisis, but not death. It might involve inheritance, debt, a health crisis, an operation, or a clearing of the decks in some area.

Death might come at an intermittent period. Let us suppose that Mars and Saturn are ninety degrees respectively from the eighth and Death at 6 Leo and 16 Libra. Obviously the circuit is not closed. I am enjoying full health.

In the month when the transiting Sun hits 6 Taurus as the Moon passes through mid Cancer, I suddenly sicken and die under the deadly

Mars-Saturn double light complex, with Moon conjunct Death square Saturn and Sun conjunct eighth square Mars.

Here another point must be made. The Parts work and as you use them you will be amazed, but not every Part shows up with its circuit closed for a given situation. The Arabian Parts form one type of yoga. For example, someone might die with the eighth house cusp and Death unaspected by conjunction. Instead, Mars-Saturn and Sun-Moon. Moon-Saturn might appear with some of his death dealing planets. A midpoint of Mars/Saturn might conjunct the Ascendant, Midheaven, Moon, ruler of the Ascendant, etc. Again, a combination of appropriate transits, synastry, progressions and solar arcs would be needed.

I do disappearance charts. Disappearance is a euphemism for an unfound body. Truly there are few disappearances despite whatever the authorities say or loved ones hope. Death is clear in these charts. I did one once where I noted that Mars and Saturn formed a close midpoint to the Midheaven. In this event chart no further work was needed. I didn't waste time doing Arabian Parts.

In another chapter I will deal with the orbs of these conjunctions, but I will note here that my Moon is within conjunctive orb of the Part of Death according to Al-Biruni. Mars obviously is conjunct the eighth house cusp.

I break stones and mount them in walls as a stonemason—my career of thirty years. During this same period I have also been involved with fighting cocks. Most of my astrology involves eighth house matters, including female clients who are involved in obsessive attractions.

In my chart note Mars, Saturn, and Uranus in the eighth house with a mutual reception bringing Venus there. Never underestimate the value of planets as significators when you delineate your charts: Mars-fighting cocks, Saturn-stones, Uranus-astrology, Venus-women—all in an eighth house context.

As for me, I've spent much of my life following obsessions—Venus/Pluto = Mars in eighth house. Work the conjunct midpoints.

I came to appreciate the potential of the Arabian Parts as they punched in on event charts. Of course I had many phantom hits by squares and oppositions, etc., that did not close the circuit before I understood what I'm attempting to explain.

Department Store Collapse

As I come across deadly charts I continue to punch the Parts in. Above is the chart of an event we all followed courtesy of *The Moun-*

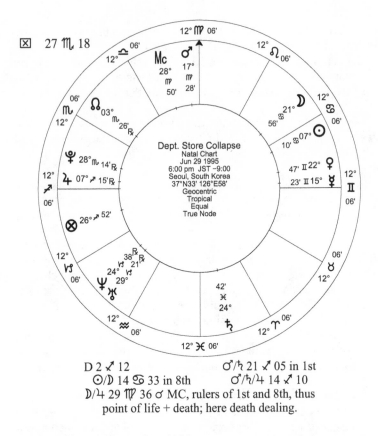

⊠ 27 ♏ 18

Mc ♂
28° 17°
♍ ♍
50' 28'

12° ♎ 06'

12° ♏ 06'

♏ ♌ 03°
♏ 26' ℞

♇ 28° ♏ 14' ℞

12° ♐
06'
♃ 07° ♐ 15' ℞

⊗ 26° ♐ 52'

12° ♑
06'
℞ ℞
38° 21° ℞
24° ♑
♆ 29° ♑

♅

12° ♒
06'

12° ♓ 06'

Dept. Store Collapse
Natal Chart
Jun 29 1995
6:00 pm JST −9:00
Seoul, South Korea
37°N33' 126°E58'
Geocentric
Tropical
Equal
True Node

12° ♍ 06'

12° ♌ 06'

☽ 21°
56'

12° ♋
06'

☉ 07°
10' ♋

♀ 22°
47' ♊
☿ 15°
23' ♊

12° ♊
06'

06'
42'
♓
24°

♄ 12° ♈ 06'

12° ♉
06'

D 2 ♐ 12   ♂/♄ 21 ♐ 05 in 1st
☉/☽ 14 ♋ 33 in 8th   ♂/♄/♃ 14 ♐ 10
☽/♃ 29 ♍ 36 ♂ MC, rulers of 1st and 8th, thus
point of life + death; here death dealing.

tain Astrologer, November 1995.

In this death chart the two circuits are closed with Jupiter, the first house ruler, conjunct Death in the first house and Sun/Moon conjunct the eighth house cusp. Here Sun/Moon from the eighth house are quincunx the Ascendant with Moon sesquisquare the Ascendant and the Sun quincunx Jupiter.

Note that Mars is conjunct the secondary axis as I'll term the point where the Arabian Part complex has its common midpoint. Note that Saturn opposes the same. Note the easy opposition Mars opposition Saturn trine Sun/Moon with the outlet in the eighth house.

Midpoints of oppositions may be read in either or both squares. Here, Mars/Saturn falls in the first and/or the seventh house: Mars/Saturn 21 Sagittarius 05, Mars/Saturn/Jupiter 14 Sagittarius 10, Sun/Moon 14 Cancer 33.

There is the deadly complex as well: Mars, Saturn, Sun, Moon, and first and eighth house cusps all in exact quincunx from the eighth and the ruler of the first, Jupiter, involved.

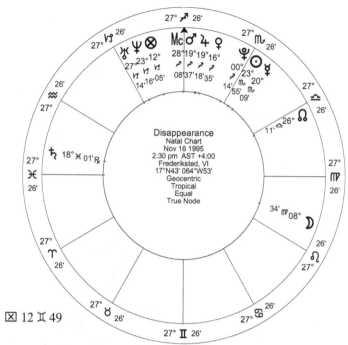

Death ASC + 8th (EH) - ☽ = D 16 ♉ 18 D, 8th without conjunction
☌ ♂/♄ 3 ♓ 49   ☉ ☽ ♂ ♄ integrate

Both the Arabian Part of Death and the Mars-Saturn-Sun-Moon yoga were perfectly closed. This illustrates another important point with the Parts. It usually takes more than just the Part contacted by conjunction to bring about a major matter.

Disappearance of Two Sisters

Recently two sisters disappeared on the island of St. Croix, U.S. Virgins Islands. They were Palestinians and the older sister drove to school to pick up the younger. The time used is when they left the school, the last time they were seen.

I have not done this chart and we'll let the chips fall where they may. Because of environmental and cultural perspectives I have a sense of foreboding. I also know the car and possessions were found

Note Mars square Saturn, then same with mutual reception Neptune making the violent triad. Venus, Ruler of the eighth house, in degree of hunting, as is Pluto (15 Sagittarius, 0 Sagittarius). Mars, Jupiter, and Saturn all in eighth duad.

Other violent degrees include Moon in death in the street—body in the ditch degree; Neptune, ruler of Ascendant, in abuse of power degree.

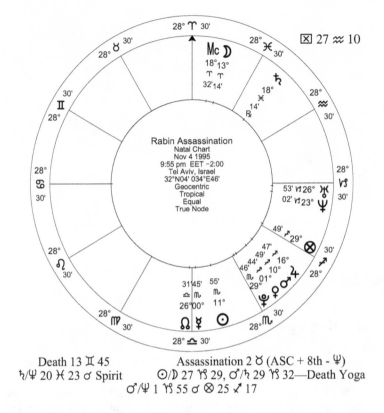

Death 13 ♊ 45   Assassination 2 ♉ (ASC + 8th - ♆)
♄/♆ 20 ♓ 23 ♂ Spirit   ☉/☽ 27 ♑ 29, ♂/♄ 29 ♑ 32—Death Yoga
                           ♂/♆ 1 ♑ 55 ♂ ⊗ 25 ♐ 17

Sun/Moon in degree of deliberate execution quincunx Saturn from the
eighth cusp. Mars-Saturn-Sun-Moon integrate; Mars square Saturn, Sun
trine Saturn, Moon square Mars, and Sun/Moon quincunx Saturn.

Here Death is not conjuncted; nor is the eighth house cusp. The
North Node is itself a point.

Rabin Assassination

Another chart that struck a strong chord in the psyches of several
countries was the assassination of Yitzhak Rabin.

Death at 13 Gemini and Assassination (ASC + 8th - Neptune) have no
conjunctions. Saturn/Neptune or the victim is conjunct Spirit. This states
he was a karmic victim. Note the complex falls on the cusp of the eighth.
Note ASC/Sun 18 Virgo 14, exactly opposition Saturn within one minute
of orb. Note Mars/Saturn, Sun/Moon hovering around the Uranus-Neptune conjunction, everything in opposition to the Ascendant from the Descendent cusp. This is the death yoga for this chart. Death to a leader of the
people through political/religious confusion in public.

When the Part of Death does not kick in, move directly to Mars, Saturn, Sun, Moon. Note how the mutual reception Saturn-Neptune enhances the entire statement, mutual reception Neptune trine Ascendant for victim by beliefs, and mutual reception Saturn/Mars/Saturn = Neptune for violent death (Mars Saturn Neptune).

Yes, the assassin is a patriot, not a psychotic as seen by the mutual solstice points of Venus to Mars/Saturn and Mars/Saturn to Venus. Mutual solstice points are extremely powerful. Note Mars-Uranus in the train wreck chart and Uranus-Pluto in my natal chart.

Before moving on to the final chart in this chapter, I do not believe that points of any sort will work without conjunctions. Try this. You will see immediate results. In passing, a conjunction to a point may have a wide orb because if functioning within a midpoint complex *the orb is halved*.

The methodology of the charts in this chapter is simple. I did not research my files for perfect charts. Nor am I interested in scientific or statistical points of view. Those boxes are too small for astrology.

I have made my case from several recent events that the reader is familiar with as well as just another unfortunate disappearance.

School Bus Hit by Train

The entire nation and CNN viewers everywhere moaned the loss of the seven children in the bus at the railroad crossing. I was without television, but still managed to conjure graphic mental images.

Note 29 degrees rising. Not good. The Part of Death at 9 Taurus 33 fails to make a conjunction to the eighth. A horribly afflicted Venus ruler of the Ascendant in Scorpio in the eighth duad in the terrible degree (eighth duad) with Moon just over it, also in the eighth duad at 19 Scorpio.

Spirit at 11 Libra is conjunct Mercury, ruler of the twelfth, here in the Libra first. In an event chart the ruler of the twelfth is not burdened with socially redeeming qualities.

Note that the ruler of the Ascendant, Venus, is also the ruler of the eighth. It is the planet of life and death. Venus/Saturn is at 18 Capricorn conjunct Neptune, Venus/Mars = Moon/Pluto.

We move to Mars/Saturn, which falls between the Uranus Neptune conjunction. Mars/ Uranus = crash, Mars Saturn Neptune = violent death, Saturn/Neptune = victims, and Uranus/Neptune = confusion, sudden fuel failure.

Sun/Moon is at 10 Scorpio within orb of Fortuna. Neither light is happy here.

Now for some linkage. Sun/Moon seventy-five degrees from Mars/Saturn. Seventy-five degrees is an aspect of excess; check it in

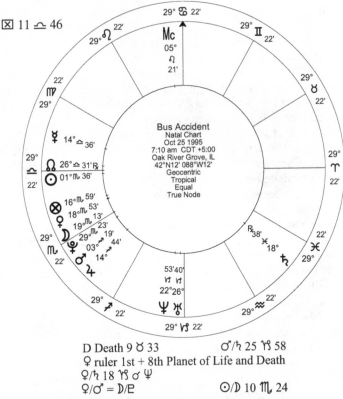

⊠ 11 ♎ 46

29° ♋ 22'

Mc
05°
♌
21'

29° ♊ 22'

29° ♌ 22'

22'
♍
29°

29° ♉ 22'

☿ 14° ♎ 36'

Bus Accident
Natal Chart
Oct 25 1995
7:10 am CDT +5:00
Oak River Grove, IL
42°N12' 088°W12'
Geocentric
Tropical
Equal
True Node

29°
♎
22'

☊ 26° ♎ 31' ℞
☉ 01° ♏ 36'

29° ♈ 22'

⊗ 16° ♏ 59'
♀ 18° ♏ 53'
19° ♏ 23'
29° ♏ 19'
29°
♏
22'
03° ♐ 44'
☽ ♇ 14°
♂
♃

℞ 38'

22'
♓ 29'

♄ ⚸ 18°

29° ♐ 22'

53'40"
♈ ♈
22°26°
♅ ♆

29° ♒ 22'

29° ♑ 22'

D Death 9 ♉ 33   ♂/♄ 25 ♑ 58
♀ ruler 1st + 8th Planet of Life and Death
♀/♄ 18 ♑ ♂ ♆
♀/♂ = ☽/♇   ☉/☽ 10 ♏ 24

your flies. Seventy-five degrees is also the midpoint distance from an
equal house eighth house cusp to the Ascendant.

All cusp Parts were used with equal house originally. This always
gives whole and midpoint aspect angles to the Ascendant of thirty degree multiples or fifteen degree multiple remainders. It is historically
known that house systems came after the Parts. The second part of the
statement is arithmetic.

So once again we did not find the Part of Death in conjunction but
we hit a good Mars/Saturn complex as well as the deadly Mars, Saturn,
Sun, Moon. Once again note the deadly enhancement of mutual reception Saturn-Neptune.

But there is an even better one: the mutual solstice points of Mars
and Uranus where they fall on each other to the minute; solstice Mars,
26 Capricorn 41; solstice Uranus, 3 Sagittarius 19.

This chart is reexamined with Fortuna and Spirit.

Thank you Grant Lewi wherever you are. You patronized the
wrong Aquarian. And thanks to Danuta Miller who always talks about
solstice points.

The Parts of Jupiter

I n describing the twenty-two major Parts, there are four Parts of Jupiter.

ASC + Jupiter - Sun, reciprocal ASC + Sun - Jupiter

ASC + Jupiter - Moon, reciprocal ASC + Moon - Jupiter

Reading the works of Zoller and Granite you will see that ASC + Jupiter - Sun appears under various names. Why not? You can symbolize many things with either Sun or Jupiter and even more in combination.

This is important to remember in dealing with the Parts. As noted, Death does not always refer to physical death. It is also simply the lunar Part of the eighth.

You may assess a person's overall luck with these four Parts, remembering that each is different. Solar and lunar Fortuna differ and their reciprocals alter polarities of action and circumstance. C is the dynamic planet in the equation which seeks the planet conjunct the Part to complete the complex or close the circuit.

ASC + Jupiter - Sun. The lucky man is aided by solar force. This is physical and soul protection. This is confidence applied to his natural luck (ASC + Jupiter, A/B). According to the planet that conjuncts the solar Part of Jupiter, the deeds or circumstances would vary, as would the luck. Saturn conjunct Point D would represent a devastating attack on this type of luck.

With the reciprocal, here Jupiter C being dynamic, the action is more Jupiter or jovian—the charmed life, favorable circumstances etc. Again Saturn attacks. Another example would be Venus conjunct the point. Here matters would occur through charm or diplomacy or in a social setting. Mercury might relate to studies and the like.

Sun-Jupiter relates to sons in the Vedic tradition. Mars to Sun-Jupiter Parts is not necessarily malefic. The fire planets all aid each other. The complex Sun, Mars, Jupiter is a war signature in a mundane chart, or that of a soldier. It is also the signature of great enterprise and accomplishment.

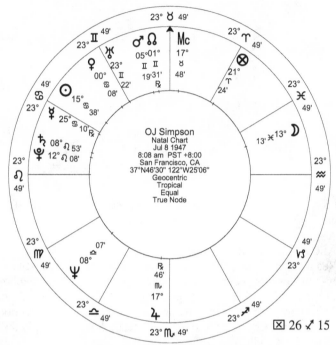

Trial and Verdict ♃ 9-10 ♐ ♂ OJ Spirit 15 ♐
Trial/Verdict ♃/♅ 2-3 ♑ ☍ U.S. Independence ♀, 2 ♋ and Jupiter, 5 ♋
OJ Fortuna 21 ♈ ♂ Trial ASC 20 ♈ (monthly transit ☽, transit ☉ early
Apirl 1995. Also ☿ and ♀ transited both in Spring 1995.
Trial Fortuna 28 ♑ ♂ trial ♅ 26 ♑ with
trial ☉ 4 ♒ ♂ both; ☉ rules OJ's Asc.
Trial ruler of Asc, void-of-course ♂ 29 ♌ ♂ OJ's Asc.

Such a fire enterprise when it fails will fail for fire reasons; for example, Sun, hubris; Mars, violence or destruction or recklessness; Jupiter, excess, overconfidence.

ASC + Jupiter - Moon is both day-to-day luck and karmic luck. All lunar Parts are thus both common and karmic rewards, the easy life. It also represents family luck. Moon-Jupiter is the pot of gold and happiness. Sun-Jupiter is ten feet tall and bulletproof according to Travis Tritt.

The lunar reciprocal would be a very passive form of luck, but one who complains.

Should the Parts not kick in by planetary conjunction, seek midpoint conjunctions to them. Failing this, seek other planetary complexes or yogas (involving at least three planets and/or conditions, e.g. the Mars-Saturn-Sun-Moon complex in death work).

In O. J. Simpson's chart, ASC + Jupiter - Sun = solar Part of Jupiter at 24 Sagittarius 45 conjunct his progressed Moon at 24 Sagittarius 32 at the time of the murders; Jupiter/ASC at 6 Libra 11 conjunct natal Neptune at 8 Libra 08, Moon/Jupiter at 21 Capricorn 40 conjunct transiting event Neptune retrograde 22 Capricorn 46. Note that O. J.'s natal eighth house cusp is Pisces, ruled by Jupiter—luck in a deadly situation. Mars/Jupiter at 26 Leo 53 is conjunct his Ascendant at 24 Leo 36. Finally his Sun/Jupiter "my ass is saved" is 17 Virgo 10, the degree of mentally unbalanced attack which also figured in Lizzie Borden (Barbara Watters).

You may set up his other Jupiter Parts for yourself. The man is lucky. But an examination of his Cancer midpoints from twelve to twenty-seven degrees leads me to believe that he will not regain his popularity.

Note Uranus/ASC at 24 Cancer 01 conjunct U.S. Independence Mercury.

His acquittal may also be seen in his early Cancer midpoints with U.S. Venus at 2 Cancer and U.S. Jupiter at 5 Cancer. The void-of-course Moon is also indicative of getting away with things, as is Jupiter-Uranus and mutual receptions; these last two are a factor in his event charts (trial and verdict).

Great U.S. superstars and the most notorious U.S. crimes and criminals will usually show extremely heavy Cancer—my vote for the Independence chart.

What Does A Part Mean?

The Arabian Part is A + B - C = D. In any midpoint book C/D = Planet B will give you the planetary meaning of the Part. The genius of the Arabian system is that C/D energy brought to A/B is brought to the Ascendant by planet B.

Thus, ASC + Venus - Mars = D (conjunct transiting Saturn) might mean a violent lovers quarrel or the robbery of money - a personal Venus event of an unfortunate nature either way. In using the midpoint book, seek the proper type of event or meaning before finding B on the opposite page. The above is Mars/Saturn = Venus.

The Parts as named represent only one or some of the Parts potential. Learn midpoints and you will automatically know the Parts. For example, Death covers other eighth house matters in terms of the Moon.

The planets of the Parts may be read by house rulership or sortilege, planetary energy, or as significators of things or qualities. Example: Sun as ruler of the third house is brother, perception, as energy, life force, will, and significator of ego and gold.

I do not use the fancy names, but try to understand the energies. With three planets it can be subtle—and revealing.

Using once again Al-Biruni's lurid Part of Torture, 9th + Saturn - Moon, the reader now knows that this refers to a soldier on the losing side or a captured spy.

Analyzing it, it simply says the worst (Saturn) of luck (ninth) in the now (Moon) and for a losing soldier that was torture. Today this means being forced off the corporate board. Note that as a cusp Part, two conjunctions were needed.

The closure of D by conjunction in the above might mean escape (D conjunct Jupiter), or the more dire consequence if Mars, Saturn, or the ruler of bad houses (eighth or twelfth) made the conjunction.

Remember, you don't need all the parts at once. If you wish to avoid learning how to write many new glyphs, just write out the formula and name.

1. ASC + Sun - Jupiter = Spiritual undertaking
2. ASC + Sun - Jupiter = War

Both D's are conjunct transiting Mars (ASC/Sun = Jupiter/Mars).

1. Spiritual undertaking for the soul
2. Violent expansion by leader

Read the lists of Parts. Work the midpoint books. With what you've read here it will come together quickly.

If you have the computer zodiacal midpoint sort, look for the Ascendant midpoints. Those midpoints conjunct or in opposition (C/D) form Arabian Parts to the Ascendant midpoint A/B.

Already complete natally, the transit conjunction to one of the C/D poles would certainly activate these planets through the Ascendant. Since at a glance you may not know which is C or D, set up the calculation. Since the natal planet has itself activated the complex, the important planet is C or the "in terms of" planet which defines the nature of the overall complex.

Visually the line AD = BC will allow the finding of C.

Examples We're All Asking About

Hillary Clinton

Why are they picking on poor Hillary? Will Whitewater ever go away?

I received this chart from another astrologer and unfortunately do not have a source. I believe it is correct.

Hillary Clinton's Fortuna falls in her sixth at 26 Scorpio. Her natal Mercury/Jupiter is conjunct Fortuna. Much of her success in life is based on her mental efforts, which must always show as the three Ascendants are involved.

At the inauguration of Bill Clinton, transiting Pluto was at 22 Scorpio conjunct Mercury, Hillary's Ascendant ruler. The long and short of it is that through the Mercury/Jupiter midpoint transiting Pluto has never been away from her Fortuna during the entire Clinton presidency. In a general sense Pluto always means complications, and usually involves power used to dominate or financial matters. Here in the sixth, the tenth of the ninth of law, it accurately describes Whitewater.

The transit of Pluto in Sagittarius will not help. Transiting Pluto conjunct her natal Jupiter pits this conjunction against her first house.

The action cannot be favorable. Jupiter on the sixth house side of the seventh, Pluto, ruler of the sixth, is the ruler of the Scorpio twelfth to her Sagittarius seventh.

I do not know the moment that her Whitewater papers were found. I'll assume transiting Uranus was still at 29 Capricorn. As it passed into Aquarius she was in the news again every day. Note her Spirit at 3 Aquarius. The consequences of this find will follow her throughout 1996—contacting three Ascendants. Spin control fails. No one controls Uranus.

Her progressed Fortuna in 1995 (ASC + Moon - progressed Sun) is

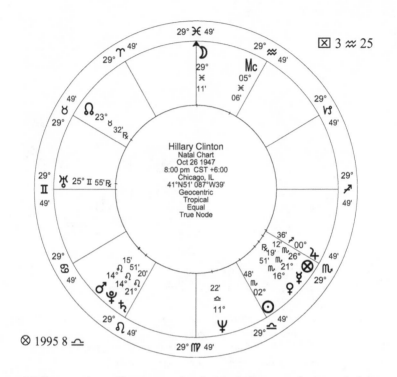

at 8 Libra, conjunct Neptune and under the influence of a strongly karmic Moon at 29 Pisces. The progressed Fortuna conjunct Neptune
cannot be positive. It relates all Ascendants to the career tenth
house—money problems (Moon ruler of the second house) that she
can do little about (twenty-ninth degree). Synthesized, it also symbolizes marital problems.

Mars-Saturn-Pluto is the signature of the control freak. From her
third house, she is one. The staffer told the truth regarding the White
House travel agency when he said he felt her words were orders. (A
mini generation of control freaks arose at this time due to the long stay
of Mars in Leo. The house is the key to synthesis. I know one with this
in twelfth who does not know and will not see or believe that he is one.

Our ancient astrologer flying his magic carpet through time, having
received an hour or two of instruction on Uranus, Neptune, and Pluto,
would advise Hillary to lay low for the duration, knowing full well she
won't with Mars, Saturn, and Pluto in the Leo third.

The time to watch is late March/early April 1996 as transiting Saturn arrives at her Moon. Transiting Pluto at 3 Sagittarius forms a midpoint with Mercury at 27 Scorpio, her Fortuna.

This is written on January 21, 1996. The principle illustrated here is
the power of the transit when the three Ascendants are involved. Hil-

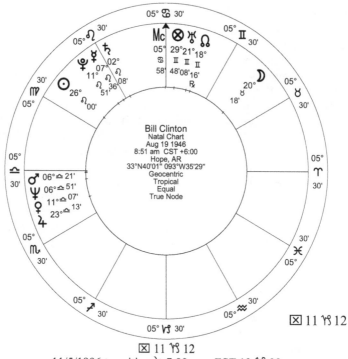

Bill Clinton
Natal Chart
Aug 19 1946
8:51 am CST +6:00
Hope, AR
33°N40'01" 093°W35'29"
Geocentric
Tropical
Equal
True Node

☒ 11 ♑ 12

☒ 11 ♑ 12
11/5/1996 transiting ♃ 7:00 a.m. EST 13 ♑ 32
ASC + ♃ - ☉ = 2 ♐ (♂ transiting ♇)
11/5/1996 transiting ♀ 8 ♎

lary twists and turns. Whitewater endures. (Around September 14, 1996, she was hit with a multimillion dollar suit over Whitewater.)

Bill Clinton

Will President Clinton be reelected?

While many may not like to hear this, a bit of luck is as good a way to get elected as any. I saw Clinton winning his first term because Bush's Moons were bad.

Clinton has quite a bit of luck in his chart: exalted Moon, Sun in its rulership Leo, the ruler of the Ascendant in the first (this alone is unusual). Jupiter/Uranus = Sun, with Jupiter strong in Fire. He escapes most of his scrapes.

Ruler of the tenth in the eighth: Here, Clinton's Moon, is often an assassination signature. However, his Moon is exalted and the Moon/Jupiter the midpoint of luck is conjunct the Part of Assassination. He will not be assassinated.

Mars-Neptune, especially in Libra, is bad. Mars is in detriment and

Neptune is eight houses from its rulership Pisces. It is an aspect of mis-timing. One fights when he should retreat and vice versa. One can see no error in the action in progress.

In the first house it invites attack and means the native continually brings it on himself. Only Mars-Neptune in Libra in the first would de-cide to take on the problem of gays in the military at his inauguration.

Mars, Jupiter, and Neptune together, especially by sign, indicate one time big trouble. Note Venus in the equation. Clinton in the first half of January 1996, learned that the Jennifer Flowers sexual harass-ment case could go forward and suffered the embarrassment of the dis-covery of the Hillary Whitewater papers.

But Venus is in Libra, in his first house with Jupiter. He will escape. His progressed Venus in 1996 at 26 Scorpio is conjunct Hillary's pro-gressed Fortuna, which has been afflicted. Here he affects her.

Returning to the Parts, Fortuna and progressed Fortuna are not con-junct Jupiter or Saturn. But turning to Spirit we see that transiting Jupi-ter is conjunct Spirit in late January and remains there throughout 1996, being direct in its final sweep at 13 Capricorn on election day. This is Moon/Jupiter = Sun applied to Ascendant—as lucky as you can get.

Meanwhile, throughout the year transiting Pluto is conjunct the so-lar Part of Jupiter: ASC + Jupiter - Sun = solar Jupiter at 2 Sagittarius. This is Sun/Pluto = Jupiter applied to the Ascendant, the signature of major accomplishment.

Clinton wins. The upset of Uranus is his winning. Opposite his Sat-urn, it is defanged by a series of easy oppositions.

Note that with the entry of Pluto into Sagittarius came his get-tough policy in Yugoslavia (late November/December 1995). He'll stay tough because he'll be lucky with that (transiting Pluto conjunct solar Part of Jupiter).

A glance at Clinton's Cancer midpoints also reveals his power, with many conjunctions to the U.S. Independence Chart.

On Election Day 1996 transiting Venus at 8 Libra has just swept over his Ascendant, Mars, and Neptune. In context it must be viewed positively. Hopefully there will be no new woman trouble.

Prince Charles

Will Charles be king?

The question of Charles' succession to the throne has been dis-cussed in astrology circles for years. I understand the consensus is that he will not be king. I have not read the articles or heard the lectures so I'm not familiar with the reasoning.

My attempt to answer the question will be done using the Parts.

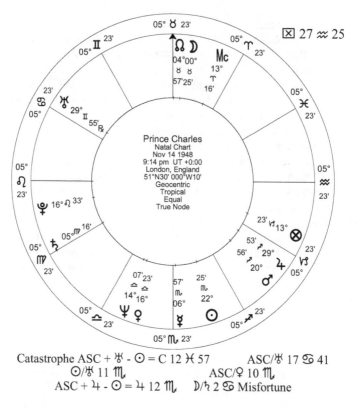

05° ♉ 23'

☒ 27 ≈ 25

05° ♊ 23'

05° ♈ 23'

Ω ☽
04°00'
♉ ♉
57'25'

Mc
13°
♈
16'

05°
♓
23'

23'
♋
05°

♅
29°
♊
55' ℞

05°
♌
23'

Prince Charles
Natal Chart
Nov 14 1948
9:14 pm UT +0:00
London, England
51°N30' 000°W10'
Geocentric
Tropical
Equal
True Node

05°
≈
23'

♇ 16°♌ 33'

05°♍ 16'

23' ♑ 13°
⊗

05°
♍
23'

♄

53'
56' ♐ 29°
20°

23'
♑
05°

07'23'
♎ ♎
14° 16°

57' 25'
♏ ♏
06° 22°

♂
♃

05° ♎ 23'

Ψ ♀

☿ ☉

05° ♐ 23'

05° ♏ 23'

Catastrophe ASC + ♅ - ☉ = C 12 ♓ 57   ASC/♅ 17 ♋ 41
☉/♅ 11 ♏   ASC/♀ 10 ♏
ASC + ♃ - ☉ = ♃ 12 ♏   ☽/♄ 2 ♋ Misfortune

Presently he is in line to be king. He has woman trouble—big time; mother, wife, and mistress. Is there astrological evidence indicating his failure to rule?

The overthrow or abdication of a ruler is covered by Sun/Uranus or Sun-Uranus combinations and aspects.

I'm quite sure that strong developments took place in the Charles-Diana saga as transiting Saturn conjuncted Spirit at 27 Aquarius and later Catastrophe or the solar Part of Uranus at 12 Pisces. I'm not lazy. I just haven't saved my *National Enquirers*.

What is interesting is the transit of Jupiter to conjunct his Fortuna at 13 Capricorn through 1996 with the final direct transit in November 1996. Will Charles liberate himself? Uranus is now in his seventh of marriage, which is also the tenth of the tenth of rulers and kings.

The energy of Sun-Uranus, when expressed, is sudden and leaves no way back. The pivotal issue of his becoming king is women. The following are Parts and planetary pictures of this situation:

ASC + Uranus - Venus = 18 Aries 59

Sun + Uranus - Venus = 5 Leo 57, conjunct Charles' Ascendant

Moon + Uranus - Sun = 8 Sagittarius 07

ASC + Venus - Sun = 29 Gemini 16, conjunct Charles' Uranus, this the solar Part of Venus involving two Ascendants; Venus is the ruler of the tenth.

Finally, natal Sun/Uranus at 11 Virgo is conjunct ASC/Venus at 10 Virgo and the solar Part of Jupiter (ASC = Jupiter - Sun) at 12 Virgo. This would need to be set off by fast planets.

Solar arc Moon/Uranus of volatility passed over his natal ASC/Uranus in 1995, and is in orb for two more years.

Misfortune, the practical essence of Moon/Saturn, is at two Cancer. This forms a yod to transiting Uranus early Aquarius and transiting Pluto, early Sagittarius in 1996. He may rebel against the entire matter.

Charles is extremely fixed—Ascendant, Moon, Sun—so he may need a lot of time to turn around. In late 1999 and 2000, repeated simultaneous conjunctions of transiting Neptune, ruler of the eighth house, to his Descendent and transiting Pluto to his lunar Part of Saturn (ASC + Saturn - Moon) may bring about abdication. This final picture is not one of power. Pluto/Moon = Saturn brought to the Ascendant.

Camilla Parker Bowles, the other woman, was born in London at 7:00 AM DGDT, July 17, 1947. (*The Mountain Astrologer,* March 1995 Data page, from biography (B). (I subsequently used her chart in the Fortuna Spirit examples.)

Her Part of Spirit at 16 Leo is conjunct Charles' natal Pluto at 16 Leo. The following midpoints by synastry are present:

Charles	Camilla
Moon/Saturn	Neptune
Mars/Neptune	Jupiter—one time big trouble
Moon/Uranus	North Node
Sun/Uranus	Mars
Moon/Saturn	Moon/Uranus
Venus/Mars	Jupiter
Mars/Jupiter	Venus/Mars

I'm betting on love.

Arabian Parts
and Midpoints

A natal or transiting midpoint influences a Part when it conjuncts it. The natal midpoint functions on a character level. The transiting midpoint actively mixes the planetary energies and brings events.

Parts and midpoints may be noted together. What is important is to know what you're seeking so that cumbersome pictures are not built up.

The designated Part is always at the Point, D, where it awaits the influence of the transit conjunction or, as noted, some other type of conjunction, e.g. synastry or progression. The significance of this is immediately seen with clear examples.

Let us say that Venus/Mars, sexuality, diplomacy, love, relating is conjunct Fortuna. Influencing three Ascendants on a character level this would in some way form significant patterns in the native's life—of course, modified by house, sign, and chart. The transit of Saturn to Fortuna would stifle these patterns, as the transit of Jupiter would make them flourish.

Make no mistake. The Arabian System is midpoints par excellence. With the fatalistic mindset of their culture, fate was not merely to be accepted, one would seek out his luck as well. If he could not avoid fate, he meant to enjoy fortune anyway.

One of the interesting facets of the Parts is that when the Moon is utilized, there is a period for any Part every month. It would be the better portion of a day encompassing full moiety or average orb of six plus degrees approaching and separating with emphasis on the partile conjunction as one of four choices. The other two would be an aspect as the transiting Moon approached or separated. The fourth would be stimulation through a proliferation, but this would involve planets other that the Moon. Not many would look for this, unless you're the type who progresses your Moon to go to the supermarket.

By this simple method our astrologer could set up the appropriate times for practically anything. This was important as much of his work involved lunations and planetary entrances into signs. Such practical knowledge was indispensable in horary work.

This now clear, it is easy to see that the ancient astrologers used the Parts they needed in terms of the matter at hand, in the main for immediate practical results.

Another way to increase opportunities is the transiting midpoints. If not Mars or Jupiter to Fortuna, perhaps he could project Mars/Jupiter.

Ascendant + Moon - Sun = Fortuna conjunct Mars/Jupiter and we have our warrior aspect—or that of great enterprises.

Can you make a Part from a midpoint? The idea occurred to me after reading Noel Tyl's work on solar arcing midpoints. I was working on disappearances then, and had not yet understood the parts.

Most disappearances are violent. I began with the midpoints of the violent triad Mars, Saturn, and Neptune which are:

Mars/Saturn Death
Mars/Neptune Attack, attacker
Saturn/Neptune Victim
ASC + Mars/Saturn - Sun = solar Part of Death
ASC + Mars/Neptune - Sun = solar Part of Attack
ASC + Saturn/Neptune - Sun = solar Part of Victim.

I also did the lunar series. The midpoint pairs are Ascendant/Mars/Saturn (A/B) and Sun/Point degree awaiting conjunction (C/D). The reader knows I had results with these for the matters and energies were brought to two Ascendants, Ascendant and Sun, or Ascendant and Moon.

I never got beyond generally using the Sun and Moon at C—in terms of the Sun or Moon, but if I went back I could use Uranus for random attacks or gunshot, Pluto for crimes involving power, sadism or control, for example rape, serial murder or terrorism; Jupiter for thrill crimes or those involving religion or beliefs. While terrorism has a belief core or motive, it is primarily an act seeking to alter the balance of power—thus Pluto.

In passing I've chosen Mars, Saturn, Neptune as the violent triad after much reading and work.

Alone they can mean:
Mars—violence, killer
Saturn—death, victim, dharma
Neptune—karma, astral body
Repeatedly, murderers who are psychically ignorant describe out

of body experiences at the time of violence (Mars/Neptune). In the victim, Saturn, Saturn/Neptune is a complete description of the victim's condition. In death, Saturn of dharma and lessons meet karmic Neptune. The other planets modify or describe the violence.

Should you come across a Mars, Saturn, Uranus combination, say gunshot or air plane crash, look at the condition of Neptune. You will be able to tie it to these planets.

Presently, midpoint work is heavily influenced by the Uranian schools. Any midpoint system works when used skillfully and judiciously. What I wish to point out is that the Arabian system emphasizes the power of the conjunction.

In your Uranian trees, move to just the conjunction and oppositions. You will have ninety percent of the matter.

If you can solar arc a midpoint can you solar arc a Part? Yes, but remember it arcs conversely because you have Ascendant + Planet - Sun (progressed to show solar arc). The higher degree Sun means a lower degree solar arc Point (D). The C Planet is the appropriate one to arc because it is dynamic. In position B it would be passive.

Any Solar Part can be arced conversely at a degree a year. Today we use the progressed motion of the Sun as the solar arc. I've achieved such results with Fortuna that I seldom go further. Any Part can be arced conversely at a degree a year. Remember that were you actually doing a computation, the solar arc increase would appear at C.

The arcing or directing of Parts to a higher zodiac degree is an error. The formula proves it. The forward direction of D cannot yield the midpoint C/D. Here let us say C is progressed Sun and D its Fortuna. Now A/B = C progressed/D converse.

Of Apheta
and Anareta

T hese are the ancient terms, I believe in Greek. Apheta means life dealing [planet] and Anareta death dealing [planet]. During the coming years we'll hear a lot about them as the old texts are studied and published, in particular by Project Hindsight.

What follows are my insights after finishing this work on the Parts—where I am today.

There are three planets and three points of Apheta. There are three planets and three points for Anareta. They are the same.

The planets are Sun, Moon and Ruler of the Ascendant. The ruler of the Ascendant is a third choice here unless powerful. See Bill Clinton's Venus. The ruler of the Ascendant may be any of the seven planets, but within that chart it will be Apheta, Anareta, or neutral. The points are Ascendant, Fortuna and Spirit, the last two for containing the three Ascendants.

In order for death to come, the Ascendants must be hit hard. Charles Carter noted that it takes a "train" (of afflictions, progressions, transits, etc.) to kill.

Simply stated the Apheta is the best and the Anareta the worst of these placements. Bill Clinton's chart is an interesting example.

The Apheta are chosen first by position twenty degrees below the Ascendant, ten above; ten degrees below the Descendant, twenty above, twenty degrees after the tenth or the Midheaven and twenty degrees into the ninth. This is the conventional rendering. De Vore's (*Encyclopedia of Astrology*) system is slightly different—twenty-fifth degree of the eighth house to the twenty-fifth degree of the eleventh house; from the twenty-fifth degree of the twelfth house to the twenty-fifth degree of the first house; and from the twenty-fifth degree of the sixth house to the twenty-fifth degree of the seventh house.

Thus Bill Clinton's Fortuna is Apheta, as is his Venus. His Sun and

Spirit are neutral. His Moon is Anareta. His Ascendant would be taken out of the equation Apheta by position; it is attacked by Mars and Neptune and enhanced by Venus and Jupiter.

Venus conjunct the Ascendant is attacked by Mars and Neptune, and also rules the eighth.

Moon is Anareta but exalted. An exalted Pluto and Sun in Leo do less harm that usual by their squares.

Fortuna is Apheta but when transited by conjunct Saturn, Mars, and Neptune are awakened at the Ascendant. Saturn conjunct Fortuna unites the violent triad Mars-Saturn-Neptune and of course the three Ascendants—Ascendant, Sun, Moon. Here it is clearly the best—with a Jupiter conjunction—and the worst— with a Saturn conjunction.

Am I delineating here? Not quite, just giving the reader a glimpse into a concept that is not as easy as it seems, which is one of reasons it has fallen into disuse and confusion.

Whatever the detail, Fortuna and Spirit, by integrating the three Ascendants, clearly have Apheta or Anareta properties according to their condition.

My approach: Look for the best and the worst and work accordingly. Transiting Saturn conjunct Fortuna and Spirit are the worst. Transiting Jupiter conjunct Fortuna and Spirit are the best. Both are true because of the enhanced Ascendant and the exalted Moon in the eighth house.

I would say Clinton has good times and bad times, rather than good planets versus bad planets. His basic luck will prevail most of the time; Sun, Moon, Venus in good signs.

His Sun, though not in an Apheta position, is the least subject to affliction. It is also backed by Jupiter/Uranus at 22 Leo conjunct Sun. Round and round we go.

My conclusion right here is that there can be more than one of each, Apheta or Anareta and that a given one can switch hit (Bill Clinton's Fortuna). Round and round we go.

Orbs and the Arabian Parts

The November 1995 edition of *The Mountain Astrologer* carried an interesting article on aspect orbs by Irish astrologer Maurice McCann. Evidently working from Al-Biruni through Alan Leo, he documented the use of wider orbs until the mid-twentieth century use of narrower orbs came to be accepted. This probably occurred under Vedic, Uranian, and computer influences. (While the Vedics often use narrow orbs in some of their work, they also call a planet within orb for the major aspects when it is in the appropriate sign. Thus Venus at 1 Aries would be square Mars at 29 Cancer.) While the article covers the matter in detail, including some small disagreement on the size of wider orbs, generally the disagreement is within a degree or two.

In ancient times separating aspects were acknowledged, some even holding them as slightly more important and wider in orb. Separating aspects have lost attention in contemporary astrology.

Regarding the Arabian Parts, McCann writes: "The Arab astrologer Al-Biruni was the first to write that the planets had orbs." Since Al-Biruni was probably a compiler of data as opposed to an originator, we may assume he drew his conclusions about the orbs from his studies or travel—simply that he noted and perhaps refined earlier orb use.

The orbs of Al-Biruni are as follows: Sun, 15 degrees; Moon, 12 degrees; Mars, 8 degrees; Jupiter, 9 degrees; and Saturn, 9 degrees. Mercury and Venus are 7 degrees. Al-Biruni goes further, noting that the orb between any two planets depends on their *moiety*. This means their average orb. The moiety of a Sun-Moon aspect is 13.5 degrees. A Mercury Jupiter aspect has a moiety of eight degrees.

McCann notes that the French astrologer Claude Dariot (1533-1594), giving an example of moiety using a Moon-Saturn sextile, implied that the orb retained its size with minor aspects. He further notes that Alan Leo, king of orb studies in the late nineteenth century and early twentieth century, neglected to deal with the semisextile and the quincunx.

Implicit in all this is the possibility that orbs exist independent of aspects. It is one step further to the argument proposed by others that all zodiacal distances are some form of aspect. This is the implicit position of midpoint practitioners who hold that energy between two planets gathers at the midpoint zodiacal distance. Implicit again here would be sign relationship. Thus an out of sign conjunction carries the nature of a semisextile. This would be the position of a Vedic astrologer.

The Arabian Parts then would seem to be part of a general system of astrology that allowed wide orbs. My burnout triggered when transiting Saturn was at 12 Pisces, nine degrees from my Fortuna at 21 Pisces.

In the predictive system of the Arabian Parts it would then appear that the transit conjunctions of the Jupiter Fortunes and the Saturn Lots were in effect at nine degrees before and after Fortuna and Spirit.

Since these were the foundation of long term forecasts, it is clear that a period of time was being blocked out, that the person or event would be under a Jupiter or Saturn influence during that time, and that finer, more careful astrological work could be done at that time when matters at hand might be somewhat known. At that time both the overall astrological tradition and the proliferations could be brought to bear on the framework* and its matters.

All astrology being viewed from a horary perspective at that time, a narrowing of choice would have been automatically sought by the astrologer.

Framework—my term for the Jupiter or Saturn conjunction to Fortuna or Spirit, the timing of the highs and lows in a life. This also refers to their intermittencies, the trines of Jupiter, and the squares and opposition of Saturn.

It was clear to our astrologer that matters did not happen at a precise moment in all cases, but rather that he should capture the flow of the entire matter. For example, a marriage between two royal heirs involved negotiations, engagement, marriage, honeymoon and marital adjustment as well as the resolution of all the side deals involving property, titles, and political favors given and received. The moment of "I do" in the ceremony like the precise position of Fortuna is more a reference than a defining reality of what is actually a process. Such a referent would be used for future forecasts.

Similarly, a trip involved purpose, preparation, the casting off of the ship, or leaving the city gates followed by the trip—its events and final success or failure with its consequences.

Take death as a final example. The cessations of life would be preceded by loss of luck, danger, or illness, and followed by a settling of estate and certainly by effects on the family, or perhaps an indication of recognition or the potter's field. Again the moment of death is actually a reference point.

Today, horary practitioners look for a concentration of factors indicating a given matter as well as exact aspects. Nor do they look only for exact aspects by planets, angles, houses, and signs. Partile aspects are an aid and at times give precise timing, but they are only one tool.

When transiting Saturn approaching Fortuna triggered my burnout as indicated by progressed Sun to Pluto, the resultant C/D or Sun/transiting Saturn energy was four and a half degrees off the A/B or Ascendant/Moon midpoint. It would intensify in the coming months.

The Arabian Parts system, ever pragmatic, noted a period of time and returned to deal with it. "Death stalks you in your twenty-fifth year. Return for a reading on your twenty fifth birthday."

Partile aspects, always important, are never all important. Transit conjunctions to Arabian Parts work like Robert Hand's analogy of the approaching plane that not everyone hears or sees at the same time. The plane passes overhead and then recedes into the distance.

Natal conjunctions to the Parts relate to character. They remain with the person or event. Orb, approach, separation, house, sign and aspect define them. Progressions may modify them and transits trigger them.

Conjunctions to the Parts by synastry are dynamic and their influence begins immediately. Certainly close and partile conjunctions in synastry are the strongest, but allow some orb in your interpretations. Alfred Witte's Saturn at 21 Pisces 42 is conjunct my Fortuna at 21 Pisces 36. Whatever I do I am not entirely comfortable with the man or his system, this despite his Mercury-Venus-Moon conjunct my Mercury. Joel Steinberg's Pluto was opposite Lisa Steinberg's eighth house cusp in her Part of Death, but picking up the monthly transit of the Moon to the eighth, it supplied one of the two necessary conjunctions.

Progressing and Enhancing the Parts

s with my first book I continue writing even as the manuscript is being edited and typed for publication. One of the remaining tasks was to write something on the conjunctions to the Parts themselves. This fell into place with some small paragraphs at the end of a small chapter on planetary orbs.*

For a moment it seemed natural to write a paragraph on progressed planetary conjunctions to the Parts, in particular Fortuna and Spirit. I realized in the last months I'd put together more than could be listed under orbs.

Fortuna is ASC + Moon - Sun, a solar Part as noted by the Sun at C. To progress Fortuna, subtract the progressed Sun. The position of Fortuna is now zodiacally lower in degree as it moves backward though the signs. You may do this with any of the solar Parts. I hold this as the origin of converse directions. As noted elsewhere I don't believe there is any justification for converse progressions in the ephemeris.

Spirit is progressed as a reciprocal, ASC + progressed Sun - Moon. It moves forward in the zodiac, as would the reciprocal of any progressed solar part. The relationship of the Part and its reciprocal to the Ascendant axis is preserved.

It is possible and unprovable, but in the example of converse progressed Fortuna it might be said that converse directions came before forward directions or that solar arcs developed from the Arabian Parts. An interesting thought and a fool's errand.

The above is covered elsewhere in this book but I wanted to join it with an inherent factor of solar arcs and progressions. Their degrees are themselves just points. Progressed Sun or a progressed or solar arced planet conjunct Fortuna is nothing conjunct nothing until transited by an actual planet or contacted by a synastry conjunction.

In the instance of progressed Sun conjunct Fortuna, the awaited planet by conjunction at D, or Fortuna, would have the same effect but be filtered through the progressed Sun, indicating a solar emphasis.

A + B - C = D

A + B - C + Fortuna conjunct progressed Sun conjunct transiting Mars

The key to synthesis then moves to the nature of progressions and arcs. Progressions tend to indicate changes over time, the bend in the river. Solar arcs are generally considered to represent activity and change in the material world. Progressions are change in character and modify both the solar arc and transits.

Note the difference between a progression or arc to a Part and the arcing or progression of a Part. Based on the dynamic C, the Part moves conversely through the zodiac, but that direct motion is achieved with the reciprocal.

As noted elsewhere, I only progress Fortuna and reciprocal Spirit. I get all I can handle. Time is against us all. Those of you who choose to go for overkill, may you enjoy the fruits of your efforts.

I recently found the chart of Alfred Witte in Sylvia Sherman and Jori Frank-Manski's *Uranian Astrology Guide Plus Ephemeris*.

His natal Fortuna is 5 Libra 48. In 1919, the year for publication of his seminal masterpiece, progressed Fortuna had moved to 24 Leo conjunct his North Node at 22 Leo conjunct Uranus at 20 Leo 47, well within orb of a conjunction to Uranus. (According to Sherman and Frank-Manske, this was a presentation or private printing of *Rules for Planetary Pictures* before it was formally published in 1928.)

In 1919 he was 41 years old. Unless the work was laid aside and the manuscript stashed, we may assume *Planetary Pictures* was strongly under the influence of transiting Uranus opposition natal Uranus.

His progressions for 1919 at his birthday, April 12, 1878, were Sun at 23 Aries, Moon at 20 Leo, Uranus retrograde at 23 Leo, Saturn at 26 Pisces, Jupiter at 4 Aquarius, Mars at 15 Gemini, Venus at 8 Pisces, and Mercury at 11 Taurus.

Note that the progressed Sun trined his progressed Uranus, which brought his natal Uranus closer to Fortuna. Sun-Uranus indicates genius. Fortuna conjunct Uranus was itself further enhanced by solar energies.

The transits themselves are more revealing and are noted for July 1, 1919 as I do not know the month of publication—Jupiter at 4 Cancer, Saturn at 25 Leo, Uranus retrograde at 1 Pisces, Neptune at 7 Leo, and Pluto at 6 Cancer.

Thus his midpoint work also was influenced by the conjunction of Saturn to Fortuna. Alan Leo called Saturn the planet of astrology. Note an exalted Jupiter squares his progressed Sun and he was under the

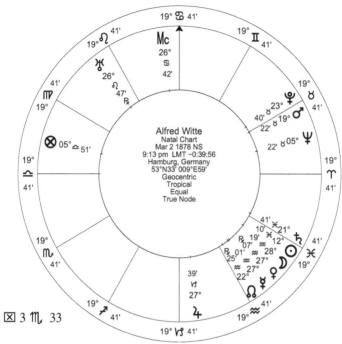

ASC + ☽ - solar arc ☉ 1919 = solar arc ⊗ 24 ♌
7/1/1919 transiting ♄ 25 ♌
4/12/1919 progressed ⛢ 23 ♌, progressed ☉ 24 ♌

In Sherman and Frank Manske's book the time 9:42 p.m. LMT is given. With this program that time gave a 24 ♎ 39 Ascendant. I elected to go with my original work. There is a variation in computer program Ascendants. I encountered it elsewhere. *Rules for Planetary Pictures* was formally published in 1928. 1919 from Sherman and Frank-Manske.

general influence of its wide trine to his Sun. Exalted Jupiter in Cancer was in the same sign as Pluto in his tenth house. Jupiter-Pluto is a signature of both great accomplishment and total fiasco.

For those who have had the patience to follow me this far, great enhancement of a Part occurs when the Part is triggered by conjunction and other planets are:

1. Conjunct square, opposition any of the components A, B, C.

2. When conjunct, square, opposition the midpoint A/B + C/D, the secondary axis.

3. When the reciprocal is itself transited by conjunction and a planet is conjunct square or opposition the Ascendant-Descendent axis.

Do the Parts
Always Work?

T he Parts do not always work in the sense that they belong to a fore-casting system based on the triggering of the Part in question. The Parts foretell the time to attempt, undertake, or avoid certain activities, or to mitigate certain states.

If a Part is not natally conjuncted, it is not in general operation. Two things must be remembered at this time. Any Part conceivable in a chart is conjunct the Moon for one day a month. Second, any general activity or state as indicated by a picture, that is a midpoint to a planet whether based on A/B or C/D, can in some charts show the same activity by other aspects and placements generating the same general energies.

Vedic astrology lists many such combinations called yogas or slokas with three or more part combinations indicating conditions generally categorized by houses. For example, a signature for death or wealth or marriage might involve three or more combinations which in themselves have at least three components each.

Regarding death, Charles Carter called it a "train of directions."

Transit conjunctions triggering Arabian Parts are only one tempo-rary yoga or sloka. The reading of some Vedic house yoga lists would clarify this matter for the reader. It is for this reason that I have little faith in so-called scientific or statistical astrology when carried too far.

Both perspectives also fail to take into consideration the nuances of what I've called the rolling signature; that is, the ever-changing posi-tion of the planets. I recently read that it has been more than 700 years since a Saturn-Pluto square had both planets in their respective signs.

Our astrologer bypassed much of this with his system. The frame-work of the Fortunes and Lots or Jupiter to Fortuna and Spirit and Sat-urn to Fortuna and Spirit are the true genius of his heritage. Jupiter or Saturn bear on all three Ascendants, Ascendant Sun, Moon for a gen-eral period of good or ill.

The Misfortunes of Fortuna

Somewhere in this text I noted that Fortuna was misnamed. I suspect this happened deliberately, for by misdirecting with a name involving luck the secret of the three Ascendants would remain hidden. This was highly successful, continuing right up to the present as the reader now realizes.

One of the many definitions of Fortuna that I've read is "a point of ease." That also is not quite correct. The position of Fortuna is always active, the Moon bringing the three Ascendants together about thirteen times a year. There is also a yearly conjunction of Sun, Mercury, and Venus, along with possible Mercury and Venus retrogrades and returns as a further possibility. Usually a person finds that whatever house Fortuna occupies is active, even in the absence of natal planets. Should the astrologer also use Spirit, the above would also apply.

Those who use Fortuna and other Parts have long noted their relationship to the ruler of the sign that Fortuna is in. This has nothing to do with Fortuna or the Part and everything to do with the transiting planet or synastry contact. The answer is the well known, but often forgotten "a ruler influences its sign and house." To which I will add: The ruler of a sign and house acts in accordance with planets in its rulership sign and house. This is according to J.H. Bhasin to whom I am also indebted for the Vedic concept of sudarshan where the Sun and Moon are read derivative house style as co-equal Ascendants. Saturn in Taurus or Libra means that the chart Venus is at all times under the influence of Saturn. The ruler of the sign and house with a stellium is another interesting example.

Moving directly to errors, Fortuna is generally considered to be fortunate. This is not so if the Ascendant, Sun, and Moon, notably two or three of the Ascendants, are heavily afflicted. A transit conjunction to Fortuna would then supercharge these natal afflictions.

Several years ago I formulated a list of violent degrees and published the findings in *Today's Astrologer*. Subsequently, in *Astro*

Data V by Lois Rodden I saw that almost all violent charts have at least two of the Ascendants in violent degrees. Three Ascendants in violent degrees is common. Ivy Goldstein-Jacobson notes that Fortuna is Misfortuna in the eighth, twelfth, Pisces, and Scorpio. I would add to that Capricorn and the Vedics would surely add the sixth. She was correct.

She was not correct in directing Fortuna forward in the zodiac. It directs conversely because the subtracted Sun increasing in degree leaves a smaller zodiacal remainder. I am indebted to her for her practical use of the Parts.

Stumbling along as we all do I made my own special mistakes, those beyond not using Fortuna or holding her to some strict interpretation. Much of my work is in eighth house matters where I made the erroneous conclusion that because Fortuna was related to good luck, it had little bearing in charts of evil and tragedy. The immensity of the mistake becomes clear when the concept of the three Ascendants is understood. When this book is behind me, I'm looking forward to reviewing some of my eighth house studies and charts. (There are now examples with event charts keyed to Fortuna and Spirit.)

I also often left Fortuna out of event charts, mistakenly thinking that a human chart was requisite. I suspect many of us do this with the new Moon where Fortuna-Spirit are exactly conjunct the Ascendant. In the full Moon, Fortuna and Spirit are naturally exactly conjunct the Descendent.

As all of us do, I haphazardly noted aspects other than the conjunction to Fortuna. They are of course real when Fortuna is activated by conjunction.

I am aware that the Vedics note aspects to empty houses. My considered answer would be the same. Much, and certainly enhanced, activation occurs at the time of the Moon's passing through the sign and house. Since the empty sign would hold no ricochet effect, moving the energy to A, B, C, I would continue to maintain that the conjunction is necessary. If the third house from Saturn, where Fortuna is, is aspected by Saturn, thus receiving a Saturn influence, Fortuna with no conjunction remains inactive. (The Vedic would maintain that the ruler of the sign and house was influenced by this Saturn). Gilbert Navarro forced me to refine and prove this which I did.

Introduction to
Practical Forecasting

What follows are the practical forecasting techniques as I believe they were used. I would say that our astrologer and those who came after him acquired special insights into the new Moon and worked Fortuna as noted.

This long usage allowed both to survive. There are no examples in this section because they are not needed. We all have natal charts and the lunations roll on. Do the work. See the results yourself. In general, use only degrees. Learn the zodiac by number.

There is only one Arabic Part Formula, for only A + B - C = D yields the dual midpoint complex A/B = C/D.

The Parts remain independent of any astrological traditions. Rather, they reveal highlighted planets, planetary pictures, and times as present in the chart at hand.

There is no reason why the Parts may not be used in the Vedic system. Since the ayanamsa affects all zodiac positions equally, the results are the same.

I hear the Trans-Neptunians exist and I hear they don't exist and I noted that someone said they were derived from Arabian Parts. I was not able to find any evidence of the last; thus, one could make Parts with them. And the asteroids too.

The Parts require hands-on work. Every planetary Part is precisely defined in midpoint books as C/D (conjunct planet) = B. No wrestlers' names are needed. You read from the completed Part—that is, with the specific conjunction planet of D.

The dynamics of the Formula A + B - C = D are as follows: A influenced by B in terms of C is triggered by D which unites the energies and carries them to A by dynamically completing a midpoint complex. They become clear with an understanding of the terms, the formula, and the D Point conjunction.

Fresh Look at the Lunation

Historically the lunation, in particular the new Moon has always been important. I feel certain the court astrologers of old erected it for their patrons, giving it a personal mundane context. A few astrologers use the lunation with people. Jan Spiller writes a lunation emphasis personal column in *Dell Horoscope* and I'd venture without asking my friend Sophia Mason that she does so routinely.

Coming from mundane work, I've attempted it, usually in my natal chart. I put it aside for reasons of time and mainly because I never got a clear fix on it.

I interpret a lunation strictly. The forward transits of the Sun and Moon and transits to the lunation Sun and Moon. Then, as we all do, note highlights and houses.

Did the ancients know something about lunations that we don't? I would answer yes and certainly that our astrologer did.

Each and every lunation, new, full, or quarter Moon, somewhere on the earth incorporates each of the 360 degrees on the Ascendant. The new Moon is most often used. Today we say it is the beginning of matters, but long ago it was also realized that it was the most powerful position of the Moon because Fortuna is exactly conjunct the Ascendant.

As with most of the Parts, the utter simplicity of mysteries proved the best disguise for centuries.

Who has a powerful lunation? When is a lunation powerful? Two questions, same answer. Whomever, whatever, wherever, a planet or planets aspect the new Moon Ascendant by conjunction, that is the lunation to note.

Purely natal conjunctions would be relatively passive, but the combination of lunation planet or planets conjunct lunation Ascendant conjunct natal or prior event planets is the lunation that must bring about matters.

In different places all planets get a turn at being conjunct the Ascendant. This is a strong lunation in terms of that planet for that place. If you are there and have a natal planet or planets conjunct the above, it will be personally active.

Ascendant/Moon = Sun/Fortuna

There is a second degree involved of tremendous power—the Ascendant-lunation midpoint. Contacts here, as noted elsewhere, further increase the power, as do the transits of the entire lunation cycle to this point. As the Sun and Moon are involved at the midpoint any other aspect is valid. These are the lunations that bring about major events or major personal changes.

Only one small bit of arithmetic is involved—the calculation of the Ascendant/lunation midpoint. According to Al-Biruni, orbs a little larger than modern usage are allowed.

In the next chapter, a method of noting the days is put forward. This may also be used on the lunation. Both the techniques deal with isolating solunar energy, relating it to the Ascendant, and noting a trigger planet at Fortuna (conjunct D).

Highlighting the Day

If the lunation showed the general trend for the month and noted those months of more than usual personal, place, or event significance, our astrologer was still in a quandary.

His royal patron, like most kings, was not very noble or bright or patient. In the manner of kings he demanded, calling for a daily reading. Usually these were minor matters—how he was getting along with his wives, matters at court, and concern for his gambling, usually with dice.

Modern astrologer Joyce Wehrmann put forward a diurnal system. She was personally interested in gambling, which spurred her development of the system as well as giving her an opportunity to test the system at any time.

Using the birth time, a daily chart is erected for the place of residence. This would advance about a degree for a day on the Midheaven, the Ascendant varying.

The chart is energized when planets contacting angles in the diurnal make strong aspects to the gambler's natal chart. In Wehrmann's words he was "on the wheel."

By most accounts the system is effective if one takes the time to practice and work with it. Naturally it can be used for other matters. What is no coincidence is the emphasis on angles.

On April 21, 1996, I was too tired to write or edit and decided to watch movies on the VCR instead. All the work I had to do nudged me through the day and suddenly the concept of transiting Fortuna fell into place. I lay there and mentally worked a couple of Fortunas.

I noted that transiting Fortuna moved forward in the zodiac at about eleven degrees a day.

What is transiting Fortuna? Natal ASC + transiting Moon - transiting Sun. It is the simultaneous transit of solar and lunar energies to the personal Ascendant. As it moves through a personal or mundane chart of any type, each planet in zodiacal sequence is contacted by this Fortuna, giving rise to a dynamic day of the month for each planet.

Natal ASC/transiting Moon = transiting Sun/transiting Fortuna (conjunct natal planet). Such a day draws the overall transiting energies available to the natal planet conjunct this Fortuna. Restated, the transiting solunar energy is carried to the natal planet conjunct transiting Fortuna and distributed by the transiting Sun and transiting Moon to the natal Ascendant. Having just happened into this we'll be verifying it together.

Why has it not been used? To say no one ever tried it would be absurd and I believe it was part of the known system before the Parts were lost, corrupted, and turned into a mystery.

The reason why this has not been used in modern times is that the Vedics, who use the concept of the three Ascendants (Sudarshan), routinely do not use the Parts.

Conversely, Western astrology, using the Parts, has failed to see the three Ascendants importance of Fortuna and Spirit and instead endlessly redefines them. Many definitions are true enough. The error is often an implied one—that such a definition is definitive. Fortuna varies from person to person and with each person from time to time, be it natal, progressed or transiting. By now the reader understands this would apply to Spirit and any other Part as well.

In the daily chart any other Part may be used as required by what is sought. One might use the proliferations. As in modern methods, there can be overkill. All the energy that is needed can be found in transiting Fortuna. If a transiting planet conjuncts the natal planet to be conjuncted by Fortuna, it is a far more dynamic Fortuna than the natal.

Natal ASC + transiting Moon - transiting Sun = transiting Fortuna (conjunct natal planet conjunct transiting planet)

Today there are few transitists. I have heard that Grant Lewi was one. During the time when I used horary a lot I used only transits, with good results. How do I think these transitists worked? By the horary law of three indicators to bring a matter to pass. At times a modern transitist would note three indicators. Another time he would have a hit with only one indicator. Another time he would have a miss, say with two indicators, and wonder why. In the last two examples the presence or absence of transiting Fortuna, or another Part conjunct one or more of the planets in question, might be the answer. Note that the yoga of transiting Fortuna can generate frequent times for activity involving any planet once a month. These times may be enhanced by whatever other planetary energy is present, for example transiting Fortuna conjunct your natal Saturn which is simultaneously aspected by transiting Mercury and transiting Mars.

The triggering of an Arabian complex of three parts, A, B, C, is more easily accomplished by one conjunction to D. This can occur at regular time intervals and can be looked for easily.

The triggering of a single planet by simultaneous transits, here at least three, occurs far less frequently. Nor would this triggering event be the planetary picture sought, and it would not necessarily have great personal significance as keynoted by the Parts use of the Ascendant.

Bear in mind that the Arab, Vedic, and horary astrologer all viewed planets as rulers of houses. If Mercury rules your twelfth house it will on occasion bring twelfth house type experiences in terms of its signs, Virgo or Gemini.

Again, the Parts are pictures or yogas or slokas, at least three factors indicating the potential for completion.

The Vedics who have used yogas for millennia know certain things. There is more than one yoga to indicate a matter. There is usually more than one such yoga in the chart. The chart for a rich man or a disaster may well each have several yogas denoting wealth or disaster.

Everything about the Arabian Parts, beginning with nomenclature (Fortunes, Lots, Fortuna), indicates that it was a pragmatic forecasting system. It apparently arose and was used in a culture that even before Mohammedanism believed in fate. The notion that those who believe in fate are weakened in their will or fail to act is a mistaken western psychological cliché, repeated so often that it is assumed to be true. The system of the Arabian Parts and the struggle of the Palestinian people over the last generation show that a belief in general fatedness is not in itself the fall into apathy. Fate and free will are flip sides of a coin. It's how we spend the coin that creates our destiny. Most understand this on some level. It is only religion ever seeking to manipulate the minds of men that says the coin has only one side.

In calculating a transiting Fortuna there are several approaches, all of which involve the Moon. Fortuna could be based on ephemeris time, time of transiting aspect, or the time of a past occurrence.

As a forecasting tool, ephemeris time with only the degree of the Sun and Moon is all the accuracy needed. This will yield the Fortuna of the day. The moon may be mentally moved forwards or backwards a degree every two hours.

It is important that you do it this way or you will not use it. Having made the rough calculation if an exact future time is needed (for example, to buy a lottery ticket), erect an exact chart or do the necessary calculations. Similarly, transiting Fortuna may be calculated exactly in an event chart.

April 28, 1996

Personal Ascendant 6 Libra	186
+0GMT transiting Moon 1 Virgo	151
	337
-0GMT transiting Sun 8 Taurus	38
0GMT Fortuna 29 Capricorn	299

Late afternoon and evening AST, April 28, 1996, transiting Fortuna will conjunct my natal Sun at 10 Aquarius. My only calculations would be the five numbers above. There is no need to write or note or connect anything else. It is done mentally. Transiting Fortuna is conjunct my Sun as I write.

When this book is behind me I'm looking forward to reviewing some of my charts in the light of this year's work on the Parts. There will be no second book.

Historical Sketch that Makes Sense

I haven't read too many books on the Arabian Parts but I suspect that a few historical notes form a more or less traditional early chapter. I'll continue the tradition. Observations scattered here and there in the text hopefully will add to the credibility of this history.

I believe the Parts were discovered by one Arabian astrologer. Knowledge of algebra plus immersion in astrology led to an intuitive breakthrough. Intuitive breakthroughs occur throughout history in human experience. This is often called the creative process, the muses. Sometimes the word Eureka! describes it. Often in such breakthroughs the actual moment is described. My breakthroughs are often of this type, occurring as I perform common tasks.

History indicates an almost certain oral tradition. Probably our astrologer taught several pupils. He or a successor probably formed a school with initiates and students.

All oral traditions are subject to distortion, incompleteness and manipulation. The Arabian Parts would prove no different.

There is a parlor game where the first player whispers something to a person next to him who in turn does the same. Usually played around a large table of people, by the time it returns to the ear of the first player, considerable change in content has taken place. The same occurs with rumor and gossip.

This distortion occurred over some period of time, generations or millennia—it does not matter. By then, this distortion, so widespread, became its own distorted tradition. Such was the situation by the time Al-Biruni collected the known parts in the early eleventh century. Al-Biruni himself was probably not an Arab. Certainly an astrologer, he may have collected Parts as today's astrologers collect data. He may well have had little more understanding of the Parts than a modern astrologer. That said, the debt owed to him is inestimable since his collection of the Parts and their subsequent resurgence kept them from vanishing. As I hope to show, they were fragile in their simplicity. In an oral tradition what is written is by nature incomplete and subjective. What is written is in effect lecture notes. Left out of such texts are the obvious or easily understood. I believe the Parts of the Ascendant were lost this way, too easily understood to be noted.

At the other extreme, the real secrets of the Parts were deliberately left out by or kept unknown from the writer. These secrets would be the conjunctions, the framework, and the proliferations, as well as some forecasting techniques. And unwittingly I see I have dealt with incompleteness, another generic problem of oral traditions.

Finally all oral traditions are subject to manipulation—leave out this, add that in, change that, place a slant here. The usual motive is power, whether ideological or economic. Take for ideological manipulation those teachers who believed or created semi-divine origin for the Parts. Take for economic reasons, the omission of knowledge of the conjunction. This single omission would lead to poorer forecasts. The initiate with knowledge of the conjunction would hold sway. This applies to other secrets of the Parts, the framework, proliferations, and the so-called unused Parts. As noted by De Vore, they were the lunar parts of Mars and Saturn.

The above is a brief essay on the corruption or change of any oral tradition.

Before the Parts were "lost," more precisely grievously misunderstood, two other factors occurred: one involving the basic formula of the Parts $A + B - C = D$, the second involving the very terminology of the Parts.

We have walked through swamps at night without lights for at least two millennia since the time of Manilius whose pseudo-Parts indicate the Parts were already lost by his time, at least to Manilius.

Al-Biruni faithfully listed all the variations known to him; by his time the formula had been set. As Al-Biruni wrote: "All Fortunes involve the beginning of the matter, the end of the matter and the casting off point or catalyst" (*The Fortunes of Astrology*, Robert Hurzt Granite Astro Computing Service, 1980, page 3).

Granite then reiterates using the example of the Part of Death, once in context and secondly to restate the "formula."

For the Point of Death we add the eighth cusp of Death and regeneration to the physical body of the Ascendant. Then we subtract the Moon, that giver and protector of life. So it is with all the Fortunes:

1. The beginning of the question
2. The end of the question
3. The casting off point, being the celestial body that interferes with the completion. It's like the knitted shawl of life, creation of the Universe.

Note Al-Biruni's chart, a self-sufficient and self-centered man, the success of his stratagem or inadvertency was secure with the midpoint focus to the Ascendant of Sun/Pluto and Mars/Jupiter. The combination Sun-Jupiter-Pluto was recently noted by the Magi Society as the picture for the greatest of successes. Note his Saturn just in orb of Spirit. The careful reader will note something.

We will never know if the error regarding C in the formula was error or deceit. That is a true secret. I incline to the second. Whatever else Al-Biruni was or was not, he was slick as gooseshit. He created the mystery. Confusion was complete.

The error or deceit involved C in the formula. Al-Biruni noted that a planetary energy was subtracted, not a number of degrees, but that one would take away the Sun or Moon or other planet. More than 900 years later Robert Granite repeats this error, this time surely in good faith.

First the subtraction of C is merely an algebraic function leading to the position of the unknown Point or D which becomes the designated position of the Part, completing the whole equation and giving its meaning.

Second, C is part of the dynamic midpoint C/D composed of the energy designating planet C which in the text I usually refer to as "in terms of." D is the designated Point or degree waiting for the triggering conjunction that will close the circuit of the midpoint complex: A/B = C/D. A/B is the passive or negative pole midpoint composed of the Ascendant A and a modifying energy B. C/D is the active midpoint composed of the planet C which defines the nature of the complex as in solar part or lunar part. The conjunct transiting planet, or any other type of conjunction (progression or synastry or midpoint or transiting midpoint) to D, is the trigger or closes the circuit.

Within each midpoint pair there is also positive and negative polarity.

$$
\begin{array}{ccc}
 & - & + \\
- & + & - + \\
\text{A/B} & = & \text{C/D}
\end{array}
$$

This in turn creates the spatially balanced geometric or linear version of the equation.

Line AD equals BC in zodiacal distance.

So much for the subtraction of planets.

As the Parts wandered through the near East and Mediterranean Europe they ran into linguistic difficulties which became semantic problems. Part, Point, Fortune, Lot ended up as synonyms for the midpoint complex here called Arabian Parts, the most used term. The other names are, in fact, precise terminology as utilized with the Parts system of forecasting.

Fortuna and Spirit are probably misnamed. Certainly Fortuna is as the reader will understand when he comes to the chapter on the framework. Here I have no intention of going against the tide. The terms Fortune and Fortuna are here very different.

As for the names and symbols of the Parts, they represent the most commonly applied use of the Part, a mnemonic use or plain sensationalism and good public relations like wrestlers' names.

By the end of the book I'm sure you'll know the example parts I could name Ripe Peach and Iron Staff.

Just as you're thinking that you've read several pages of highly concentrated assertion, most of the matters noted here have their own chapters in the text.

Just as unfound bodies are called missing persons and unsolved problems are called mysteries, the core issue remains the same, the failure to find the one or understand the other concealed in a euphemism.

The Mystery Was
Natural Understanding

The Parts of the Ascendant

The concept of the reciprocals and the concept of the proliferations were lost or in confusion precisely because their original users did not have to write them down since they automatically knew their positions. Anyone who has taken notes in college knows that one omits what he thinks he knows.

Carl Payne Tobey rediscovered the solar Part of the Ascendant in the twentieth century. Like many others who dealt with the Parts, he then chose to stand still. From the context of the book *Astrology of Inner Space* (Omen Press, Tucson, Arizona, 1973), he apparently only believed in the solar Parts.

The solar Part of the Ascendant is ASC + ASC - Sun = Solar Ascendant.

I interpolated the lunar Part of the Ascendant from this: ASC + ASC - Moon = Lunar Ascendant. I have used it extensively with hits and misses, not entirely understanding it until the spring of 1995.

I then realized I could make Ascendant Parts with the other planets and seeing them spread out outside my equal house natal chart I realized that D of an Ascendant Part is the point where a conjunction forms a midpoint directly to the Ascendant in terms of the planet involved, here always the C planet.

In my chart:

ASC + ASC - Pluto = Ascendant Part of Pluto

186 + 186 - 124 = 248

Note that now only three factors show in the chart. Thus a conjunction to an Ascendant Part creates a direct midpoint to the Ascendant, here Pluto, ASC Part conjunct Planet = Planet/Pluto = ASC.

Sex—wait until Venus contacts the ASC of Mars, Mars/Venus = ASC.

Anger—wait until Mars contacts the ASC of the Sun, Sun/Mars = ASC

Parts of the ASC are equidistant from the Ascendant or Descendent to the planet in question, again always C.

The Reciprocals

This is the time to show that the position of reciprocals was also naturally understood.

A reciprocal involves the switching of B and C positions in a Part:

A + B - C = D

ASC + Moon - Sun = Fortuna

ASC + Sun - Moon = Spirit

A reciprocal's position is always the same. It is equidistant on the opposite side of the Ascendant or Descendent from its counterpart. Stated another way: Part/Reciprocal = Ascendant.

Thus the simultaneous transit by conjunction to the Part and its reciprocal would mean the following:

1. Rare period or event
2. Strong enhancement of the Ascendant in terms of the Part and its reciprocal

The Proliferations

D or the Point when in the presence of a conjunction became A'.

D (conjunct planet) now A' + B' - C' = D'.

The astrologer sought the time when a particular type of energy would reach D, now conjuncted by a planet completing the original Part. *D' in turn would require a conjunction.* Using Fortuna as an example: Ascendant + Moon - Sun = Fortuna (conjunct Jupiter) Jupiter + Mars - Sun = D'.

The astrologer simply attempted to bring the energy of the entire war or great enterprise picture directly to the three Ascendants, Ascendant, Sun, Moon.

Thus it eventually came to pass that some astrologers were not told their hammers needed nails. That mixed analogy is too terrible for an Aquarian to pass up.

With seven planets forming sixty-three Parts without duplication using any given planet as D-A' formed 7 X 63 combinations. When conjuncted, D' yielded 7 X 441 possible combinations.

I have not seen Manilius' writings. Elsewhere I dismiss his text, but in a Eureka moment it occurred to me that it might be a balance chart house reading. The houses were not read "from" Fortuna but in terms of the planet aspecting Fortuna by conjunction. For example, Fortuna (conjunct Jupiter): This would yield a house by house Jupiter reading, the whole always carried to the three Ascendants, Ascendant, Sun, Moon.

From what I've read about Manilius' text, he may have kept the conjunction to Fortuna or D a secret, making it a skeleton outline. If derivative house balance charts were used from Fortuna or other Parts, surely someone also came up with the proliferations. (I had not yet read Manilius. See chapter, A Visit with Manilus.)

Lecturing at AFA 1996

D ue to work I was unable to complete this book before the 1996 American Federation of Astrologers Convention in Chicago. It began on July 17, preceeded by a flood west of Chicago and that evening TWA Flight 800 went down off Long island.

On July 18, 1996 at 1:30 CDT, I began my lecture on the Arabian Parts, effectively opening the door on more than 2,000 years of confusion and mystery. The lecture itself went fairly well with a second lecture two days later to concentrate on forecasting.

This was no longer the honing of a theory in private, but its full testing, where the idea is tossed about in strange circumstances and collides with opposing viewpoints.

The main problem that I encountered in the lecture was the conveyance of the concept A + B - C = D being equal to the midpoints A/B + C/D. For that reason I have chosen to retain their repetition in the text.

Broadly speaking, two main reactions occurred. Some felt that they already understood the Parts since many were aware that line AD equals line BC, that the Ascendant and Fortuna (AD) are the same longitudinal distance apart from each other as the Moon is from the Sun. This is the geometric result of the algebraic equation A + B - C = D.

The general perception seemed to be that this was known. This thus detracted from A/B = C/D, two pairs of midpoints, C/D completed by a conjunction to D where otherwise there is nothing-the essence of the Arabian Parts.

Attending the lecture was Gilbert Navarro, the great horary astrologer, protégé of Ivy Goldstein-Jacobson and fellow Aquarian. He refused to accept the concept of only the conjunction to D as locking and triggering the midpoint complex. Tired and unprepared for debate I was unable to give him a good answer, noting lamely that the Moon would conjunct any Part during the course of a month.

This did not satisfy him and as a parting shot he noted shock at my drawing of the Aquarian glyph without ripples. I draw two parallel lines. Here too I was forced to concede the field, not having given much thought to the devolution of my glyph drawing over the years.

So this chapter is dedicated to Gilbert Navarro, with thanks for pointing out to me something that needed clarification. I shall write of flat tires and marbles.

Gilbert maintained that by years of use he believed the Parts are activated by aspects other that the conjunction. I still maintain that the conjunction is all important.

A Part in a sign is influenced by the sign's ruler in some way, usually cause, effect, and character. The Vedics believe that empty signs are aspected. Generally speaking it is as follows: The Sun, Moon, Mercury, and Venus cast oppositions. Mars ditto with six and eight aspects or quincunxes. Jupiter casts the opposition and trines. Saturn casts the square, opposition, and three and ten aspects; that is, three and ten signs forward in the zodiac from itself—in effect the sextile and approaching square.

As a marble rolls through an empty ring, planetary energy rolls through empty signs. Given this, should a Western astrologer accept this premise which actually makes sense, a planet would move into this aspect field cast by another planet. Using the example of Fortuna, now without conjunction, it may find itself influenced by several planets. The first is naturally the ruler of the sign. But let's then say a square from Mars and a trine from Jupiter rolls through the sign, aspecting Fortuna. They do not aspect Fortuna, they influence the sign as a whole, Make no mistake, this is a dynamic influence but it cannot deflect off itself to bring energy to A, B, or C.

In the example, Pisces receives additional influence from Jupiter, its ruler, and Pisces also receives a Mars influence. Note that their rays rolling through Pisces aspect no planet. No contact or deflection occurs. But simultaneously, it happens in this example that transiting Jupiter trines the Moon and transiting Mars trines the Sun, otherwise known as B—Moon—and C—Sun. Note in this example the Sun trines the Ascendant. Thus some link exists connecting the three Ascendants. This is what happens many times when astrologers say that an aspected Part brought about a matter or defined a condition. I did it myself prior to April 1995. Now I am going through my charts working the conjunctions to the Parts. What an experience! What happens to a Part without a conjunction is that the sign itself receives additional aspect stimulation and, simultaneously, that one or both of the planets involved with the Part (for example the Moon and Sun) in Fortuna may also receive aspects from the transiting planets which also aspect the (empty) sign of Fortuna.

A watered down but similar type of combined planetary energy can thus be attributed to Fortuna. But this is not truly Fortuna in action, nor

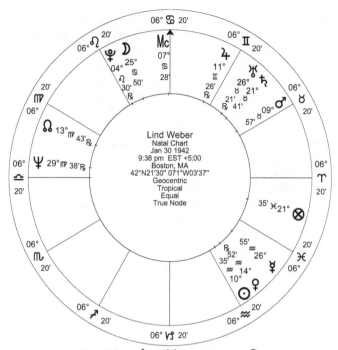

Transiting ♂ (15 ♊) in wide △ to ☉
Transiting ♃ (21 ♏) in approaching △ to ☽

is it integrated energy. Finally it is not nearly so powerful, a point I'll make with actual charts showing conjunctions to Parts.

An unconjuncted Part is a flat tire on a car. When the tire is fixed the energy centers at the crankshaft midway between the wheels. The crankshaft and the wheels need each other. The crankshaft is analogous to the midpoint axis of the Arabian Part midpoint pairs of A/B = C/D which, when aspected natally or by transit, adds power to the complex. This image shows itself most clearly when B and C are widely separated but not in opposition. When B and C are in conjunction the best image is a set of double wheels on a truck. Without a conjunction to D one tire is flat. Thus it is that a natal new Moon chart or monthly lunation when aspected by conjunction to the Ascendant is extremely powerful, especially in terms of the energy of the conjunct Ascendant planet. Both Fortuna and Spirit are at the Ascendant.

When I was a boy I played marbles for several years. Like billiards, marbles are about deflection and the ricochet, moving your marbles in a desired direction after contact. Whether explicitly or implicitly, all aspect theory deals in deflection. It is innate to any aspect other than the conjunction and the opposition. Traditional astrology, whether

Western or Vedic, uses fifteen- and thirty-degree divisions of the circle to develop the classic and minor aspects. Modern Western astrology uses divisions of five, seven, and nine, as well as colliding marble—like midpoints, indicating that planetary energies can reach each other from any angle. This energy is located at the midpoint between the two planets and can be tapped into by a third planet aspecting it from a classic angle. Midpoints, like Parts, need contact, but they are not limited to the conjunction, since two planetary energies are already present. Nevertheless, the conjunction is best, followed by the opposition, etc.

Since Arabian Parts are a system of midpoints we can now connect them to Western astrology. All modern astrologers use the T-square and grand trine. These are activated midpoint complexes as is the yod, the grand cross and others. In passing, most farmers don't believe in astrology but many have a well thumbed *Farmer's Almanac* on the kitchen table.

So, Gilbert, thank you for forcing me to clarify a point and I'll try to remember to put some waves in our glyph when you're around.

A Visit with Manilius

T wice I commented unfavorably on Manilius. When I saw an edition of his *Five Books of M. Manilius*, I realized that I owed him a hearing in the interests of fairness and objectivity. The book is at once tedious and interesting. The tedium mainly arises from the forcing of astrology lore twice into verse, first in the original Latin and then into English verse, a matter which several scholars have put their hands to. In literary style it is vague and full of literary allusions, some of which I recall from college courses and others that I'm happy to remain in ignorance of. Astrologically, it is a compendium in verse, all subjects treated in brevity, some well and clearly, others not so. He was not held to academic niceties and assertions are as prevalent as what is dealt with carefully.

I have not had time to read all five books. The book which deals with his balance chart from Fortuna is III. By today I will have read it for the third time. I also read Book Four. Of interest, there is his argument for fate as a Stoic (he was a complete fatalist) and his cookbook rendering of the Sun signs by vocations.

In Western astrology the doctrine of fate has been usurped by the doctrine of free will. I hold both as philosophical and theological absurdities.

The weaving of fate and free will yields one's destiny, a word often used synonymously with fate and one of history's greater semantic booby traps.

In gambling terms, one is dealt a hand and has some choice in how to play it.

Depending on the chart, on his overall environment, and his point in history, one is more or less fated. While chart examples of the extremes of fate or free will abound, most of us are somewhat in the middle. I agree with those who hold that great political leaders and world conquerors are fated.

Time to cut to the chase. His work on the Parts, such as it is, is in

Book Three. Here, as elsewhere, he attacks the Chaldeans. Of interest to the modern is his recognition of the zodiacal duads as still used by the West and Vedics: 0 Aries ruled by Aries Mars, 2 Aries 30 ruled by Taurus Venus, 27 Aries 30 ruled by Pisces Jupiter. Of course they used only five planets and two lights, but each sign begins with itself and ends with its twelfth sign. Manilius was not content to leave well enough alone. Instead of further dividing the duad of two and a half degrees into twelfths as do the Vedics, he assigns one planet to each half degree. Personally I disagree with this though I'll admit not having used it. I haven't had the time to go beyond duads, nor found it generally necessary.

Finally he offers in Book Four a new system of decanates which is simply beginning at 0 Aries to run the zodiac sequence three times through the zodiac: 0 Aries, Aries; 10 Aries, Taurus; 20 Aries, Gemini; 0 Taurus, Cancer, etc.

I would be dishonest if I said any less than that I think: This is nonsense. The same goes for the modern version of decanates generally used today (elements in order). They are the fifth and ninth duads, 10-12$\frac{1}{2}$ and 20-22$\frac{1}{2}$ degrees and nothing else.

As for the faces or six degrees rulerships. If anyone has ever used them, please announce yourself. I consider them nonsense too.

From use I believe in the classic duads. The planet in a given duad is influenced by and responsive to its duad sign and ruler—just a secondary rulership situation.

Regarding the Arabian Parts, Manilius calls them Lots and the translator calls Fortuna Fortune. Nowhere in the text is the term Arabian Parts or Points used.

We immediately know from reading him that the Parts preceded Manilius by some time, sufficient for true knowledge of them to have become clouded. He knows and uses the birth by night error with Fortuna; that is, he has no concept of Spirit or its difference from Fortuna.

He does not discuss Parts other than Fortuna nor does he give Fortuna by formula (A + B - C = D), instead designating it by arc AD = BC.

Regarding what I designate as the proliferations, a Part originating at Fortuna or Spirit (that is with Fortuna or Spirit with conjunct planet as A'), a possible reference appears. I've noted that I regard my work on them as a rediscovery.

The reader by now familiar with the proliferations may make his own judgment.

This way some take to fame; Thru Worlds unknown.
And things abstruse my Muse goes boldly on,

Observe all Interchange of Time, compares
The fatal turns, and views the Leagues of *Stars*
Things so remote, so intermixt and wrought
With Parts in Parts: They are too fine for thought.
To know them is too much, but to explain
How great! To bind in Verse skews more than Man.

Manilius does not know what to do with them and proceeds immediately to his system. His system is nothing more than a balance chart based on Fortuna to be read with Fortuna as Ascendant and first. He makes no note of the conjunct planets.

For the unfamiliar reader, a balance chart is a derivative house reading from a planet instead of a house. Granite puts forth a solar Part balance chart system as one used by the ancients. I disagree. Our astrologer would have simply read the planets from the charts, even as sophisticated horary readers occasionally do today and as the Vedics routinely do with the Sun and Moon in natal charts.

In his January 1995 interview in *The Mountain Astrologer*, Robert Hand, using the example of the Part of the Father, notes that this was (common and effective) usage.

I have no quarrel with reading a balance chart from a conjunct Part, that is emphasizing houses over a secondary Part, the proliferation. But like the Part, such a balance chart is not operative, at a given time without a conjunction. Without conjunction a few general matters may be observed and this has obscured the need for the conjunction.

Such a balance chart is merely another attempt or means of bringing the energies back to the Part which in turn passes them to the Ascendant through the planets used—B, C or in the case of Fortuna and Spirit the three Ascendants, Ascendant, Sun, Moon.

Manilius is keenly aware of the nature of the Ascendant, though he refers to it from the position of Fortuna.

But still the *Time* of every birth confirms
These *Lots* to Seats, and makes them change their Signs
That every *Lot* from every *Sign* may flow
And vary the *Nativity* below.

Here Lots refer to the derivative houses of Fortuna which Manilius refers to above as "fixt to Signs"—here the true enough noting of the ruler of a sign wherein a Part falls. Forthwith the houses of Manilius from Fortuna, quoted and paraphrased.

1. Fortune's the First: This name our art bestows and who it signifies the title shows.(Luck, vocation servants wealth)
2. Warfare's the next. How every Native shall in Arms succeed.

3. Civil Employments—its (problems) and *Patronage*.

4. The *Court* Concerns and Fortunes of the Bar—all related to the law as well as the natives ability to persuade and speak eloquently.

5. Marriage

6. Plenty "with Preservation." What stores of Wealth shall come, how long their stay. As *Planets* tamper with their ruling Ray:

7. The Seventh in horrid Dangers shall engage the Birth, if Planets not correct it's Rage (quoted in its entirety).

8. The Eighth Nobility pretends to claim, [honor, Fame Family Favor (notice reputation and patronage)] Generally like modern X.

9. The doubtful Lot of Children [along with parents and Guardians].

10. Acts of life. How by their *Masters* formed *Slaves* make their way (read like the sixth and servants).

11. Strength and health, [the type of medicine to use].

12. [Success in vocation and the life's work as well as its nature].

There you have them as put forth by Manilius. Personally I doubt that I'll be using them. They certainly are not part of the final Western or Vedic house traditions, both of which are generally the same with several areas of disagreement, e.g. Vedic ninth for father. Both traditions do not change the content of derivative or balance houses, only the position from where the count begins. This occurs with the natural zodiac and the precessed zodiac.

All those who have dealt with the Parts over the ages deserve credit for preserving them. In this respect Manilius deserves it too, although I personally doubt the validity of this house assignment. I believe the concept of balance chart reading from Fortuna using the conjunct planet would be extremely useful. In reading the section on the Lots (Manilius' houses) one is struck by the fact that such a nativity had to be for the well-to-do who are told how to deal with the poor. Religion is no where indicated.

We have entered the realm of that cynic, the court astrologer. I believe he sold a bill of goods to some Greek or Roman astrologer by misnumbering the houses, rather deliberately misplacing the house contents. Missing too, overall, is precision; they are vague. The individual parts as collected by Al-Biruni eleven centuries later are precise, and horary astrologers, which then meant most astrologers, were acquainted with the balance chart.

In Manilus' system there is no precise mention of luck or death in the houses. Implicitly he recognizes both in Fortuna, but our astrologer knew these were not inherent properties of Fortuna which might more properly be said to be a conductor of them, albeit a good or poor conductor.

Again our astrologer dealt with all these matters with precision, so I must close believing Manilius had to work from a corrupted system. His monumental ego, evident in the most cursory reading, would be unlikely to admit that he had been duped. Human nature does not change. The Stoic, like the modern astrologer, was supposed to have his ego in check. No such luck then or now.

Al-Biruni's great accomplishment was to maintain an interest in the Parts. This came about through their marvelously theatrical names and the hoax he created with the mystery of the Parts, the subtraction of energy. Hats off to a hoax well done. It lasted 900 years.

Bonatti in the 1300s made the Parts work and probably developed many of them as used subsequently. He used them practically, as well as trying to treat them in scholarly fashion like Zoller.

Though I came to disagree with them in some areas, English speaking astrologers and myself personally are greatly indebted to Robert Granite and Robert Zoller, who in their books personally brought the Parts into the latter part of the twentieth century as objects of interest and mysterious potential.

These men all noted the importance of Fortuna. I think it began there for everyone. It certainly was what opened up the matter for me.

The philosopher Nietzche, in one of his aphorisms, noted that a writer should be able to sum up his work in one sentence. I will rise to the challenge. The Arabian Part is two pairs of midpoints, one Ascendant-based for individualizing and timing, the second transit based by conjunction to the Part for forecasting, nothing more and nothing less.

At the Balance Chart Bazaar

I t seems that when I write, one thing leads to another. When I read Manilius I was presented with a second system of balance charts which is detailed in his chapter.

Second system, for Robert Granite put one forward too. Stated simply, his is to place the natal planet (or other, for example cusp) on the Ascendant in a separate chart. This gives a reading for that planet as an Ascendant, both its own houses and aspects. The third dimension would be its own Parts, the planet subtracted, his term or "in terms of" (my term), or simply the C planet.

Thus with natal Mars on the Ascendant using the natal Ascendant, ASC + Jupiter - Mars, would be such a Martian Part. B would change and C is always Mars. These placed outside would bring a three dimensional effect to understanding Mars.

I just reread the chapter and looked at my own set of balance charts. I note that I place natal Fortuna outside of all of them, but that Granite does not. It also seems these balance charts came somewhat by way of Wynn from *Wynn's Magazine,* January 1946.

This balance system has complete astrological validity which cannot be said for that of Manilius. Having noted that, I say that this was not the method of the ancients.

1. On the whole it expands the natal chart, and emphasizes the natal placements; its perspective is primarily of character. The ancients were interested in forecasting—period. The signs or character level were dealt with from the perspective of rulership, exaltations, and their reverse, detriments and falls, which when the dead wood of academia is hacked away means that the rulerships and exaltations perform well and detriments and falls perform poorly. Good luck and bad luck as well as generally good or poor life can begin to be assessed from this.

2. Somewhere I read early on that the Parts were invented to save papyrus or parchment. If anyone knows the source of this, please write it down and send it to me. That is not what the Parts are about, but a grain of truth exists. The ancient would not draw up seven charts more than the natal and slap in their [C] Parts. He would read derivatively, probably here giving a derivative house position to Fortuna and Spirit as well. He would use any Part, as long as it was relevant, and only such a Part. He would note the conjunctions.

Did he do 2 often? I don't think so because he had a better position and planet to read from. The clue is in Manilius and the generic names of the Parts, Fortunes, and Lots. He would read from the transit conjunction to Part planet. Example: Transiting Mercury is conjunct Fortuna. Here the matter of concern is a trading expedition. Restated, the astrologer tells his patron that this is time to buy and sell or trade.

Using transiting conjunct Fortuna Mercury as Ascendant, he creates its house system and examines the mix of all natal and transiting planets in terms of the matter at hand (here, trade). Having done this, our astrologer wants to get a bit more specific so he sets up proliferations, here emphasizing Saturn, buy cheap; Jupiter, sell high; and Venus, money itself.

While these matters could involve other Parts, transits and balance charts given that transit Mercury was conjunct Fortuna, we know our astrologer started there, realizing the three Ascendants would bring matters to pass and that the conditions of Mercury and all aspects and proliferations to Mercury having modified, enhanced, or damaged Mercury, would flow just so to the three Ascendants.

The true balance chart of the ancients began from the transiting conjunction planet to Part, and most of the time this was Fortuna and Spirit.

Reading from a planet rather than a sign is a more dynamic reading. The planet (here, Mercury) does things as opposed to the sign "in the nature of." This is the balance chart that I believe our astrologer used. The reader may make his choice.

Fortuna in the Natal Chart

W hile writing this book the question of what to do with example charts, the overall illustration of the principles, was of concern. Initially I let circumstances answer the question. I decided to omit many examples, directing the reader to do his/her own work which I find is the best way. I felt that the book was clear enough to not need many examples. Subsequently two things occurred. At the convention, the Parts were not as easily understood as I had expected. Whether the subject or my treatment and communication of it or both, it became clear during the lecture that examples were needed. They would answer the questions and bring excitement to the subject. The insight came when someone pointed out that I was expecting people to understand in an hour what had taken me years to research and understand.

During 1996, transiting Saturn is continually in orb of conjunction to my Descendent and opposition to my Ascendant. Personally, it has brought fatigue, depression and the need for extra effort in everything. Ruling my fourth house, Saturn has affected my family and the family business both positively and negatively. Conjunct the Descendant, it took me a while to pick up the most common theme. I was being affected by the problems of others. In tenth house matters, I had to put aside my stonework for a while, but my work hours were longer than ever and when I returned to stonework, the hard work level of it was emphasized. Nothing was easy.

Natal Saturn in my eighth house permitted me to continue earning well, giving validity to the Vedic principle that malefics in bad (dusthana) houses give benefits.

Saturn, planet of delay, didn't allow for the completion of this book prior to the 1996 AFA Convention but frustration was turned to enthusiasm as I began very extensive work on using what I had figured out on charts.

Before the convention, I worked the charts of famous people. Seeking natal conjunctions to Fortuna and, sometimes, Spirit. The hypothesis was simple. Having noted that Fortuna and Spirit are the two most powerful points in the chart, being the only two points that reach the three Ascendants simultaneously, then a natal planet or planets conjunct one or both of these would have profound effects on the character and life of the native.

Both Vedic astrology and Greco-Roman astrology have formats for weighing planetary energy and influence. Today they survive well-honed in the Vedic Ashtakavarga, the astrodynes of the Church of Light and the Volguine planetary tables. All have much in common and are a means of weighing planetary energy. The methods are noted in order of cumbersomeness. They cannot be used quickly, certainly not in an ordinary reading limited by time and money. Therefore, such weighing techniques are seldom used, the astrologer preferring to "eyeball" a highlighted planet or count aspects to it. In most cases this seems to work but it is not always easy to know where and when it didn't work or what would have worked better. In the first instances there is a partial or similar effect. In the second you don't find what you don't look for.

Using ten planets (eight planets and two lights), by probability theory there is a one out of 360 chance that a given planet will conjunct Fortuna. Ten planets reduce the odds to 1:36. Orb increases the chance of contact or lowers the odds in both instances. The same would apply to Spirit. Spirit is the lunar emphasis of the three Ascendants. It is only slightly less powerful than Fortuna. Since the chart has both Parts, the odds of a single contact are halved. Thus the odds of a conjunction to Fortuna or Spirit are one out of eighteen, or say fifteen when orb is factored in. The odds of a conjunction to both parts then increases exponentially to approximately 1:225. (The triple sign, Ascendant-Sun-Moon in the first is about 1:135, about five hours a month.)

The premise is that if you have a conjunction to either Fortuna or Spirit, your life and character will manifest according to the conjunct planet. Here is the true definition of the Saturnian, Venusian, Jovian or other person. The conjunct planet as planetary energy, house ruler, and significator, factors into and generally determines the life of the native.

Midpoints conjunct Fortuna and Spirit are also important. They will function on the "character" level, especially when activated. The effects may not be so clear or highly specialized, coming through as traits, highlights, or behavior patterns.

Those born with conjunctions to both Fortuna and Spirit will be unusual and often notable, whatever their overall station in life.

While Fortuna and Spirit are used as examples in this book because they are the most powerful, the above applies to any other Part, the other Parts being more specialized.

Working from this position, as the reader knows, Fortuna and Spirit are reciprocals equidistant from the Ascendant/Descendant axis, one above, one below, both on the same (east/west) side of the chart.

A person with conjunctions to both Fortuna and Spirit will bring the combined energies directly to the Ascendant-Descendant axis. This energy will pervade all of his/her personal relationships on any level.

The example of a general Part most frequently used here was ASC + Mars - Venus = Wallflower with its reciprocal ASC + Venus - Mars = Red Dress. They were used with a sexual connotation, but they also apply to salesmanship, diplomacy, war and peace, and as natural rulers of the first and seventh houses. Continuing with the sexual level of the example, a person aspected by natal conjunction on one of these Parts would be more successful using that planetary energy. Should that planet be Saturn, such a person might be counseled to wait for an intermittency or a good transiting conjunction to the reciprocal without conjunction. That person would be counseled to also remember that the Moon gives such a day once a month.

Continuing with the Wallflower/Red Dress example, a conjunction to both Parts would be the stimulation of reciprocals and both energies would flow to the Ascendant-Descendant axis. Such a person would be able to hunt and lure sexually, would be sexually charismatic, and would be very active in such matters. As noted, such a person might also opt for diplomacy or salesmanship. Success in any of these would also involve personal charisma.

Using the Parts requires discipline. Fortuna and Spirit may be placed in all charts. Other than that, have the question in mind, know the matter at hand. This will bring you down to using a handful of Parts. They may be used with any system of astrology and do not conflict with other techniques.

Some weeks after moving heavily into these charts, intuition tells me that the Arabs began with the Parts, then layered on their techniques. Restated, the Parts formed a starting point for conventional interpretation. I came to this conclusion with the examples that are shown here. The research technique was to work any random group of charts in sequence. When there was a noted conjunction to Fortuna or Spirit, the native would relate to the planet as previously stated. I ran sequences from *Astro Data II* and *Astro Data V* (both by Lois Rodden). I also ran sequences from my personal files and sequences from the unfiled folder. The conclusion was simple. A planet conjunct Fortuna or Spirit stamps the character and life of the native.

In closing, remember that conjunctions to Fortuna or Spirit are just a sloka, yoga, complex, or combination—your choice of terms. Any

131

complex may be negated in some instances. There is more than one way, more than one complex to signify a given matter. This is best illustrated in Vedic texts. Any of the combinations has at least three parts or conditions. One of Western astrology's shortcomings has been its reliance on binary concepts, planetary aspects, planets in signs, and planets in houses.

Binary concepts have a factor of four, aspected midpoints a factor of nine, and the locked Arabian Parts a factor of sixteen. Combinations at once enhance, delineate, and eliminate, streamlining interpretation. Now on to the examples.

Examples: Natal Conjunctions of Fortuna and Spirit

T he major premise put forward with these natives is simple. A natal conjunction to Fortuna or Spirit gives the purest planetary type (true Venusian, Martian, Jovian, etc.).

While other weighing systems attempt the same matter, that is to see if a planet other than the ruler of the Ascendant, and perhaps the Sun and Moon, is the strongest planet in the chart, a conjunction to Fortuna or Spirit answers the question with sureness and simplicity.

But nothing remains simple in astrology for long. Multiple conjunctions and conjunct midpoints give multifaceted characters.

Furthermore, a distant minority, which I crudely reckon at about 1:225 (This makes them somewhat rarer than then a triple Ascendant birth, 5 hours a month for about 1:135.) have conjunctions to both Fortuna and Spirit. In some manner, their lives strongly indicate both energies.

The examples as such are not carefully sought out and your own examples will corroborate these charts. They illustrate the essence of the Arabian Parts. The energy of three planets directed to the Ascendant is definitive.

Suzanne Valadon, Artist

I have a special affection for Suzanne Valadon. It was her Venusian qualities that brought the insight of these examples.

Quoting Rodden: "Suzanne Valadon, the mother of artist Maurice Utrillo, was an accomplished artist in her own right and a model for Chavannes, Renoir, Satic and Toulouse-Lautrec. As a youngster Valadon would cajole the local boys to take off their clothes so she could sketch them. Later she learned to develop her techniques from the masters for whom she posed."

Model artist, mother, lover—she is one of the few women remem-

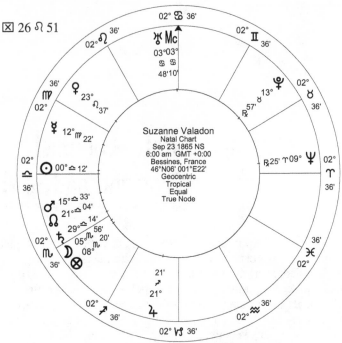

⊠ 26 ♌ 51

02° ♋ 36'
02° ♌ 36'
♅ Mc
03°03'
♋ ♋
48'10'
02° ♊ 36'

♏ 13° 57' R

02° ♉ 36'

36' ♍ 02'
♀ 23° ♌ 37'

☿ 12° ♍ 22'

Suzanne Valadon
Natal Chart
Sep 23 1865 NS
6:00 am GMT +0:00
Bessines, France
46°N06' 001°E22'
Geocentric
Tropical
Equal
True Node

R25' ♈ 09' ♆ 02° ♈ 36'

02° ♎ 36'
☉ 00° ♎ 12'

♂ 15° ♎ 33'
☊ 21° ♎ 04'
29° ♏ 14'
♄ 05° ♏ 20'
56'
02° ♏ ☽ 08°
⊗
36'

36' ♓ 02°

21'
21° ♐

02° ♐ 36'
♃

02° ♒ 36'

02° ♑ 36'

Mutual Reception ☉ 0 ♌   Mututal Reception ♀ 23 ♎
♀/♃ 22 ♎ ♂ ♂/♄ 22 ♎

bered from her milieu. Other than the rare double conjunction to Fortuna and Spirit defining her, note Moon/Venus at 29 Virgo conjunct Sun, the midpoint of the artist Venus/Saturn at 26 Virgo conjunct Moon/Venus. Note the implications of mutual reception Sun-Venus. Note Venus/Jupiter conjunct North Node. The ruler of the fifth house, Uranus, conjunct the Midheaven, shows her famous son and sexual liberation. It is also the trigger of an angular T-square.

Romy Schnieder, Actress

Naturally both Spirit and Fortuna conjunct the Ascendant, a new Moon chart. Here, without conjunction to the Ascendant, they wait and the Ascendant ruler has importance. She is a linguist and an actress.

Sun and Moon are trine by sign to the Ascendant, and Libra on the fifth house cusp. She lost a son by impalement as he fell from the home window. This may have occurred as solar arc Sun/Moon neared Venus and North Node. Venus rules the fifth house of children and the twelfth or the eighth of the fifth. Note karmic final duad on Ascendant.

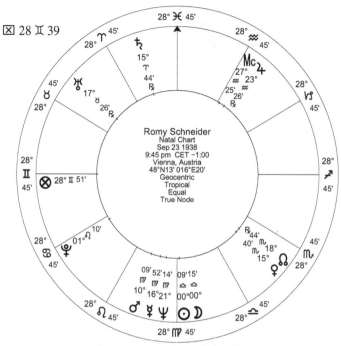

⊠ 28 ♊ 39

28° ♓ 45'

28° ♈ 45'

28° ♒ 45'

♄ 15° ♈ 44' ℞

Mc ♃ 27° ♒ 23° 25' ♒ 26' ℞

28° ♈

28° ♒ 45'

♅ 17° ♉ 26' ℞

28° ♉ 45'

28° ♑ 45'

Romy Schneider
Natal Chart
Sep 23 1938
9:45 pm CET −1:00
Vienna, Austria
48°N13' 016°E20'
Geocentric
Tropical
Equal
True Node

28° ♊ 45'

⊗ 28° ♊ 51'

28° ♐ 45'

♇ 01° ♌ 10'

28° ♋ 45'

℞ 44' 40' ♏ ♏ 18° 15°

♀ 15° ♎ 28°

28° ♏ 45'

♂ ☿ ♆ 10° ♍ 16° 09' ♍ 52' ♍ 21' 14'

09'15' ♎ 00°00'

☉ ☽

28° ♌ 45'

28° ♎ 45'

28° ♍ 45'

Point of Life + Death ☿/♄ 1 ♋ 18
Deriviative Point of Life + Death of Children ♀ 15 ♏ 40
Point of Life + Death rulers ASC/ruler 8th

Madame Du Barry, Courtesan

With Jupiter conjunct Fortuna, she became the mistress of Louis XV of France. Jupiter near her Ascendant clearly relates to her personal luck and here corroborates house rulership, ruling the seventh and fourth, her partner, the king and his elevated status. As ruler of the fourth it also rules the estate he left her at death.

Venus/Mars is at 15 Libra in the degree of deliberate execution and she died on the guillotine five weeks after Marie Antoinette.

Jupiter on the twelfth house side of her Ascendant shows that it was not all good luck, for her luck led to her undoing with Mercury/Mars as rulers of the first and eighth, the point of life and death conjunct Jupiter.

A multifaceted Fortuna near the Ascendant, she was a new Moon nativity. As such her life was one of both fortune and tragedy. The tragic side of new Moon births is noted by the French astrologer Volguine and the Vedics.

Note the dynamic, public thrust of Fortuna, the solar part as com-

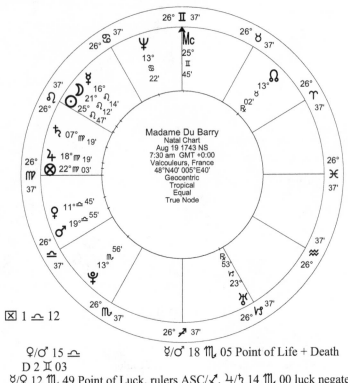

Madame Du Barry
Natal Chart
Aug 19 1743 NS
7:30 am GMT +0:00
Valcouleurs, France
48°N40' 005°E40'
Geocentric
Tropical
Equal
True Node

26° ♊ 37'

26° ♋ 37'   ♅ 13° ♋ 22'   Mc 25° ♊ 45'   26° ♉ 37'

26° ♌ 37'   ☿ 16° ☽ 21° ♌ 14' ☉ 25° ♌ 12' 47'   ☊ 13° ♌ 02' ℞   26° ♈ 37'

♄ 07° ♍ 19'
♃ 18° ♍ 19'
⊗ 22° ♍ 03'
26° ♍ 37'   26° ♓ 37'

♀ 11° ♎ 45'
♂ 19° ♎ 55'
26° ♎ 37'   56' ♇ 13° ♏   ℞ 53' ♄ 23° ♑   ♒ 26° 37'

☒ 1 ♎ 12

26° ♏ 37'   26° ♐ 37'   ♅ ♑ 26° 37'

26° ♐ 37'

♀/♂ 15 ♎   ☿/♂ 18 ♏ 05 Point of Life + Death
D 2 ♊ 03
☿/♀ 12 ♏ 49 Point of Luck, rulers ASC/♐, ♃/♄ 14 ♏ 00 luck negated

pared to Valadon who had Spirit conjunct Venus. Though Fortuna was conjunct a planet as well, it being the Moon, the lunar emphasis carried through.

Hedda Hopper, Columnist

When I saw this chart in Lois Rodden's Profiles of Women, it was too good to pass up. Given the symbology, I'll go with this birth time.

Uranus conjunct Fortuna, the ruler of the first in an equal house eighth. What could be more precise for this unveiler of sexual secrets. Note the sign, Virgo, which feels it has a right to say anything, involved with the first and its ruler Uranus, which just says it anyway.

Catherine the Great of Russia

The Parts were formulated at a time when equal house charts were used. This chart is interesting because Mercury defines the lady, not so much in terms of planetary energy as noted in most of the other examples, but by sortilege, that is rulership of the houses.

136

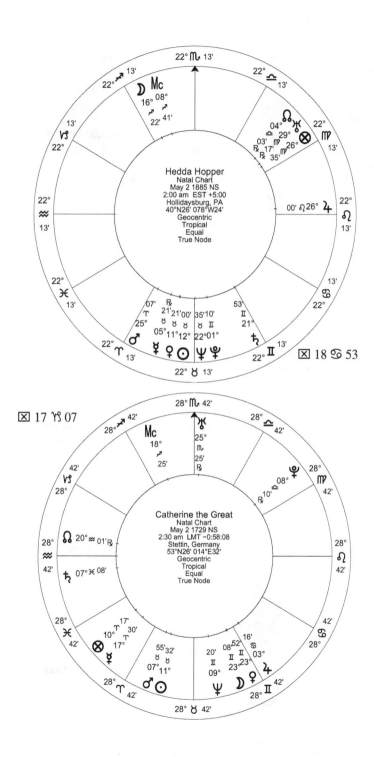

Hedda Hopper
Natal Chart
May 2 1885 NS
2:00 am EST +5:00
Hollidaysburg, PA
40°N26' 078°W24'
Geocentric
Tropical
Equal
True Node

⊠ 18 ♋ 53

⊠ 17 ♑ 07

Catherine the Great
Natal Chart
May 2 1729 NS
2:30 am LMT −0:58:08
Stettin, Germany
53°N26' 014°E32'
Geocentric
Tropical
Equal
True Node

137

Mercury rules the fifth house of love and art. She was known for her extreme love life and as a patroness of the arts. By derivative houses, the fifth is the second of the fourth or revenues from lands, estate. She probably assassinated her husband to gain the throne—fifth as the eighth of the tenth, and Virgo also ruled by Mercury.

The eighth rules raw sex, violence, and taxes, quickly noted as stable hands and soldiers, cruelty, expansion, and an increase in the tax base.

Note the stellium in Gemini, further strengthening the fifth house and Fortuna's conjunction Mercury.

That she was successful in all may be noted with Fortuna conjunct Mercury, ruler of the fifth house, the trinal house of self-extension. An exalted Jupiter in Cancer and the ruler of the first in the tenth complete the classic three indictors for a given matter—in this case, her personal success. She was not assassinated or deposed, making her a rarity among Russian rulers. (She died of apoplexy caused by a stroke in November 1796, according to Rodden.)

Can't Get It Together

Originally the man came to me regarding money and vocation. Not knowing what I know now about the Parts, I tried to read from the practical potential of the chart and approach it in a positive manner. In short I botched it.

I came across it again looking for these samples. Some seven or eight years have passed since the reading and what I've heard since has not been good—restlessness, a lack of success and looking for easy money.

He was functional for a time in the military. Those with a stellium often seek institutional jobs. This would appear to reduce the overload of the stellium.

Here the two stellia meet by midpoint in Cancer or the first, turning the whole chart into a super grand trine water, and with Sun/Moon conjunct the Ascendant, there is emotional self-centeredness—in effect the triple Ascendant plus five planets.

Neptune is conjunct Fortuna in Scorpio in the fifth house. The co-ruler of Scorpio, Mars is poorly placed in Taurus. Confusion at all times flows directly to the three Ascendants. The native travels widely seeking his lucky break (Neptune, ruler of the ninth house; Saturn present by sign).

That the outcome will probably not be positive is seen with the overall position and condition of Saturn, this corroborating the terrible affliction of Spirit.

Spirit conjunct Midheaven with Sun/Saturn and Mars/Saturn both

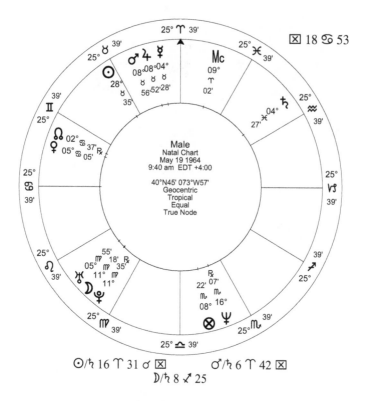

25° ♈ 39'

⊠ 18 ♋ 53

25° ♉ 39'

♂ ♃ ☿
08°08°04°
♉ ♉ ♉
56'52'28'

☉
28°
♉
35'

Mc
09°
♈
02'

25° ♓ 39'

39'
♊
25'

♄
04°
27' ♓

25°
♒
39'

☊ 02° ♋
♀ 05° ♋ 37' ℞
05'

Male
Natal Chart
May 19 1964
9:40 am EDT +4:00

40°N45' 073°W57'
Geocentric
Tropical
Equal
True Node

25°
♋
39'

25°
♑
39'

25°
♌
39'

55'
♍ 18' ℞
05° ♍ 35'
11° ♍
♅ 11°
☽ ☿

℞ 07°
22' ♏ ♏
08° 16°

⊗ ♆
25° ♏

39'
♐
25'

25°
♍ 39'

25° ♎ 39'

☉/♄ 16 ♈ 31 σ ⊠   ♂/♄ 6 ♈ 42 ⊠
☽/♄ 8 ♐ 25

conjunct and forming a midpoint bring energy concentration in their tight conjunction to the Midheaven and Spirit.

Finally, general bad luck may be seen from Moon/Saturn at 8 Sagittarius 25 square the Virgo stellium and quincunx the Taurus stellium except for the Sun itself in a final duad with a poor Mars in Taurus. In retrospect I wish I might have thought of reenlistment.

Mars/Neptune and Saturn/Neptune as midpoints in reciprocal-like positions to the Descendent caused various levels of mutual abuse in his marriage, which did not last.

The three planets are the signature of violence, here psychological. By sortilege both the children and wife are seen as victims, (Mars rules the fifth/Neptune and Saturn rule the seventh/Neptune). The native sees himself a victim as well.

Lawrence Noxon, Infanticide Victim

This is a strange and awful chart. At first glance it may seem good with the Sun-Moon-Pluto grand trine and with an exalted Jupiter in mutual reception with the Moon.

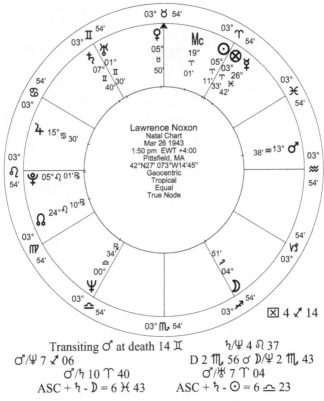

Lawrence Noxon
Natal Chart
Mar 26 1943
1:50 pm EWT +4:00
Pittsfield, MA
42°N27' 073°W14'45"
Geocentric
Tropical
Equal
True Node

Transiting ♂ at death 14 ♊   ♄/Ψ 4 ♌ 37
♂/Ψ 7 ✶ 06   D 2 ♏ 56 ♂ D/Ψ 2 ♏ 43
        ♂/♄ 10 ♈ 40   ♂/♅ 7 ♈ 04
ASC + ♄ - D = 6 ♓ 43   ASC + ♄ - ☉ = 6 ♎ 23

Born prematurely, a Mongoloid, Saturn/Neptune conjunct Ascendant conjunct Pluto and rulers of the seventh and eighth. Jupiter in degree of family execution or murder with mutual reception goes to 15 Sagittarius of hunter killer.

Ascendant in violent degree and Sun in violent degree of tragedy. Other violent degrees present.

Because of the Ascendant forming the grand trine, Fortuna is conjunct the Sun and Spirit is conjunct the Moon, both lights forming the other points of the grand trine.

Mars/Neptune of attack is conjunct the Moon, ruler of the twelfth, and Spirit. It opposes Saturn, locking in violence.

Mars/Uranus of electricity is conjunct Sun and Fortuna. His father electrocuted him on September 22, 1943.

John Noxon Jr., Father of Lawrence Noxon

Ascendant-Sun-Moon are in violent degrees. Fortuna in violent 19 Scorpio is conjunct Saturn at 17 Scorpio 35 and Uranus at 22 Scorpio

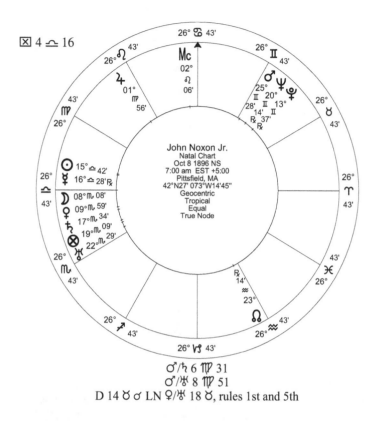

☒ 4 ♎ 16

26° ♋ 43'

Mc
02°
♌
06'

26° ♒ 43'
26° ♌ 43'

43'
01°
♍
56'
♃

26° ♊ 43'

♂ ♆ ♀
25°
♊ 20°
28' ♊ 13°
14' ♊
℞ 37'
℞

26° ♉ 43'

43'
♍
26°

John Noxon Jr.
Natal Chart
Oct 8 1896 NS
7:00 am EST +5:00
Pittsfield, MA
42°N27' 073°W14'45"
Geocentric
Tropical
Equal
True Node

26° ♎ 43'

☉ 15° ♎ 42'
☿ 16° ♎ 28' ℞
☽ 08° ♏ 08'
♀ 09° ♏ 59'
♄ 17° ♏ 34'
⊗ 19° ♏ 09'
22° ♏ 29'

26° ♈ 43'

26° ♏ 43'

℞
14'
♒
23°

26° ♓ 43'

26° ♐ 43'

☊ ♒
26° 43'

26° ♑ 43'

♂/♄ 6 ♍ 31
♂/♅ 8 ♍ 51
D 14 ♉ ☌ LN ♀/♅ 18 ♉, rules 1st and 5th

29, both violent degrees. He electrocuted his son, all that he is remembered for.

Uranus ruler of the fifth house conjunct Saturn and Spirit in the tenth of the fifth—fame through children. His Midheaven is conjunct Lawrence's Ascendant. This often occurs in event charts as closure, for example the end of a war. The synastry rendering of this was not to prove fortunate here.

Jeffrey Wolf Green

Mr. Green is an astrologer who has done much work on self-transformation and he specializes in Pluto, writing books and teaching courses on it. He hopes to start a school more or less controlled by him.

He has Saturn and Pluto conjunct Spirit (8 Leo). Saturn is the ruler of the third house of communication, and Pluto rules a strongly tenanted first house. With Jupiter conjunct the Ascendant and Pluto ruling the Ascendant in the tenth house, I'll forecast success in his endeavors.

How will Saturn-Pluto be used—for the good or not so good? Orga-

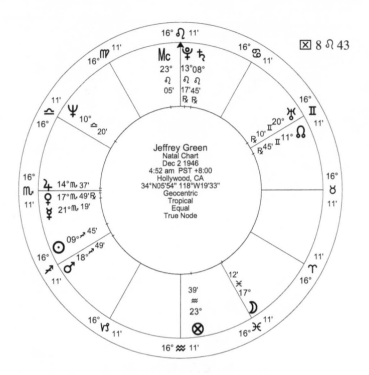

nization or control or both? An interesting question.

Any emphasized school of astrology has a lot to offer as long as it does not think it has everything. It is interesting to note that astrological schools and groups are proliferating after the Uranus-Neptune conjunction.

On a mundane level this conjunction tribalizes all systems, organizations, and governments. There is not an increase but a cutting of the pie even as some would cry out for a new pie.

The conjunction of Uranus and Neptune in 1821 brought to a close the Napoleonic Empire and the Spanish Empire in South America, and brought the Industrial Age into being. The latter was innately tribalized by self-interest, specialization, and the assembly line.

This time one notes the decline and fall of the USSR, the splintering of the U.S. Republican Party, and the possibility of a genuine third party in the near future for America.

Tribes make war (Somalia, Burundi and Rwanda); enemies make peace; England-Ireland, Israel-PLO; civil wars erupt, Czechoslovakia.

Importantly, all mundane processes drag on. It took most of the nineteenth century for South America's newly independent countries to stop fighting with each other. This was followed by a system of coup d'etats. Now a democratic system, albeit a South American version, emerges.

Astrology, Uranian in nature, will never be totally controlled by anyone. Such is the observation of an Aquarian with mutual Uranus-Pluto solstice points in fixed signs with a mutual reception of Uranus to its own sign.

Camilla Parker Bowles

I dealt with this chart indirectly at first, scanning it from *The Mountain Astrologer* for my comment on Charles, Prince of Wales. Of course I wanted it for my collection. On September 14, 1996, I copied it and punched in Fortuna and Spirit.

Sun, Mercury, Venus and Moon are conjunct Fortuna, as is the Moon by Al-Biruni's orb, and Venus is carried by the Moon. Spirit is conjunct Saturn and Pluto.

Sun/Pluto at 1 Leo 41 conjunct the Ascendant and Jupiter square Pluto unite the energies of lasting accomplishment—Sun-Jupiter-Pluto. Jupiter trines all the plants in the Cancer stellium, it being in the fourth house of the Magna Carta chart.

It is not the place to go on record with a tight forecast here. I noted that I bet on her if there is a choice to be made by Charles.

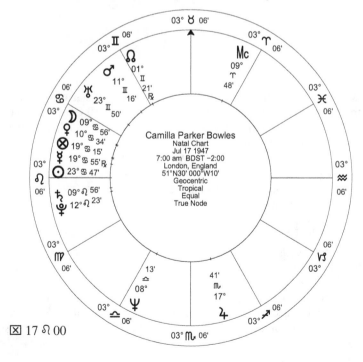

Camilla Parker Bowles
Natal Chart
Jul 17 1947
7:00 am BDST −2:00
London, England
51°N30' 000°W10'
Geocentric
Tropical
Equal
True Node

☒ 17 ♌ 00

143

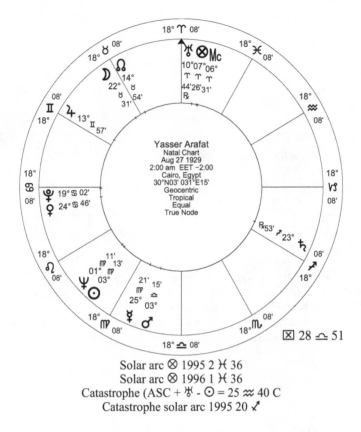

Yasser Arafat
Natal Chart
Aug 27 1929
2:00 am EET −2:00
Cairo, Egypt
30°N03' 031°E15'
Geocentric
Tropical
Equal
True Node

Solar arc ⊗ 1995 2 ♓ 36
Solar arc ⊗ 1996 1 ♓ 36
Catastrophe (ASC + ♅ - ☉ = 25 ♒ 40 C
Catastrophe solar arc 1995 20 ♐

Mars/Jupiter is at 29 Leo 59 conjunct Regula, a star often noted with kings and fate and great falls. Mars/Saturn at 10 Cancer is conjunct Venus. Mars/Neptune at 8 Leo is conjunct Saturn. Venus rules her tenth, and Saturn rules the Magna Carta tenth.

Since many astrologers are almost authorities on the royal family, I won't connect all the dots. To influence the course of royal succession in many ways and probably get the king is no small accomplishment. I direct the reader to the chart of Al Biruni who set in motion a 900-year hoax.

Yasser Arafat

The man needs no introduction after a lifetime career dedicated to getting the Palestinian people their own homeland, first by war, then by diplomacy.

The premise of these charts, that a planet conjunct Fortuna or Spirit stamps the life, is clear. Uranus and the Midheaven conjunct Fortuna. He is the revolutionary's revolutionary. Nor is he through [converse]

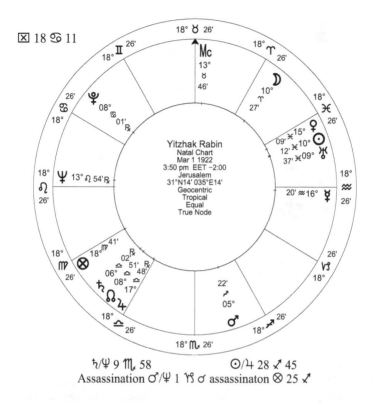

⊠ 18 ♋ 11

18° ♉ 26'

Mc
13°
♉
46'

18° ♈ 26'

18° Ⅱ 26'

☽
10°
♈
27'

18° ♓ 26'

26'
♏ 08°
♋ 01'
18° R

09' ♓ 15°
12' ♀ 10°
37' ♓ 09° ⊙ ♅

18° ♌ 26'
♇ 13° ♌ 54' R

Yitzhak Rabin
Natal Chart
Mar 1 1922
3:50 pm EET –2:00
Jerusalem
31°N14' 035°E14'
Geocentric
Tropical
Equal
True Node

20' ♒ 16' ☿
18° ♒ 26'

18° ♍ 26'
♍ 41'
18° ⊗
02° R
06° ♎ 51' R
08° ♎ 48'
♄ ☊ 17°
♃

18° ♑ 26'

22'
♐
05°

18° ♎ 26'

18° ♐ 26'
♂

18° ♏ 26'

♄/♆ 9 ♏ 58   ⊙/♃ 28 ♐ 45
Assassination ♂/♆ 1 ♑ ♂ assassinaton ⊗ 25 ♐

progressed Fortuna (ASC + Moon – progressed Sun) in 1995 was
around 2 Aquarius conjunct transiting Uranus.

Working conservatively with allowed orbs of seven degrees for Mercury and Venus, solar arc Fortuna remains with Uranus through 1997.

Yitzhak Rabin

His assassination chart is in the chapter on the Part of Death with
the midpoint Saturn/Neptune of victim or dharma/karma conjunct
Spirit.

On finding his natal chart I was surprised to see the same midpoint
in wide orb to his natal Fortuna. Spirit has the same relationship to
Pluto, here just out of orb. A slightly earlier birth time (fifteen or
twenty minutes) would place them well within orb.

It is to be noted that his chart, described as "widely used," can only
get a C or D rating.

Fortuna in this chart at 18 Virgo opposes his Pisces stellium, this all
conjunct Venus, ruler of his tenth of leaders and fate.

There is no conjunction to Fortuna by transit in his natal chart, but

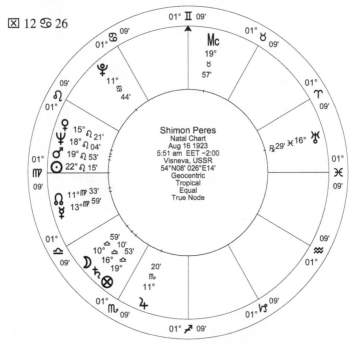

01° ♊ 09'

Mc
19°
♉
57'

01° ♉ 09'

01° ♋ 09'

09'
01° ♌

♇
11° ♋
44'

09'
♌
01°

01° ♈ 09'

♀ 15° ♌ 21'
☽ 18° ♌ 04'
♂ 19° ♌ 53'
☉ 22° ♌ 15'
♏
01°
09'

Shimon Peres
Natal Chart
Aug 16 1923
5:51 am EET −2:00
Visneva, USSR
54°N08' 026°E14'
Geocentric
Tropical
Equal
True Node

℞ 29° ♓ 16' ♅

01° ♓ 09'

☊ 11° ♏ 33'
13° ♏ 59'

01° ♎ 09'

59'
☽ 10°
10° ♎ 53'
16°
19°

20'
♏
11°

09' ♒
01°

01° ♏ 09'

♃

01° ♑ 09'

01° ♐ 09'

the Moon hammering away at his Pisces stellium every month had now done this with the energy of transiting Saturn for many months.

I would say the firm decision to kill him was made some fifteen days before the event. But I do not have to stretch to find connections. Sun/Jupiter is the point of life and death, here at 28 Sagittarius 45. This is the Scorpio duad and often involved with cutting off from, grudges, revenge. Despite my work with duads, this was driven home by noticing the general rancor of private clients with this Moon.

Natal Sun/Jupiter at 28 Sagittarius 45 is conjunct Assassination Mars/Neptune at 1 Capricorn and Assassination chart Fortuna at 25 Sagittarius. At his assassination transiting Saturn signified his downfall, set in motion as it transited his natal Sun-Uranus, the signature of leadership lost. Note the unfolding of events, again all brought to the three Ascendants.

In favor of this chart is transiting Moon over Fortuna at 18 Virgo 52 on October 21, 1995 with transiting Saturn retrograde at 18 Pisces 51.

Shimon Peres

Shimon Peres succeeded Rabin and then lost the election, being considered too moderate. He was succeeded by Benjamin Netanyahu, who played the conservative card. I hold that Sun in Taurus does not

146

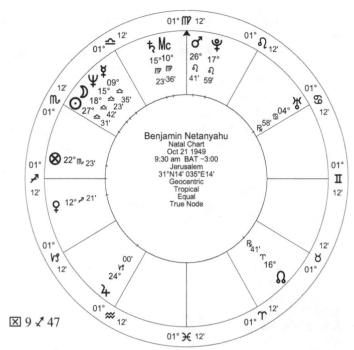

01° ♏ 12'

01° MP 12'

♄ Mc
15°10'
MP MP
23'36'

♂ ♀
26° 17°
♌ ♌
41' 59'

01° ♌ 12'

12' ♇ ♀
09°
15° ♎
♍ 18° ♎ 35'
♐ 27° ♎ 23'
01° ♎ 42'
31'

01°

Benjamin Netanyahu
Natal Chart
Oct 21 1949
9:30 am BAT −3:00
Jerusalem
31°N14' 035°E14'
Geocentric
Tropical
Equal
True Node

R58' ♋ 04° ♅
01° ♋ 12'

01° ⊗ 22° ♏ 23'

01° Ⅱ 12'

♐ 12' ♀ 12° ♐ 21'

01° ♑ 12'
00' ♑ 24°
♃

R41' ♈ 16° ♌

01° ♉ 12'

01° ☿ 47

01° ≈ 12'

01° ♈ 12'

01° ♓ 12'

⊠ 9 ♐ 47

⚷ 7 ♐ 23   Progresed ⚷ 10/12/1996 OGMT 12 ♐ 50
Progressed ☉ 10/21/1996 OGMT 14 ♐ 48
Solar arc ⊗ 1995 5 ♎ ASC + ☽ - solar arc ☉ 1995
SA ⊠ 1995 26 ♑ ♂ transiting ♀ (reciprocal) ASC + solar arc ☉ 1995 - ☽

give up its marbles and that is Israel's Sun.

Peres has Spirit conjunct Pluto and Moon/Saturn conjunct Fortuna. These midpoints then must move to his Ascendant where they contact his Sun as well because of their ``reciprocal'' positions.

Simply, this is power, deep feeling, and bad luck. It does not lend to a charismatic presentation of the self. Peres often appears stiff and dour.

Sun Pluto does not vanish or cave in. Out of sight for now he may return if Netanyahu over plays his hand. A young lion, he would do well to remember that with Arafat and Peres, he is up against leaders of the pride.

Benjamin Netanyahu

Originally I'd only included Yasser Arafat in this section because of his amazing Uranus conjunct Fortuna. I then included Yitzhak Rabin on the basis of a repetition of the Saturn/Neptune theme in his natal chart.

147

Violence broke out again in Jerusalem prior to the lunar eclipse of September 26, 1996, so I decided to include Shimon Peres and I had gotten Benjamin Netanyahu's chart a couple of weeks earlier from Theresa McDevitt, who specializes in composite charts. These define the relationship not the individual, as well as how the relationship is expressed or experienced by the individuals involved.

As with the rest of the Mideast players, Netanyahu has a conjunction to either Fortuna or Spirit. Here Spirit is conjunct Chiron and Venus in Sagittarius in the first house. Progressed Sun separates from both at 14 Sagittarius, but is still in orb.

If Chiron here means a quest, the egotistic self-centeredness of Sun-Venus progressions may not bode well. A Sagittarius Ascendant leaps before it looks, here with Chiron, Venus, progressed Sun and progressed Mercury and Ascendant/progressed Mercury = Venus/progressed Sun.

The problem here is Venus conjunct Spirit. That his desires are uppermost is confirmed by both Sun and Moon in Libra, a Venus sign and the despositor of Venus, Jupiter is in its fall as is the Sun in Libra. There is no astrological reason to expect the finest level of Venus energy. For the immediate purpose of this example he is a Venusian defined by his own desires expressed through his sixth and eleventh.

Uranus in the eighth in Cancer means he can thrive on turmoil. Natally at 4 Cancer retrograde, now by progression at 3 Cancer retrograde, it is volatile by the progressed Moon at 2 Cancer (September 1996) and 3 Cancer (October 1996). Moon-Uranus, especially the conjunction, is the signature of upset. Again, one does not control Uranus.

If this delineation is not upbeat, there is a reason. The September 26, 1996 lunar eclipse Moon at 4 Aries and Saturn retrograde at 3 Aries is conjunct the composite Jupiter at 4 Aries of Arafat and Netanyahu. Other than bringing ill luck to the relationship, it may be viewed humanistically as diminishing expectations or a mutual pessimism. Key this to a strong Uranus for both.

The lunar eclipse of September 26, 1996 featured a loose fire grand trine of Saturn and Moon in Aries, Venus and Mars in Leo, and Pluto in Sagittarius. This echoes the Israel national horoscope—May 14, 1948, Tel Aviv, 4:37 PM EET, "The State of Israel has arisen." This is the 0 Scorpio Ascendant chart. Most prefer the 4:00 PM 23 Libra Ascendant when Ben Gurion began to read the statement. Personally, I see nothing Libran about Israel.

Some Quick Takes

Much of my astrology is on eighth house matters. For me it is natural, and would be so for some other astrologers. For those of us, Lois Rodden's *Astro Data V*, which I call the Black Book, is indispensable. It is of victims and victimizers, of the unfortunate and the brutal.

Since I've used her data often I'll try and pique your interest with a few partials from *Astro Data V*.

Henry Desire Landru Fortuna—Spirit conjunct Ascendant (new Moon) seduced women and murdered them for profit. He died on the guillotine, and had an interesting grand trine.

Andrew Dalton Lee—American traitor to Russia for profit serving a life term; Saturn conjunct Spirit.

Raymond Buckey—stood trial for child abuse and was acquitted. Held in jail through trial; life ruined. Mercury, ruler of the twelfth, conjunct Spirit.

John Norman Collins—serial killer with a shoe fixation. Neptune conjunct Spirit.

Lindsey Crosby—son of Bing Cosby and suicide by gunshot. Ascendant 15 Sagittarius, Sun 15 Capricorn, Moon 8 Pisces; all three Ascendants in violent degrees, a frequent occurrence in *Astro Data V*, clearly indicating that Fortuna can be innately unfortunate. He had Jupiter, ruler of the Ascendant, conjunct Fortuna.

At the time of his death converse arc Fortuna was at 17 Sagittarius conjunct Ascendant, transiting Sun at 18 Sagittarius, transiting Mars/Neptune at 17 Sagittairus, and transiting Mars/Saturn at 18 Sagittarius.

Dennis Michael Crosby—brother of Lindsey Crosby, son of Bing Crosby, also suicide by gunshot. Natal Mercury ruler of financial houses two and eleven conjunct Spirit in the twelfth. Spirit might be unfortunate. At death, converse solar arc Fortuna was conjunct Mars.

The Part of Suicide ASC + 8th - Neptune was not aspected by natal or progressed planets. Nor did Suicide form a conjunction by converse arc in either case. I did not check the transits.

Parts are only one of various yogas or formulas for a given situation.

Restated, Ascendant/eighth (with conjunction = Neptune/Suicide) is not the only signature for suicide.

Fortuna in the Event Chart

By the time I left for the 1996 AFA Convention, I'd pretty much reached a conclusion on a natal conjunction to Fortuna and Spirit. It turned out that all that remained were additional amazing examples. I found these immediately after the convention in the binder of unfiled charts that I had carried with me. Examples were too exciting to pass up.

Most of my work involves eighth house matters. Aside from most being violent, many are also major events. The combination gives an intensity and clarity to the chart which is ideal for research. I then extrapolate or modify for kinder, gentler matters.

As noted more than once, I made all the errors with the Parts too. In an article on River Phoenix in *Today's Astrologer*, the AFA bulletin, April 17, 1996, written in early 1995), I did not draw in Fortuna or Spirit, direct Parts forward, and note Parts without conjunction.

Before "Eureka!" in April 1995, I associated Fortuna with good luck. This is not so and often poor placement indicates bad luck. Fortuna is only indirectly involved with luck. It is really the connection of the three Ascendants, Ascendant, Sun, Moon. Only Fortuna and Spirit can do this. Because I associated Fortuna with luck and Spirit with spiritual matters, I did not place them in most of my charts on violence.

In these charts violent Arabian Parts made strong aspects, including many conjunctions, It was these aspects that spurred me on. Now going back I would discount those violent Parts not aspected by conjunction. I would add Fortuna and Spirit.

Immediately I began to get amazing conjunctions. Once again not every chart could produce a conjunction but if so the chart was true to this conjunction. I soon came on two charts, the embarkation of the Titanic and the ValuJet crash in the Florida Everglades.

I have worked with the Titanic charts for years. I keep returning to them like Robert Hand returns to Nixon and Watergate. But I had never placed Fortuna or Spirit in the chart.

In Titanic Sails, Saturn was conjunct Fortuna and disappearance factors conjunct Spirit. Using only Parts I will show you the fate of the Titanic in just several moves. Very quickly I came to ValuJet. At crash time Venus was conjunct Fortuna. In retrospect, it was generally agreed that something had gone wrong with the cargo (second house) of oxygen bottles. Venus rules the second house of cargo. I returned to the Titanic chart. Saturn of misfortunes and sinking is conjunct Fortuna. A Leo rising chart, Capricorn rules the sixth, the manufacture and design of the ship, its structure, and skin. We know that the hull was gashed and there were engineering flaws in the structure of the watertight compartments.

The question was whether I could key the chart to the conjunctions of Fortuna or Spirit. Apparently the answer is yes. The story could be extracted from Fortuna and/or Spirit. Moreover, the rulership of the houses as the planet of that activity was confirmed.

The Aries or natural zodiac rulers are also significators. For example, in Titanic Sails the twelfth of disappearance is Cancer ruled by the Moon. It makes a noteable aspect to Neptune, the natural ruler of disappearances.

In using the Parts to determine a matter, use the house ruler to denote a matter as well as the natural midpoint pairs. For example, Mars/Saturn is death but so are the rulers of the first and eighth as the points of life and death. In the Titanic Sails chart with Leo ascendant, Sun/Jupiter and Sun/Neptune are death points. Disappearance is Neptune/Pluto, the natural rulers of the twelfth and eighth. (Elaboration may occur in the examples). In Titanic Sails, the midpoint Moon/Neptune, the chart rulers of the twelfth and eighth, are conjunct Spirit. These are the chart and natural rulers respectively of disappearance.

A Church Blows Up

Many readers who have not seen this chart know the story. I have heard and read it at least three times, in radio's *The Rest of the Story, Fate Magazine*, and *The Weekly World News Tabloid*.

The choir consisted of about a dozen members, all noted for being present and on time. On this evening all were late and thus no one was killed. The explosion from the heating system was such that the death of all or most would have been a forgone conclusion.

Saturn of delay rises, but Moon/Jupiter of luck trines it approaching from the sign of the ninth and Moon energy in Taurus is exalted—a lucky delay. Circumstances for the explosion are readying them-

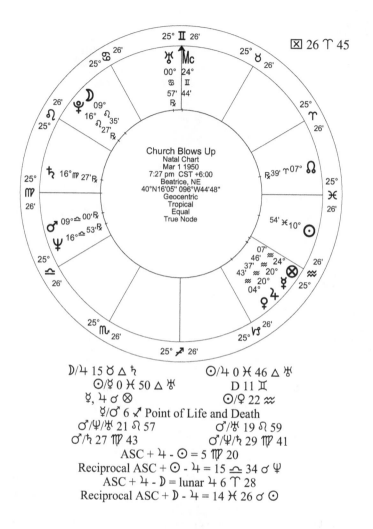

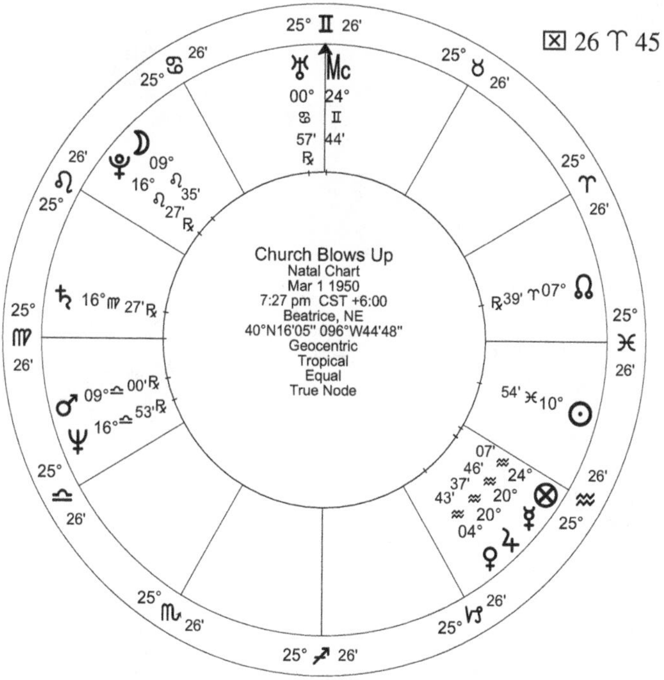
Church Blows Up
Natal Chart
Mar 1 1950
7:27 pm CST +6:00
Beatrice, NE
40°N16'05" 096°W44'48"
Geocentric
Tropical
Equal
True Node

☽/♃ 15 ♉ △ ♄ ☉/♃ 0 ♓ 46 △ ♅
☉/☿ 0 ♓ 50 △ ♅ D 11 ♊
☿, ♃ ☌ ⊗ ☉/♀ 22 ♒
☿/♂ 6 ♐ Point of Life and Death
♂/♆/♅ 21 ♌ 57 ♂/♅ 19 ♌ 59
♂/♄ 27 ♍ 43 ♂/♆/♄ 29 ♍ 41
ASC + ♃ - ☉ = 5 ♍ 20
Reciprocal ASC + ☉ - ♃ = 15 ♎ 34 ☌ ♆
ASC + ♃ - ☽ = lunar ♃ 6 ♈ 28
Reciprocal ASC + ☽ - ♃ = 14 ♓ 26 ☌ ☉

selves: Mars/Uranus at 19 Leo 59, and Mars/Neptune/Uranus at 21 Leo 57.

Simultaneously, Fortuna was conjunct Jupiter and Mercury, here the Ascendant ruler conjunct Jupiter of good fortune. At the time of the explosion it had already departed (increased Ascendant equals greater zodiac degree). This is simply incredible luck in action, its energy carried to the Ascendant, Sun, and Moon.

Mars/Saturn of death at 27 Virgo 43, Moon/Saturn of misfortune and Mars/Neptune/Saturn of violent death at 29 Virgo 41 are all in later degree and void-of-course. Note that the part of Death at 11 Gemini is without conjunction, as is the cusp of eighth.

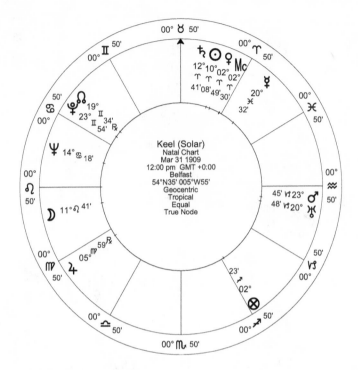

Note that the only midpoints to Death—Moon-Neptune/North Node—do not exist. There is nothing at a Node. It too needs a conjunction.

Uranus at 0 Cancer 58, taken as a balance chart, saved their lives. Sun/Jupiter on its ninth is in exact approaching trine at 0 Pisces 46.

Such is the wonder and simplicity of rulerships midpoints and Parts, themselves midpoints. Such is the power of Fortuna, here directing the benefits of Jupiter to Ascendant, Sun, Moon and Ascendant ruler Mercury, itself conjunct Jupiter.

The keynote of this chart is good luck. This is defined by the conjunction of the first house ruler and Jupiter to Fortuna.

The Sinking and Disappearance of the Titanic

This is one of my favorite series of event charts.

Mundane tradition has for millennia noted certain beginnings. The king is dead, long live the king, the laying of the cornerstone or the ground breaking, and the laying of a ship's keel. While the last two were sometimes done at elected times, the first obviously was not. The maxim of astrology in operation is to look to the first chart. These three events would have a second chart, specifically coronation, launching,

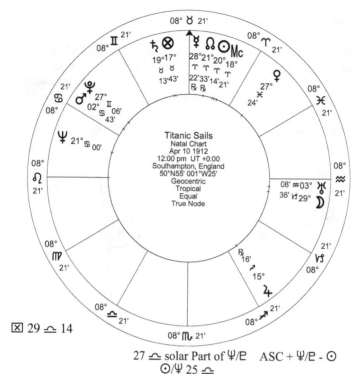

08° ♉ 21'

08° ♊ 21'

♄ ⊗ 19°17' ☿ ☊ ☉ Mc 28°21'20° 18'
♉ ♉ ♈ ♈ ♈
13'43' 22'33'14'21'
℞ ℞

08° ♈ 21'

21' ♋

08°

♂ ♇ 27° 02° ♊ 06' 43'

♀ 27° ♓ 24'

08° ♓ 21'

♆ 21° ♋ 00'

Titanic Sails
Natal Chart
Apr 10 1912
12:00 pm UT +0:00
Southampton, England
50°N55' 001°W25'
Geocentric
Tropical
Equal
True Node

08° ♌ 21'

08° ♒ 21'

08' ≈03' ♓ 36' ♑ 29° ☽

08° ♍ 21'

℞ 16' 15° ♃

21' ♑

08°

⊠ 29 ♎ 14

08° ♎ 21'

08° ♏ 21'

08° ♐ 21'

27 ♎ solar Part of ♆/♇   ASC + ♆/♇ - ☉
☉/♆ 25 ♎
Spirit ⊠ 29 ♎ The Disappearance Complex
☉/♃ 17 ♓ 45 ♂ ASC lunar Part of Ascendant 17 ♓ 06

and dedication, but the timing of the earlier phase remains of great significance.

I do not know the time that the Titanic's first keel plate was laid, so I'll just make a speculative noon chart. A glance at the ephemeris says much.

Note the terrible T-square, its trigger position closed by the wide orb of the Sun and mutual reception to Mars at 23 Aries and mutual reception to Saturn at 12 Capricorn. Two sides of the T-square now hold Mars-Saturn or death. Neptune in the third leg reads to Mars-Saturn-Neptune or violent death. Of course all energy moves to the trigger sign Aries ruled by Mars and the Sun of the entire matter seals it.

I cannot make Arabian Parts or read houses with no Ascendant, but I can use a few judicious midpoints.

Mars/Saturn of death at 3 Pisces
Saturn/Neptune of victims and sinking at 28 Taurus
Moon/Saturn of bad luck at 11 Gemini
Jupiter/Saturn of luck negated at 24 Gemini

Mars/Jupiter of recklessness at 14 Scorpio
Mutual reception Mars/Sun/Saturn at 17 Aries
The Titanic set sail on her maiden voyage at 12:00 PM GMT from South Hampton on April 10, 1912. Some 2,500 souls were aboard, more or less half and half the cream of English and American wealthy high society and steerage class. Separated on board, many would become equal in death.

I'll now punch in some embarkation aspects to the above midpoints.

Keelplate	Sailing
Mars/Saturn, 3 Pisces	Part of Peril, 4 Pisces
Saturn/Neptune, 28 Taurus	See Pluto, Venus, Moon
Moon/Saturn, 11 Gemini	Mars/Saturn, 10 Gemini
Jupiter/Saturn, 24 Gemini	Saturn/Neptune, 20 Gemini
	Lunar Part of Neptune,
	24 Gemini
	Mars/Pluto, 29 Gemini
	Pluto, 27 Gemini
Mars/Jupiter, 14 Scorpio	Trine Sun/Uranus, 11 Pisces
	This square Mars/Saturn
	Trine Neptune, 21 Cancer
	(Mars-Jupiter-Neptune
	One Time Big Trouble)
Mut Recept Mars/Sun-Saturn	Mars/Uranus, 18 Aries, MC
17 Aries	17 Aries

Such was the terrible birth of the Titanic.

For the purpose of this study I want to key the event to the Parts, specifically Fortuna and Spirit. I only punched them in after having previously left them out of tragic charts, not understanding their nature—carrying energy to the three Ascendants.

From the embarkation or sets sail chart: Fortuna at 19 Taurus 13 conjunct Saturn of sinking at 17 Taurus 43; Spirit at 29 Libra 13 conjunct Solar Part of Neptune/Pluto at 27 Libra, the natural zodiac midpoint of disappearance, conjunct Moon/Neptune chart and zodiac rulers (twelfth and eighth) of disappearance.

There above is the sinking and disappearance of the Titanic and my point is made. Moving for a little overkill, Ascendant ruler/eighth house ruler is the point of life and death. Here Jupiter as the ancient ruler of Pisces is a death dealing planet. Indeed the first cause of death was hubris (Sun/Jupiter). Here Sun/Jupiter is conjunct the lunar Part of the Ascendant at 17 Aquarius. Restated, decoding the Part conjunct Sun/Jupiter/Moon = Descendant and the death dealing energy flowed to the Ascendant.

This chart is too good to walk away from. In 1985 when the Titanic was found by Robert Ballard, progressed Sun, ruler of the first house, and progressed Venus, ruler of the tenth house, had come to Mars, ruler of the ninth house of luck.

Nothing is more open than the union of the first and tenth house rulers, and the Titanic was found and seen by the world.

Ivy Goldstein Jacobson observed that the chart continues after death. As transiting Uranus made its return in Sets Sail, plans were underway for a new movie. It's scheduled for summer 1997 after transiting Uranus makes its final (C) return. I forecast a blockbuster.

TWA Flight 800 Mysteriously Breaks Up

At first glance Fortuna and Spirit are not aspected, but Pluto and Uranus form a midpoint at 1 Capricorn 41 conjunct Fortuna at 1 Capricorn 42. I do not use change by night. The midpoints work in conjunction and this one somewhat defines the nature of the matter. Can we key to this? First a digression.

I hand calculated this chart the same evening, coming up with an Ascendant of 27 Capricorn 02 supposedly for crash time at 8:40 PM EDT. Somehow I made a twenty-minute error in the Ascendant according to Matrix and my chart inadvertently became correct for the runway time.

In this chart Neptune may be said to rule fuel. In the equal house Pisces third, it rules the tenth of the sixth of engines. I read catastrophic failure for the following reason: possible fuel error, Sun (captain) heavily to Neptune and the Ascendant-Descendant.

Mercury rules the manufacture and the "sickness" of the craft, and the crew. Earlier in the day Mercury made and separated from an opposition to Uranus, this same planet triggered by the Moon less than two days earlier.

Note that Sun and Saturn rule the eighth and the first—their midpoint that of life and death. Both are in poor signs for their energy, Saturn in detriment, and the Sun in its twelfth sign.

Note the actual midpoint Sun/Saturn is at 3 Gemini 05. Mundane astrologers often refer to this as the point of weakness. It may be stated as limitations (Saturn) of the whole (Sun). The Sun is also the captain here.

At this time the Part of Death at 3 Aquarius 12 was conjunct Uranus retrograde at 2 Aquarius 51 by equal house, as the ancients worked. With Placidus cusps it is at 19 Aquarius. Note that the above Sun/Saturn trines this and that the midpoint Saturn/Pluto is conjunct Death and Uranus.

157

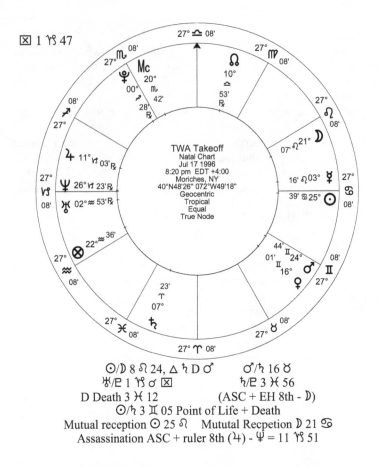

⊠ 1 ♑ 47

27° ♎ 08'

27° ♏ 08'
Mc
♇ 20°
00° ♏
♐ 42'
28' ℞

27° ♍ 08'

☊ 10°
♎ 53' ℞

27° ♌ 08'

27° ♐ 08'

07' ♌ 21° ☽

♃ 11° ♑ 03' ℞

27° ♑ 08'
♆ 26° ♑ 23' ℞
♅ 02° ♒ 53' ℞

16' ♌ 03' ☿ 27° ♋ 08'

39' ♋ 25° ☉

TWA Takeoff
Natal Chart
Jul 17 1996
8:20 pm EDT +4:00
Moriches, NY
40°N48'26" 072°W49'18"
Geocentric
Tropical
Equal
True Node

22° ♒ 36'

27° ♒ 08'
⊗

44' ♊ 24°
01' ♊ 16° ♂
♀

27° ♊ 08'

23' ♈ 07'

27° ♓ 08'
♄

27° ♉ 08'

27° ♈ 08'

☉/☽ 8 ♌ 24, △ ♄ ☽ ♂   ♂/♄ 16 ♉
♅/♇ 1 ♑ ♂ ⊠   ♄/♇ 3 ♓ 56
☽ Death 3 ♓ 12   (ASC + EH 8th - ☽)
☉/♄ 3 ♊ 05 Point of Life + Death
Mutual reception ☉ 25 ♌   Mututal Recpetion ☽ 21 ♋
Assassination ASC + ruler 8th (♃) - ♔ = 11 ♑ 51

So much for the catastrophic failure scenario. "[The Boeing 747-100 is a] bulwark of rugged dependability with one anomalous exception. On May 9, 1976 a Continental Boeing 747-100, the same model as TWA Flight 800, leased by the pre-Revolutionary Iranian Air Force, exploded in flight and crashed near Madrid, killing 17 crew members."

I am almost certain that quote came from *USA Today*. The content is indisputable and verifiable.

I find the idea of many old planes with metal fatigue or other catastrophic failure potential far more frightening than an occasional terrorist attack. The government to date has not been able to prove what it wishes to prove. On September 12, 1996, the government announced it might blow up an empty 747 to further the investigation. My thoughts on that are somewhat unprintable.

Nevertheless in the interest of objectivity I decided to look at the

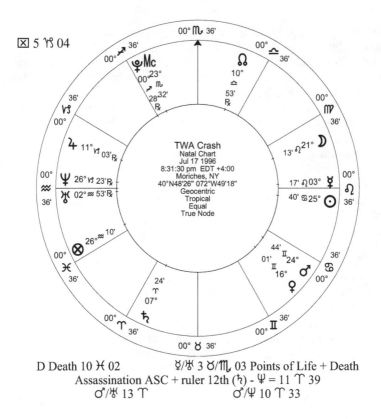

⊠ 5 ♑ 04

00° ♏ 36'

D Death 10 ♓ 02   ☿/⚷ 3 ♉/♏ 03 Points of Life + Death
Assassination ASC + ruler 12th (♄) - Ψ = 11 ♈ 39
♂/⚷ 13 ♈   ♂/Ψ 10 ♈ 33

terrorist scenario. First let's note the time sequence as it relates to the Parts and either scenario.

By crash time Jupiter was within four or five degrees of Spirit (conjunct it) and the Ascendant was Aquarius. This is an afflicted Jupiter, sign, retrograde, twelfth—not always good and squared by a stronger (stationary) Saturn in violent detriment.

The natural movement of time has now brought Aquarius to the first and Scorpio to the tenth—in short, the original midpoint to earlier Fortuna, Uranus/Pluto is slamming into action. On the angles the possibility of this taking on a sabotage connection grows especially with Saturn/Pluto conjunct Uranus and Sun/Saturn trine them.

Regarding either scenario, Death is locked, Death conjunct Uranus, and Moon and mutual reception Sun are conjunct the eighth. Moon itself is enough with the influence of the ruler of the eighth, the Sun.

Returning to the 8:20 chart, on the runway, the Part of Assassination, Ascendant and the ruler of the twelfth, Jupiter (Neptune), Neptune equals Assassination at 11 Capricorn 51.

A case may be made for both scenarios and I simply have not come to a conclusion. It eludes me at the moment. The ambivalence continues. I incline to catastrophic failure. My original reading. Mars/Uranus at 13 Aries is clearly both crash and explosion, but Mars/Neptune at 11 Aries is both fuel fire and attack. Both are brought to Saturn by the South Node and both afflict the poor Jupiter.

Finally Venus is in a sneak attack degree and Moon/Venus at 18+ Cancer equals Jupiter/Neptune at 18+ Capricorn. Moon-Venus-Jupiter is the signature of massacre.

Regarding the known case of catastrophic failure May 9, 1976, the Sun there was in the same degree as Titanic Saturn, at 19 Taurus for the duration of the flight. The reader should glance at the ephemeris. Spain, Mars/Saturn at 26 Cancer, with natural conjunction Long Island, Mars/Saturn at 16 Taurus.

ValuJet Crash

The ValuJet crash was the first event chart that I attempted to key to Fortuna and Spirit. It was pretty self-evident, supplying the insight. FAA investigations concluded that the cargo oxygen bottles exploded or that an oxygen fire flared up.

Venus, ruler of the second house of cargo, is conjunct Fortuna. It also rules the ninth house of luck. The Part of Catastrophe (ASC + Uranus - Sun) is conjunct the Sun. The midpoint of life and death (rulers of the first and eighth), Mercury/Mars, is within orb of Sun.

There never was a question of sabotage so I did no violent Parts. Between the Moon and Saturn in the seventh, unpleasant midpoints clump.

Mars/Jupiter, 12 Pisces—carelessness
Mars/Neptune, 17 Pisces—gas activity
Mars/Uranus, 20 Pisces—crash, explosion, fire
Moon/Saturn, 22 Pisces—misfortune
Mercury/Neptune, 27 Pisces—rulers of the first and seventh, the matter opposed

No conjunction is formed with the Part of Death. Mars/Saturn at 20 Aries is conjunct Sun/Moon at 16 Aries. All are conjunct the South Node, this confirming negativity. The Nodes are solunar points.

Note the Moon besieged (between) Uranus and Saturn, that ancient horary axiom. Mars is the death dealing planet, as ruler of the eighth house it brings bad luck to the ninth where it also is in detriment and in a Venus sign.

Take off time some ten or so minutes earlier would have brought Fortuna close to partile with Venus and Catastrophe in 18-19 Taurus, a degree present in Titanic Sails and TWA 747 crashes in Spain.

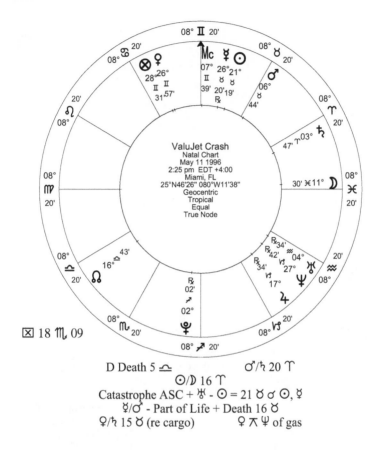

ValuJet Crash
Natal Chart
May 11 1996
2:25 pm EDT +4:00
Miami, FL
25°N46'26" 080°W11'38"
Geocentric
Tropical
Equal
True Node

⊠ 18 ♏ 09

D Death 5 ♎   ♂/♄ 20 ♈
          ☉/☽ 16 ♈
Catastrophe ASC + ♅ - ☉ = 21 ♉ ♂ ☉, ☿
        ☿/♂ - Part of Life + Death 16 ♉
♀/♄ 15 ♉ (re cargo)   ♀ ⚻ ♆ of gas

Two Sisters Disappear

On November 16, 1995, two Palestinian sisters disappeared on the island of St. Croix, U.S. Virgin Islands. The older sister had come to pick up her younger sister at school. Over the next few days the newspapers gave varying times. They were last seen at the school and I picked a time.

Earlier in the text I dealt with this event in delineating the Part of Death to show that it does not always kick in—an important lesson for all Parts. I decided to go back and reexamine the chart in terms of Fortuna and Spirit.

In this chart Spirit is without conjunction, as is Fortuna. I'll put aside its conjunction of mutual reception Saturn at 18 Capricorn in order not to muddy waters. Personally I've had some interesting results with the degrees of mutual receptions. For now, let us say point to point (MR Saturn to Fortuna) equals nothing to nothing.

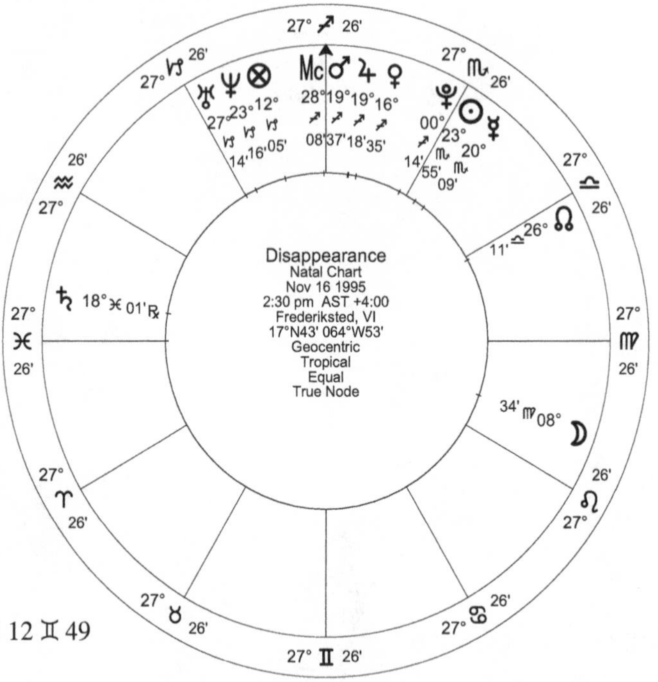

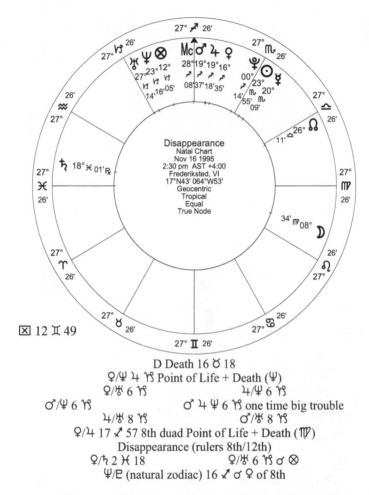

☒ 12 ♊ 49

D Death 16 ♉ 18

♀/♆ 4 ♑ Point of Life + Death (♆)

♀/♅ 6 ♑ ♃/♆ 6 ♑

♂/♆ 6 ♑ ♂ ♃ ♆ 6 ♑ one time big trouble

♃/♅ 8 ♑ ♂/♅ 8 ♑

♀/♃ 17 ♐ 57 8th duad Point of Life + Death (♍)

Disappearance (rulers 8th/12th)

♀/♄ 2 ♓ 18 ♀/♅ 6 ♑ ☌ ⊗

♆/♇ (natural zodiac) 16 ♐ ☌ ♀ of 8th

Midpoints are actual dynamic energy points. The chart leaps to life. Whatever the precise time of abduction, these midpoints conjunct Fortuna and Spirit and with one other set of points, the whole story is laid bare.

Venus/Neptune at 4 Capricorn, usually the wrong type of love or attraction, is applicable, but more importantly they are the point of life and death (rulers of first and eighth). Venus/Uranus at 6 Capricorn is a forceful attraction. Jupiter/Neptune is at 6 Capricorn and they are rulers of the Ascendant—the event is sure to happen. Mars-Jupiter-Neptune bring one time big trouble here tied to the ruler of the eighth house of death. Jupiter/Uranus at 8 Capricorn is a reckless undertaking.

Mars/Uranus at 8 Capricorn is sudden violence, an out of control event.

What may have began as an attack escalated out of control. That there were two, or the younger sister was a factor, and that the relatives would seek revenge may also have been a consideration.

The planet of death, Venus, is in the duad degree of the hunter-killer 15-17.5 Sagittarius.

The Sagittarius stellium is of sexual excess. Here Moon/Saturn is at 13 Sagittarius. Sun/Mars is at 5 Sagittarius, concentrating the deadly Sun-Moon-Mars-Saturn at 9 Sagittarius conjunct Venus/Pluto of obsession at 8 Sagittarius; Venus rules the eighth. The assailant was capable of murder and may have been a stalker.

Finally moving to Spirit, Moon-Saturn of worst luck conjuncts it.

Here the interweaving of energies brought about the tragedy of disappearance. Simple rape would have been terrible in itself, but not as bad. This is akin to those ancient soldiers who would have seen slavery as salvation over death by torture.

As of September 14, 1996, they have not been found, though the car and some personal effects were found shortly afterwards. That I believe them dead is my personal conclusion as drawn from this single chart. The midpoints for disappearance are Neptune/Pluto (natural) and Venus/Uranus rulers of the eighth and twelfth houses. The transit of the Sun to Jupiter, ruler of the first and tenth, or the progression of Jupiter to the actual Midheaven some years from now may solve the mystery. I know the Midheaven is not exact. The Moon is in a body in the ditch or street degree, as is the concentration of the Sun-Moon-Mars-Saturn and Venus/Pluto.

These are first/fourth house ruler combinations, the self and the grave. All have some connotation of being hidden or final. I do not see an early resolution. Mercury/Jupiter is at 4 Sagittarius between Venus and Pluto; Mercury/Neptune is at 21 Sagittarius conjunct Neptune/Pluto; and Moon/Mars (natural) at 29 Libra is played out.

The Trial and Verdict of O.J. Simpson

Trial Begins has Fortuna conjunct Neptune, Uranus, and the Sun. The transiting Moon's first aspect some ten hours later is to conjunct O.J.'s Jupiter at 17 Scorpio.

In the Verdict, O.J.'s Fortuna is barely conjunct Saturn. I wonder what might have happened if the deliberations had continued another half hour.

Spirit appears without conjunction. Not so, as it is conjunct O.J.'s Sun at 16 Cancer and Verdict Mars conjunct the Ascendant is conjunct O.J.'s Jupiter 17 Scorpio. Mars co-rules Scorpio. Verdict Sun/Moon is conjunct Verdict Jupiter.

Trial Begins Saturn at 10 Pisces is conjunct Verdict Fortuna at 11

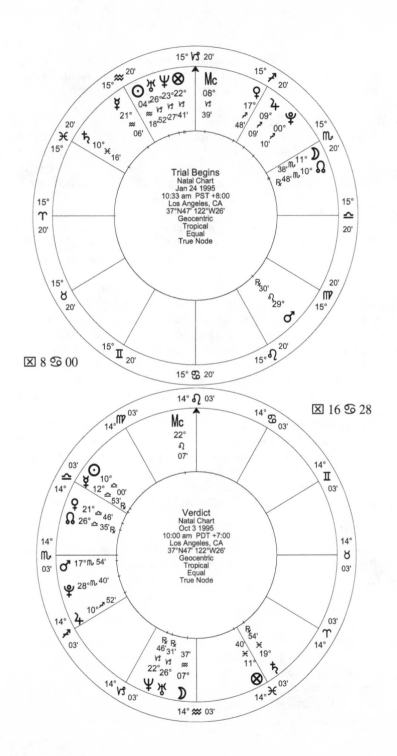

Pisces. I have not figured that one out yet. (In the spring of 1997 I saw the obvious—Saturn ruler of Trial Begins; tenth also involved in a mutual reception.) Trial Sun/Verdict Sun = 6 Sagittarius conjunct Sun/Moon = Jupiter. O.J. Sun/Verdict Sun = 28 Leo conjunct Trial void-of-course Mars at 29 Leo and ruler of the Ascendant and O.J. No, I did not forecast this one. I dropped the matter for lack of time and without using astrology in the final days I thought he'd be found quilty. Personally I never thought the verdict had much to do with O.J. I cynically see it as a vote against sequestration, overbearing marshals, and racist cops. O.J owes Mark Fuhrmann a thank you note.

Astrologically, these charts are a study in luck. For those who believe O.J. got away with it, those indicators are present—mutual receptions, void-of-course planets, strong Uranus or Jupiter-Uranus and planets in good signs.

For those who await a comeuppance, don't hold you breath. Sun trine Jupiter is the survivor. Progressed Sun reaches Neptune when he is about eighty-three years old. The damage of future transiting Uranus and Pluto are offset as each finds itself with "easy" oppositions—his Mars, Saturn, and Pluto, receiving trines with the oppositions from the opposing planets themselves.

His Sun/Moon midpoint is at 21 Taurus close to the Midheaven at 18 Taurus 47, a degree that has turned up tragically several times in this study. The ruler of the first and tenth is a winner and the Moon is exalted in Taurus, here as Sun/Moon.

O.J.'s Luck

Violence Mars/Neptune 6 Leo 43 conjunct Sun/Ascendant 5 Leo 36, Mars/Neptune conjunct Saturn at 8 Leo 54. Saturn/Pluto 10 Leo 36—violence as a control freak. Note involvements of two Ascendants—a good bet to happen; Mars/Neptune of attack, Mars-Saturn-Neptune violent death, Mars-Saturn death, Saturn/Neptune victim, Saturn/Pluto control, Mars-Saturn-Pluto control freak for personal power Ascendant/Sun.

Violent degrees—I will not do all but only highlight 15-17.5 Cancer degree of domestic violence, murder, execution of family. Mars/Ascendant 15 Cancer, Saturn/Uranus 16 Cancer, Sun 15 Cancer 39. When placed with Mercury/Venus 13 Cancer, Uranus/Neptune 17 Cancer 48 (8th duad), Venus/Saturn 20 Cancer 11, Sun/Venus 20 Cancer 37, Venus/Pluto 21 Cancer 46, all centered at 16 Cancer.

Neptune 8 Libra Vindemiatrix—suffering women, suffering through women 7.5 plus cardinal, tragic-violent death of a noted person, here Neptune of victim. Jupiter/Ascendant 6 Libra cardinal 5-7.5

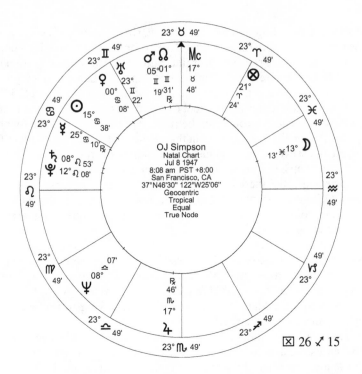

OJ Simpson
Natal Chart
Jul 8 1947
8:08 am PST +8:00
San Francisco, CA
37°N46'30" 122°W25'06"
Geocentric
Tropical
Equal
True Node

tragic, here ruler of eighth; Jupiter, Ascendant, self; and Libra, relationship.

7.5-9°59' mutable—body in the ditch or street degree, Saturn/Neptune of victim 8 Virgo 34, Venus/Jupiter of excessive love 9 Virgo 33. Note Jupiter and Neptune here rulers of eighth, Venus ruler of third, eighth of eighth, and tenth of fate.

O.J.'s natal Parts of Jupiter are ASC + Jupiter - Sun = Jupiter 25 Sagittarius 45; reciprocal ASC + Sun - Jupiter = 23 Aries 27; ASC + Jupiter - Moon = 16 Aries 46; reciprocal ASC + Moon - Jupiter = 19 Sagittarius 16; ASC Part of Jupiter, 21 Taurus 27; Sun/Mars 26 Gemini 18 Point of Luck, rulers of first and ninth; Moon/Jupiter luck 21 Capricorn 40; Sun/Jupiter luck (protection) 16 Virgo 42; Sun-Moon-Jupiter grand trine water in water houses. This enhanced by Sun, ruler of first, Sun in Cancer of Moon, Juiter in Mars sign Scorpio with Mars, ruler of fourth and ninth.

Death work—Sun/Jupiter 16 Virgo 42, Point of Life and Death rulers first and eighth; Sun/Neptune 27 Leo 22, Point of Life and Death rulers of first and eighth; Mars/ Saturn 7 Cancer 31.

Part of Death—4 Virgo 25, ASC + 8th (equal house) - Moon. Part of Assassination—ASC + ruler 12th - Neptune = 28 Capricorn 55. Part of Suicide—ASC + 8th - Neptune = 9 Aquarius 31.

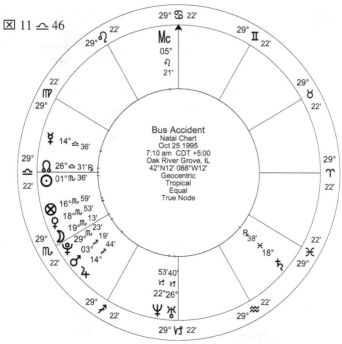

⊠ 11 ♎ 46

29° ♋ 22'

29°♌ 22'

Mc
05°
♌
21'

29° ♊ 22'

22'
♍
29°

29° ♉ 22'

☿ 14° ♎ 36'

Bus Accident
Natal Chart
Oct 25 1995
7:10 am CDT +5:00
Oak River Grove, IL
42°N12' 088°W12'
Geocentric
Tropical
Equal
True Node

29°
♎
22'

☊ 26° ♎ 31' ℞
⊙ 01° ♏ 36'

29°
♈
22'

⊗ 16°♏ 59'
♀ 18°♏ 53'
19°♏ 23'
☽ 29°♐ 19'
♍ 29°♏ 44'
♂ 03°♐ 14°

℞
38'
⚷ 18°
♓
♄ 29°

29° ♏ 22'

29° ♐ 22'

53'40'
♃ ♑
22°26°
Ψ ♅
29° ♑ 22'

22'
♒
29°

Saturn/Pluto 10 Leo 55, stimulated intermittently by transiting Moon conjunct S in Aquarius, Saturn/Pluto control, Mars-Saturn-Pluto the control freak, Mars/Saturn-Pluto energy center of control freak 8 Cancer 28 conjunct Sun/Venus 8 Cancer 58, Sun/Venus solipcism, narcissism, loss of perspective, ego cravings, blind desire. Blind desire for control—Sun/Venus, here point of fate, rulers of first and tenth.

So I ended up doing the whole ball of wax. I do not believe O.J. innocent. There was too much rage in the murders. Having said that, I hope he is acquitted in the civil suit. It is double jeopardy and a bad precedent in law. The sacking of Panama to capture Noriega, drug confiscation laws, double jeopardy, sooner or later everyone is a victim.

School Bus Train Accident

I could go on and on, but I may as well end soon. Hopefully the reader wants to start checking his own charts. I am confident his results will match mine.

America was disturbed by this accident. When the school bus stalled on the train tracks, seven students were killed when the train hit it.

There was a 29 degree Ascendant, the ruler was in a bad sign for it, and it was too late to help the matter. The ruler of the Ascendant, Venus, conjunct Moon in the "terrible" degrees of horary 18-19 Scorpio—bad signs for both as well. Spirit at 11 Libra was conjunct the ruler of the twelfth, Mercury, in the first sign, twelfth house side—bad.

Venus and the Moon in Scorpio were conjunct Fortuna. These afflicted planets have been collecting Saturn energy through the Moon. Note that in Libra rising, Venus is the life and death point.

The Part of Death has no conjunctions, not the eighth or itself. Move to Sun/Moon at 10 Scorpio 75 degrees from Mars/Saturn at 25 Capricorn.

Seventy-five degrees is an aspect of excess and more or less fated in most charts. It is also the midpoint distance between the first and the eighth houses in the equal house chart. Sun-Moon-Mars-Saturn is the death picture or yoga.

For those who use antiscia or solstice points, Mars and Uranus form perfect to the minute mutual antiscia.

Venus/Saturn at 18 Capricorn, death dealers in the eighth duad, Sun in Leo conjunct a midpoint to Neptune from Uranus. Mars/Saturn is between Neptune and Uranus in orb of conjunction to both. The pictures are all there in synthesis; Venus-Neptune fuel problems. Venus-Mars-Saturn is death, with Neptune violent. Mars/Uranus crash, emphasized with solstice point Mars.

Saved by Washing Dishes

I acquired this chart from the *National Enquirer* or *The Weekly World News*. I know I was tired because I failed to get the source once again.

Other than enjoying these tabloids and watching clerks twitch when I carefully hide the local newspaper inside *The Weekly World News* (that's the one with the Elvis and Hitler sightings), I have found them a consistently good source of data over the years.

Anyway it seems that Mrs. Ptasinski was very adamant about husband David doing the dishes that morning. This made him late for work and saved his life. Due in his office at 7:00 AM, it blew up at 7:15.

This is reminiscent of the church explosion and besides being upbeat and positive, I thought I should check it out with the Parts.

This chart is not as clear or intense. After all, the gods were only saving one henpecked husband and blowing up his office was nothing more than kicking the cosmic trash can.

Fortuna, Spirit and Death are without planetary conjunctions. I managed to place Jupiter/Pluto in wide conjunction to Spirit, well

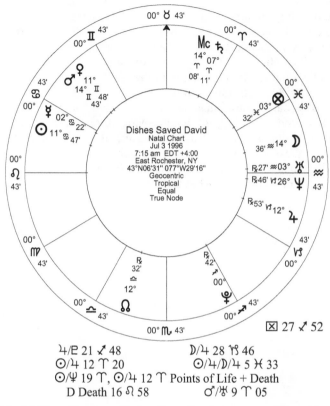

00° ♉ 43'

00° ♈ 43'

00° ♊ 43'

Mc ♄
14° 07°
♈ ♈
08' 11'

43'
♂ 11°
14° ♊
♊ 48'
43'

00° ⊕ ♓
32' ⚹ 03' 43'

00°
43' ♀

00°
♋

☿ 02° ♋ 22'
☉ 11° ♋ 47'

Dishes Saved David
Natal Chart
Jul 3 1996
7:15 am EDT +4:00
East Rochester, NY
43°N06'31" 077°W29'16"
Geocentric
Tropical
Equal
True Node

36' ≈ 14° ☽

00°
♌
43'

℞27' ≈03° ♅
℞46' ♑26° ♆

00°
≈
43'

℞53' ♑ 12° ♃

00°
♍
43'

43'

00°
♐

00°
♑

℞
32'
♎
12°

℞
42'

00°
♐

⚷
00° ♐ 43'

00° ♏ 43'

♗ 27 ♐ 52

♃/♇ 21 ♐ 48   ☽/♃ 28 ♑ 46
☉/♃ 12 ♈ 20   ☉/♃/☽/♃ 5 ♓ 33
☉/♆ 19 ♈, ☉/♃ 12 ♈ Points of Life + Death
D Death 16 ♌ 58   ♂/♅ 9 ♈ 05

within Al-Biruni's orb and bring the midpoint energy of the midpoints Sun/Jupiter (save your ass) and Moon/Jupiter (good luck) to their own midpoint, which is conjunct Fortuna on the cusp of the eighth house.

Sun/Neptune and Sun/Jupiter are the points of life and death here. It appears they opt for life. Both fall in Aries, favorable for the Sun and Jupiter. Mars/Uranus of fire and explosion also falls there conjunct Sun/Jupiter. It is sextile Moon/Uranus the sudden, the volatile, the turn around, in its own sign. That is, all four planets Sun, Jupiter, Mars, and Uranus are in favorable signs. This is a strong factor in favorable outcomes.

What about the Moon? The closest aspect is an immediate approaching trine to Mars, ruler of the ninth house of luck. Mars is a good planet for a Leo Ascendant. Sun is semisextile Mars and Mars is semisquare Ascendant.

All three Ascendants are influenced by luck. The Moon has also completed a recent trine to Venus, ruler of the tenth.

Now it remains to examine death in the chart. The Part of Death has no conjunction. It is not locked. Move to Sun-Moon-Mars-Saturn.

Note that they are not connected. The nearest they come is the weak sextile of Mars and Saturn, but Mars itself tones down Saturn here. While they influence each other, Saturn is weak and malevolent in Aries. The ninth, being strong for the overall synthesis, is favorable. Not only are these four planets not integrated, neither are their midpoints Sun/Moon or Mars/Saturn.

Finally Mars/Saturn square Death equals Mars/Saturn square nothing. Traditional astrology is favorable here. Moon trine Mars, Sun opposition Jupiter, and Pluto trine Ascendant, all approaching—for the last time these trines involve three Ascendants.

All in all this was an unusual event and I hope Mr. Ptasinski doesn't get roped into doing the dishes too often.

Closing Comments

Working with these example charts I decided to go full steam ahead with something that I'd begun earlier. The midpoint of the Ascendant ruler and a given house ruler are the point of the matter of that house as it connects to that person or event or horary question. I am satisfied in the results.

This midpoint at times may not be a midpoint. For example, my chart has Libra rising. Thus the midpoint of life and death is Venus itself.

Similarly in my own chart, Mercury rules the ninth house of luck and the twelfth house of misfortune through self-undoing. In the end all eagles come to earth. In the meanwhile fly and don't worry about it.

Sagittarius or Pisces as ruler of the sixth, eighth, or twelfth will give both good and bad. Bad might be cancer, carelessness, hubris; the last two are either the eighth or twelfth.

Indira Gandhi died because she had the temerity to sack a Sikh temple. A young male TV star, John Hexum, shot himself in the temple with a blank gun and died. These were Jupiter deaths.

At the AFA I promised Ann Parker something if she attended my lectures. At conventions we are somewhat the passing ships though we share at least three astrological interests: alcoholism, Arabian Parts, and earthquakes.

So here it is Ann. After the convention I punched Fortuna and Spirit into a bunch of my timed earthquake charts and came up with significant conjunctions to Moon, Mercury, Mars, and Uranus. In my book on earthquakes I designated these as trigger planets. Like many earthquake aspects, these conjunct Parts were often separating. (During a given day, there are times when both move forward zodiacally since the Ascendant increasing numerically more rapidly then the Sun or Moon is always on the increase side of the equation $A = B - C = D$).

Research into this may yield some hope of time of day for a major event. Populations and economies have grown over the centuries.

Thus, body counts and economic ripples will also increase. These are not my concerns.

I have one earthquake concern: A 6+ Richter or larger quake rising up beneath a nuclear power plant making Chernobyl look like the shorts to the movie.

In this text, the reader may have noted my use of three-planet pictures, not necessarily midpoints, but connections. Some are vaguely noted in midpoint books, some not. These are not the only meanings and they require a relevant chart.

Connections include minor aspects, midpoints of two planets in aspect with the third—conventional midpoints, a fourth planet in aspect to all three. These planets in same sign line up the energies. Forthwith:

Moon-Venus-Jupiter—massacre, extreme violence

Mars-Saturn-Pluto—the control freak

Mars-Saturn-Neptune—violent death found in victim or culprit's chart

Mars-Jupiter-Neptune—one time big trouble changing the life

Sun-Mercury-Mars—in an author, prolific and/or acerbic, in an athlete, the natural

Venus-Mars-Jupiter—plenty of sex, the playboy or playgirl, marriage

Venus-Mars-Saturn—sexual problem or lasting love

Ascendant-Moon-Sun (the components of Fortuna and Spirit)—when activated simultaneously by a fourth planet something must happen

Sun-Saturn-Pluto—power

Sun-Mars-Jupiter—war, religion, the great enterprise undertaken

Moon-Saturn-Neptune—unfortunates

Sun-Jupiter-Pluto—noted by the Magi Society for lasting achievement or success. I agree.

There are others. These are just the ones I work with routinely.

Disappearances are always of interest. First check for death. If you find it, then you have unfound bodies. Outside of runaway children or spouses and AWOL soldiers, most disappearances involve death. Planes crash in obscure places or over the sea. Ships sink. The sea, the desert, and the jungle hide many bodies.

Working with disappearance charts, I believe the signature is Neptune-Pluto, usually by midpoint. These are the zodiac or natural rulers of the twelfth and eighth houses. Similarly, use the Ascendant chart rulers of the twelfth and eighth. Aspects between any of these merely confirms the matter. Usually they aspect the Ascendant, Sun, Moon, Midheaven, or Ascendant ruler strongly.

Having pointed out how I know the body is misplaced, is there any hope of finding it?

The discovery of the Titanic offers a solution which I have not had time to work with elsewhere. In the Titanic Sails chart the progressed rulers of the first and tenth (Sun and Venus) are conjunct Mars at the time of discovery in 1985. Mars here rules the fourth of the grave and the ninth of luck. The symbology of the houses in question taken together needs no explanation and I will work forward from here.

The Arabian Parts did not arise as spiritual or psychological astrology, but as a forecasting technique. Since they are actually nothing more than two pairs of midpoints, appropriate Parts may be used in psychological or spiritual astrology.

Regarding spirituality in astrology, it will not find bodies, though one can quickly note the karma involved in many violent charts. Again karma is not spirituality, but a debt. Personally, I think some murderers and victims are playing tag.

At the conventions I've found astrologers who do not know the Golden Rule: "Do unto others as you would have them do unto you."

This is the only common tenet of the great religions. They seldom mention it in the latter days of the twentieth century. Regarding the Golden Rule, the Buddhists note that if you practice it you don't need to read the [spiritual] book.

Forecasting is the essence of astrology. If you can do some forecasting, you can probably manage the rest.

It is a known fact that Picasso of the contorted faces was a master draftsman.

Regarding the astrology of midpoints, in general Saturn is important. Conjunct Al-Biruni's Fortuna, transiting Saturn came to Witt's converse progressed Fortuna and Uranus at publication. I had my breakthrough on the Parts with transiting Saturn conjunct Fortuna. The English astrologer Sepharial notes Saturn as the ruler of astrology.

I did finally visit with Manilius. In that chapter what I wrote followed the AFA convention. After some reflection I decided to let the earlier comments stand as they were not far off the mark.

Tripping on the tent peg, our astrologer rose from the dust and brushed the camel chips from his robe saying, "I'll reach the Ascendants all at once and more often." He was about to find Fortuna. ASC + Moon - Sun = Fortuna (conjunct transiting Jupiter).

The astrologer came from a lunar people, both by psyche and belief in its powers. He began to work this in with the intent of marking time with the Moon and Sun. ASC + Jupiter - Moon = Lunar Jupiter.

It wasn't exactly transiting Jupiter conjunct the Ascendant, but it was pretty close and he could get it every month—a lucky time each month: ASC/Jupiter = Moon/lunar Jupiter (conjunct transiting Moon). His time of misfortune: ASC + Saturn - Moon, or ASC + Mars

- Saturn. Danger: ASC + Saturn - Mars, all to the transiting Moon.

Today we have the slow planets. None of us ever gets to experience all of their conjunctions. Would you like a taste of the Neptune-Pluto conjunction of the late nineteenth century? ASC + Neptune - Pluto = Part (conjunct transiting Moon) or ASC/Neptune = Pluto/transiting Moon. There Pluto is the dynamic planet. With its reciprocal you can feel it through Neptune.

Our astrologer gave us the richness of all planetary combinations in all charts to be experienced personally through the Ascendant with one simple formula: A + B - C = D.

The End
September 15, 1996
6:27 PM AST
St. Thomas, U.S. Virgin Islands

The Astrology of Missing Persons

O n June 1, 1937 a plane left Miami airport at 6:00 a.m. EST flying into the rising Sun. Aboard were Amelia Earhart, the world's first lady of aviation, and her co-pilot Fred Noonan, accomplished navigator and alcoholic.

The purpose of the trip was to be the first woman to fly around the world. There would have been relief as they flew into the Sun, for a May 21, 1937[1] attempt from Los Angeles had aborted in Hawaii when she broke the wing while landing. In less than six weeks she had refitted. Breaking aviation records was a high pressure, deadly business.

Neither beautiful nor vain, most pictures show her slouched in flight garb. Nevertheless her sex appeal was immense—confirmed by Mars conjunct Jupiter square Moon, Moon/Venus midpoint conjunct Pluto. Neptune here in the Gemini stellium lent a mystique to her.

Mars-Jupiter is the signature of courage. Hers is both real and legendary, but it is also the signature of carelessness—here in Virgo surely not admitted. Hawaii was not her first scrape and her navigation ability had also been questioned.

She would not have known that the solar part of Jupiter (ASC + Jupiter - Sun) was conjunct her Moon. Solar Jupiter protects; lunar Jupi-

---

1. An earlier March 17, 1937 trip date has surfaced as bad data. This trip ended in Hawaii. The correct date was May 21, 1937. Unfortunately Claire Stickel had both flight and birth times wrong, the 1898 date of her birth first appearing in the *National Astrological Journal* in 1938. This date was subsequently reinforced when an anthology of the journal, articles taken from the 1930s, was published in the early 1980s. Should anyone be in doubt, simply move her birth date forward one year and attempt to do what I do here. Stickel subsequently came up with a rectified 6:15 a.m. 1897 chart, this now held wrong by time. I use the chart developed by Mrs. Yerrington who quoted data from Amelia Earhart when she attended the National Women's Convention, same data in Lovell's *Sound of Wings* (*Profiles of Women*). I got the Yerrington chart from *American Astrology*, August 1992. The data for both flights, Miami and Lae, New Guineau comes from "Untold Stories: The Search for Amelia Earhart," Discovery Channel.

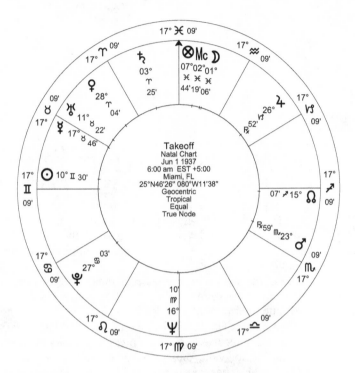

Takeoff
Natal Chart
Jun 1 1937
6:00 am EST +5:00
Miami, FL
25°N46'26" 080°W11'38"
Geocentric
Tropical
Equal
True Node

ter delivers goodies. As she stepped unharmed from her wrecked planes, she always managed to get a new one.

As she flew into the Sun, she did not know that this Jupiter was finally estranged, as eventually it is from those who take risks and that one morning thirty-one days later, it would choose to remain behind in the jungles of Lae.

Amelia Earhart's horoscope is remarkable. A Gemini stellium and two close and approaching conjunctions are interconnected by the Moon square Mars-Jupiter and 165 degrees from Saturn-Uranus. Venus carries the stellium energy to the Sun, itself in wide conjunction to Mercury which is semisextile the Mars-Jupiter conjunction.

It is beyond the limits of this chapter to fully explore her chart, but the Moon and Mars-Jupiter conjunction by aspect angle to Saturn and Uranus (165 and 75 degrees) show an implacable and inevitable path.

The Gemini stellium, obviously the key to her incredible appeal during her life and following her disappearance, is also a complete disappearance signature in itself; this was squared by the Mars-Jupiter conjunction of her courage itself, through the Moon. Mars and Jupiter, as rulers of the twelfth and eighth, also function as a disappearance signature.

This fully integrated chart carries all energies to the Sun through

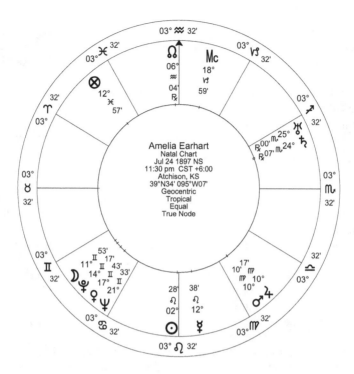

Amelia Earhart
Natal Chart
Jul 24 1897 NS
11:30 pm CST +6:00
Atchison, KS
39°N34' 095°W07'
Geocentric
Tropical
Equal
True Node

her Ascendant ruler Venus. If not too high like Icarus, she would in the end fly too far and disappear.

So much for Amelia Earhart. We all know the rest. I will use her charts and two others to show how to work disappearance in a chart using a personally tested technique and examining the difficulties of solution, noting some unproved but astrologically correct possibilities.

Coldly stated, people don't disappear. They die and their bodies are not found. Unfound bodies disturb the general psyche to the extent that we have invented the comforting concept of disappearance. Heroes and arch villains like Elvis, Hitler and Amelia Earhart live on.

Periodically I work on disappearances. I sensed early on I had to get beyond aspects because a lot of people had the same ones. The techniques that follow intensify the individuation of the chart. Their presentation is self explanatory.

A plane flying over the ocean disappears. Available landing areas amount to a fraction of a percent of the surrounding water. The plane runs out of fuel and falls and sinks.

The situation is clear. First we look for the death potential in natal and event charts.

1. The death aspects and signatures are always multiple and require sufficient progressions, solar arcs, and transits or strong synastry.

2. Arabian Parts are nothing but a system of midpoints. They are active only when a conjunction is present with the Part.

3. Planetary midpoints function like planets and may be used in other ways than set forth by the Uranians.

4. Houses are extremely important. They deliver to and limit the action of their rulers. They also permit any planetary energy or combination to vary from beneficial to deadly.

Most of us know the above to some degree or other, so I'll throw a curve. The ruler of the Ascendant forming a midpoint with the ruler of a house defines your life in terms of the house in question. With some combinations only one planet is involved. This also works for inter-house rulers. While all planets and combinations will function on their zodiacal and energy levels, they also function on this one for the individual.

The death combinations are Mars/Saturn, midpoint of the rulers of the first and eighth, strongly afflicted Fortuna, Spirit, Ascendant or Midheaven by conjunction .Combinations of Sun, Moon, Mars, and Saturn, the Part of Death formed by ASC + equal house 8th - Moon when 8th and Death are with conjunction.

Amelia Earhart: Mars/Saturn of Death, 17 Libra, conjunct Mars/Uranus of plane crash 17 Libra.

With a Taurus Ascendant, the rulers of the first and eighth become the point of life and death; here Venus/Jupiter at 29 Cancer 00, also involving Mars. In the end Venus/Jupiter will kill you. Remember this Venus-Jupiter. It is conjunct Mars/Neptune of fuel problems at 1 Leo.

Notably, Fortuna, the solar part of the Moon, ASC + Moon - Sun, is not aspected by conjunction; but Spirit, the lunar part of the Sun (ASC + Sun-Moon) is conjunct Neptune, a natural zodiacal disappearance planet.

Sun, Moon, Mars, Saturn distribution is not striking but Sun/Moon 7 Cancer 11 is in a degree of tragedy, the third house, and squares Sun/Saturn, the planetary point of weakness at 3 Libra 18 in the sixth (technology.). But Mars/Saturn, Mars-Uranus, both at 17 Libra are also here by house. Solar arc Mars-Jupiter is at about 19 Libra at death. Remember Mars-Jupiter.

Natal Fortuna is 12 Pisces 51. Fortuna arcs conversely and at Amelia's disappearance it was at 2 Aquarius without a natal conjunction. The nearest midpoints within orb are Miami, Jupiter 26 Capricorn; Miami, Mars/Saturn 28 Capricorn; Lae, Mars/Saturn 27 Capricorn; Lae, Moon/Mars 5 Aquarius.

Natal Spirit conjunct Neptune, when solar arced with the solar arc Sun, moves forward in the zodiac, here coming to 3 Leo. The midpoint of midpoint Neptune/Pluto and Mars/Jupiter centers its energies at 29 Cancer.

The true significance of Fortuna and Spirit—we all have them both—is that when conjuncted they distribute that planetary energy simultaneously to the Ascendant, Sun, and Moon. I conclude she is dead but I want a clincher. Transits are often the answer.

Using an old horary and mundane rule I turn to the beginning of the journey or Miami. Moon/Saturn of misfortune square her natal ruler Venus at 17 Gemini. Mars at 23 Scorpio 59 is tightly conjunct her natal Saturn 24 Scorpio Uranus 25 Scorpio, forming a transit picture of death by plane crash.

The clincher for this is the 10 Gemini Sun of Miami conjunct natal Moon, setting the whole matter ablaze.

Amelia Earhart died when her plane went down.

Bodies float to the surface, they drift to shore. Hers was never found, nor was the plane. We return to the natal chart. Can disappearance show there? The answer is yes. Over the years, working with several dozen charts, I came up with a solution.

Disappearance is signified by the rulers of the twelfth and eighth, thus the signatures are as follows: the midpoints of Neptune/Pluto and the chart rulers of the twelfth and eighth by midpoint.

I also made Arabian Parts of these: ASC + Neptune - Pluto and ASC + ruler of the 12th - ruler of the 8th. This translates to the body (Ascendant) lost (ruler of the twelfth) in death (ruler of the eighth). The purpose of all Arabian Parts is to connect the planetary energies to the Ascendant.

Those with the potential to literally lose their body from their fellow man will have these strongly configured to Ascendant, Midheaven, Fortuna, Spirit, Sun, Moon and ruler of the Ascendant.

It is that simple. There are refinements on this: the rulers of the first and twelfth and Parts of the twelfth/eighth midpoint rulers using the Sun and Moon, but these are redundant.

A clear death reading also makes unnecessary the reading of luck .

Turning to her natal chart, Neptune and Pluto are part of a Gemini stellium which is a continuing conjunction. The energy of the stellium centers at 16+ Gemini. In short, Neptune and Pluto are conjunct the Moon and her Ascendant ruler Venus.

The Miami Ascendant is 17 Gemini conjunct her Venus and the stellium center.

The rulers of disappearance in her equal house chart are Mars, rulers of the twelfth, and Jupiter, ruler of the eighth. Natally they are eight minutes apart by conjunction in her fifth equal house of self-expression and risk. Her natal Part of Disappearance, ASC +Mars - Jupiter = 3 Taurus 21 conjunct her natal Ascendant. At Miami this was triggered by Venus/Uranus at 4 Taurus. The natal potential was strong and activated at Miami take-off.

Such a person making certain choices and repeatedly taking risks in flying over water would in the end lose her body. It was not fate or free will, but the weaving of the two into destiny.

So much for the natal chart. An event chart involving the disappearance will indicate the matter in the same way.

Miami rulers of disappearance are Neptune/Pluto (zodiac) at 21 Leo 37 and Venus/Saturn, rulers of the twelfth and eighth at 15 Aries 45. Remember, Venus is her personal ruler. Venus/Saturn semisextile Venus/Jupiter, Sun,/Node, Moon/Saturn and Saturn/MC. Jupiter is a natal disappearance planet. The Midheaven and North Node are accentuated.

Miami Neptune/Pluto 21 Leo 37 is square Jupiter/Neptune and Mars (Scorpio), square Sun/Venus, Venus/ASC, Sun/Uranus (Taurus), and opposition Mars/Uranus, Mercury/Mars, and Venus/Node (Aquarius).

First you die. Miami Mars/Saturn conjunct Jupiter; Saturn/Pluto square Moon, Midheaven and Fortuna and Moon/Saturn is square the Ascendant, the position of her natal ruler, Venus. Her Miami Part of disappearance is ASC + Venus - Saturn at 21 Cancer conjunct Pluto.

Going back to her natal chart, Miami Mars is exactly conjunct her Saturn-Uranus. Her natal Neptune/Pluto with Moon and Venus (her super disappearance configuration) is conjunct Miami Ascendant. Miami Venus/Jupiter, her natal life and death planets at 12 Pisces conjunct natal Fortuna, oppose natal disappearance Mars and Jupiter, both at 10 Virgo. A cardinal t-square of Jupiter opposition Pluto to Venus involves her one natal disappearance planet Jupiter, one zodiac disappearance planet Pluto—this to her Ascendant ruler Venus, played out, and in detriment, deposited by deadly Mars making an exact conjunction to natal Saturn and Uranus. Mercury/Saturn, here the Miami life and death point (rulers of the first and eighth), is conjunct Miami Venus at 26 Aries, forming a terrible square to the afflicted Jupiter = Mars/Saturn. Note Miami Moon conjunct Midheaven and Fortuna. Jupiter/Saturn (luck ran out) at 0 Pisces conjuncts the Moon and (widely) natal Fortuna. The Jupiter energy in this confers lasting fame (Moon-Jupiter). Venus/Jupiter at 12 Pisces 28, her rulers of life and death, exactly conjunct natal Fortuna at 12 Pisces, is widely conjunct Miami Fortuna at 7 Pisces 48—an eerie foretelling of the fame she would receive in death, her life's work carried forward in time by the mystique of disappearance.

The important point in Miami is that the disappearance and death can be noted in the same way in the event chart. Naturally such an event chart will integrate with the natal chart of the victim, but it can stand on its own. The three Amelia Earhart charts woven together tell quite a tale. Where the natal chart and the event chart are used to delineate a disappearance, various linkups of the relevant rulers are enhancement factors. Note that the basics were present in both charts.

There were stowaways on that flight from Miami, a tired Jupiter and eager Death. Jupiter would get off in Lae. He had had enough of Amelia Earhart.

In Lae she considered herself on the homeward leg. As I recall the documentary, there were no special problems, though both Earhart and Noonan were tired and had had stomach trouble.

Again, Noonan was a crack navigator and also an alcoholic. Earhart's Mars/Jupiter was not only the signature of her incredible courage but also the signature of carelessness, here unadmitted (Virgo).

What most likely happened is that they did not properly calculate slippage, the aviational equivalent of leeway. That is, there is a sideways slippage from wind striking the side of the plane or ship. Over aviation distances this can amount to hundreds of miles to the side of a destination. As her fuel ran out, there was little or no land in sight. The U.S. Navy felt they knew the general area. The best she could hope for was coming down in a coral lagoon.

One of the problems with great charts is that you cannot do them justice in an article. You have the charts. Please work them.

At 10:00 a.m. in the morning they left Lae. Once past the Solomon Islands, all land between there and California shows as dots on a map. Only two of the Hawaiian Islands, two thirds of the way to California, are big enough to roughly draw.

She ran out of gas, came down and died, most likely immediately. Death may have been a mercy—Mars/Saturn conjunct Jupiter, even closer than Miami. Mercury/Mars, the Lae planets of Life and Death, form a midpoint at 11 Virgo 12. They are conjunct the Ascendant with Sun/Mars, the Lae planets of disappearance (Sun ruler of the twelfth, Mars ruler of the eighth) as well as natal Mars-Jupiter planets of disappearance, square natal Moon and Miami Sun. Venus/Mars as rulers of the ninth/eighth—read crises in luck or death on trip—are in the twelfth at 22 Leo 05 exactly conjunct zodiac disappearance Neptune/Pluto. Both are tightly conjunct the Part of Death at 23 Leo 10. Mars at 19 Scorpio is widely conjunct Spirit, bringing its energies to Ascendant Sun and Moon. Fortuna at 17 Gemini 47 ties to Amelia's now terrible Gemini stellium—and is conjunct Miami Ascendant with its Sun.

Death is locked and triggered with these conjunctions and the conjunction of Saturn at 5 Aries to the eighth. The Part of Peril is activated strongly in this chart at 21 Aries 09 conjunct the Moon at 20 Aries 50. Finally, the Part of Disappearance at 27 Aries 12 is conjunct Jupiter/Pluto, a great fiasco, and conjunct Miami Venus at 28 Aries, the ruler of her natal Ascendant.

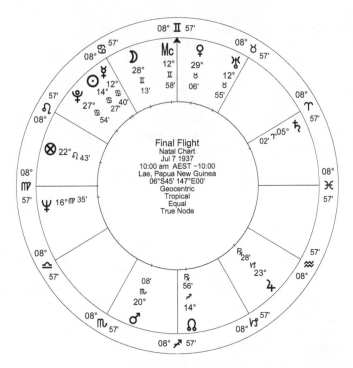

Final Flight
Natal Chart
Jul 7 1937
10:00 am AEST −10:00
Lae, Papua New Guinea
06°S45′ 147°E00′
Geocentric
Tropical
Equal
True Node

Note the interweaving of death and disappearance in this final chart. From birth to Miami to Lae the tumblers were clicking into place. Her tale was over less than twenty-four hours out of Lae. Her legend was just beginning and continues to this day.

Did you notice that Miami Sun is conjunct her Moon. Both are on my Jupiter and my Sun/Moon midpoint is 3 Taurus. Perhaps this is why I sit here....

My work is not over. I offer two randomly selected charts from my files for a control study. One needs no introduction and the second is just another everyday tragedy of the air and sea.

On December 15, 1945 a fighter squadron took off from Fort Lauderdale, Florida at 2:10 p.m. EST on a routine training flight. It was a triangulation flight, one leg out, one across, one back. The entire squadron vanished. No pilot or plane were ever recovered. This event thrust the Bermuda Triangle into the public eye. The full tale of this flight is in any Bermuda Triangle book or TV documentary.

The Part of Death at 10 Scorpio 14 has no conjunctions, not at Part or eighth. Sun/Moon at 19 Sagittarius 04 forms a quincunx with Mars/Saturn at 20 Cancer (Sun Moon Mars Saturn). The planets of life and death are simply Mars (old) or Mars/Pluto (new). Mars is conjunct Pluto and both conjunct the Ascendant Part of the Moon (ASC + ASC

- Moon), meaning Moon/Mars-Pluto sits on the Descendant opposing the Ascendant. This placement by ladder or continuing conjunctions involves Neptune, Sun/Pluto 12 Libra, Jupiter/Neptune 14 Libra, Moon/Pluto 18 Libra. This is conjunct Catastrophe 18 Libra 07 (ASC + Uranus - Sun), meaning these energies mixed with Sun and Uranus are carried to the Ascendant. Moon/Saturn at 2 Libra and Venus/Pluto at 5 Libra influences Neptune 8 Libra.

Mars/Uranus of airplane crash at 9 Cancer is conjunct Saturn at 7 Cancer.

Let's conclude death and move on.

Neptune/Pluto zodiac disappearance at 9 Virgo is conjunct chart disappearance Mars/Jupiter 12 Virgo. Out of fuel Mars/Neptune 5 Virgo centers all these energies on Neptune/Pluto.

Note that Mars rules the Ascendant.

The Part of Disappearance (zodiac ASC + Neptune - Pluto) is at 12 Gemini 30 conjunct Uranus 15 Gemini 31. Chart Part of Disappearance 3 Cancer 43(ASC + Jupiter - Mars) is conjunct Saturn which is conjunct out of fuel Mars/Neptune. This means the energy of both Parts since they are conjuncted brings all mentioned planets to the Ascendant.

Thus both the Ascendant and its ruler Mars are clearly tied to disappearance planets.

Those who live by the sea are accustomed to disappearances—small boats and small planes vanishing with their passengers. Many of the charts used in this study were Caribbean vanishings—fishermen and passengers of commuter or freight flights. Once again it is important to distinguish two factors in order to accomplish the astrology: death and a lost body.

Such a plane with five passengers vanished, having departed from Roseau, Dominica en route to St, Croix a few hundred miles to the west.

The plane came down about twenty minutes later (Mars/Neptune Uranus 21 Libra fuel gone, crash) conjunct Mercury 21 Libra, and the solstice point of Saturn 22 Libra conjunct the lunar part of Mars/Saturn 24 Libra (ASC + Mars/Saturn - Moon). The Part of Death at 27 Libra is conjunct all the above as well as Mercury/Venus at 0 Scorpio, rulers of the first/twelfth, the body lost. The Part of Death also has its necessary conjunction at the eighth, Mars/Saturn. Venus, life and death planet, is in detriment in violent 8 Scorpio. Mars/Saturn and Moon/Saturn center their energies at 14 Aries, exactly on the Descendant and conjunct Fortuna at 12 Aries and Spirit at 18 Aries. They died.

The planets of disappearance are Mercury, ruler of the twelfth, and Venus, ruler of the eighth, with Venus doubling as the life and death

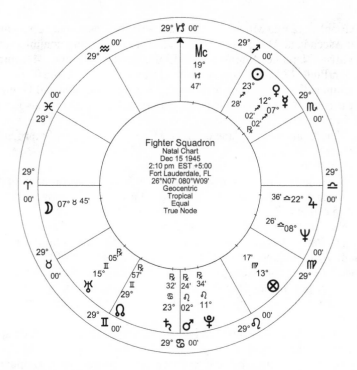

Fighter Squadron
Natal Chart
Dec 15 1945
2:10 pm EST +5:00
Fort Lauderdale, FL
26°N07' 080°W09'
Geocentric
Tropical
Equal
True Node

planet. Both are conjunct an active Part of Death by midpoint and as such bring their energy to the Moon and Ascendant.

The zodiac planets of disappearance, Neptune and Pluto form a midpoint at 23 Sagittarius conjunct Sun/Moon 24 Sagittarius.

The Part of Disappearance, Ascendant + ruler of the 12th - ruler of the 8th (chart rulers Mercury and Venus) is at 27 Virgo 08 conjunct Sun 26 Virgo 18.

The Part of Disappearance at 10 Sagittarius 19 with zodiac rulers Neptune and Pluto does not make a conjunction.

You can make a Part from a midpoint. Here, solar Neptune/Pluto (ASC + Neptune/Pluto - Sun is at 22 Capricorn, conjunct Neptune at 20 Capricorn and Uranus at 22 Capricorn. Solar Neptune/Pluto means this energy is carried to the Ascendant and Sun, also picking up that of Uranus. Fortuna carries the three planetary energies to Ascendant Sun and Moon.

Disappearance factors have been brought to all Ascendants and Ascendant ruler Venus repeatedly.

The more of these connections there are, the less likely the matter will be resolved (craft or bodies found). Here they fell into one of the deepest trenches in the world's oceans. Unlike Amelia Earhart, no one will ever search for them again.

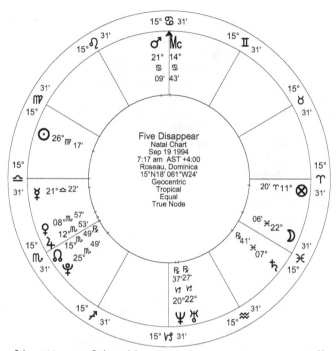

15° ♋ 31'

15°♌31'

♂ Mc
21° 14°
♋ ♋
09' 43'

15° ♊ 31'

31'
♍
15°

15°
♉
31'

☉ 26° ♍ 17'

Five Disappear
Natal Chart
Sep 19 1994
7:17 am AST +4:00
Roseau, Dominica
15°N18' 061°W24'
Geocentric
Tropical
Equal
True Node

15°
♈
31'

15°
♎
31'

☿ 21° ♎ 22'

20' ♈ 11° ⊗

♀ 08° ♏ 57'
12° ♏ 53'
♃ 15° ♏ 49' ℞
♂ 25° ♏

06' ♓ 22°

℞ 41' ♓ 07'

☽ 31'

15°
♏
31'

♇

℞ ℞
37'27'
♑ ♑
20°22°

♄ 15° ♓

15°
♐
31'

♆ ♅
15° ♒ 31'

15° ♑ 31'

♂/♄ 14 ♉ ♂ 8th, ☽/♄ 15 ♓ ♂ 6th—centering at Descendant 15 ♈;
Fortuna 12 ♈, Spirit 18 ♈

Nevertheless relatives and the collective psyche desire a resolution. What follows is unfinished work in progress with tentative conclusions.

Regarding missing children examine the charts of those found alive: Concentrate searches on those charts where the death factor is low when evaluated.

I am sure the finding of a body may be astrologically isolated along similar lines. Work from such finds. It took seventy-three years to find the Titanic and 130 plus to find the Confederate submarine. At the time the Titanic was found, using the embarkation chart, Leo Ascendant, progressed Sun and Venus, rulers of the first and tenth, made a conjunction to Mars.

Such bodies may be found in some cases using horary principles. Some are found by chance. But someone must search for or chance upon them.

The revelatory planets are Sun, Mars, Jupiter, Uranus and the rulers of the first and tenth.

The Part of Peril (Ascendant + ruler of the 8th - Saturn) and the Part of Catastrophe (solar part of Uranus ASC + Uranus - Sun) may be used

185

as death sign factors in appropriate charts. They were not used regularly here since death was otherwise evident.

Amelia Earhart's Perils were :

Natal: 19 Aquarius 40 conjunct Miami Mars/Uranus (plane crash) 17 Aquarius 41, conjunct Miami Mercury/Mars 20 Aquarius 43, rulers life and death Lae.

Miami: 17 Gemini 10 conjunct Ascendant, conjunct Miami Sun, natal Moon, Venus, Neptune and center point of Gemini stellium—16 Gemini; 15 Gemini is the duad of surprise attack which here may be rendered death by surprise or unexpected death.

Note that both of these form a grand trine to natal midpoints, Mars/Jupiter and Saturn/Uranus, both pairs strong by natural conjunction, all centering at 17 Libra and activated by the deadly Miami Mars to natal Saturn Uranus.

Lae: Peril is at 21 Aries 50 conjunct Lae Moon 15 Aries and Miami Venus; the Ascendant ruler remains the Ascendant ruler with its secondary rulerships in other charts. To anyone who doubts or has ignored the Ascendant ruler, please note:

Lae Venus opposes natal Saturn Uranus.

Natal Venus is conjunct Lae Fortuna; Miami Venus is conjunct Lae Part of Disappearance.

In solving an astrological problem the house rulership properties of the planets are most important. Just ask General Custer, triple Sagittarian with Jupiter-Moon as his planets of life and death. His luck ran out one sunny summer day.

Arabian Parts work only by conjunction. They are then midpoint combinations reaching the Ascendant.

Fortuna and the Scorpio Independence Chart

Finding the correct chart for America is now an astrological cottage industry. Since one chart ties to the others, each can work; but I believe the Independence chart works best overall.

Cutting to the chase I like the Scorpio Ascendant chart. Rather than endlessly dither about exactly when our founding fathers did what from July 2-6, 1776, the Scorpio Ascendant chart of July 4 reflects the psyche of the country and gives a true picture through the houses.

First house ruler Pluto, old ruler Mars—power, greed, money riches, cooperation, vengeance God on our side; ruler Pluto in the third house—transportation and communications, invented and pioneered by us—made here the biggest and the best; old ruler Mars in the eighth house—violence and other people's money. America is the most violent of first world countries and the richest and the most creative in methods of finance.

Ninth house ruler Moon with Sun and Jupiter in wide conjunction in the house of luck and foreign affairs; Sun/Jupiter in Cancer trine the Ascendant. Truly we are a fortunate nation. Mercury and Venus also function from this house. Foreign policy by food—the Marshall Plan and endless groceries since then. Foreign policy that lasts until lunch time—Cancer; Sun/Mars 2 Cancer = Venus ruler of the seventh house of war. We attack by surprise (Mars/Uranus 15 Gemini) and then give money and are willing to let bygones be bygones. We do not see ourselves as starting hostilities, though our neighbors do.

Eighth house Mars and Uranus in Gemini, by midpoint, are on the degree of surprise attack—one man killing another by gunshot with roads and walking and transportation; frontiersman and Indians on the forest trails, gunfighters dueling and murdering on frontier streets, today's gang members doing drivebys. Truly, death by gunshot is the American way of death. Perhaps we have made little moral progress,

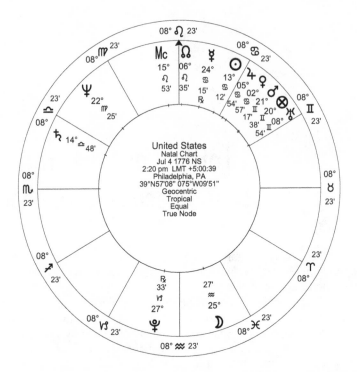

but if measured in bullets we are doing well, 1-6-15/30 respectively.

All astrologers know Neptune is big in the stock market, though they cannot quite say why. Actually, it rules the fifth house. It is opposite the eleventh house of corporate earnings in the sign of manufacturing, as in Dow Jones companies.

Neptune in the eleventh house also gives us a perfect ego projection. Every Scorpio needs a bogeyman. Slavery, prohibition, communists, drug users and dealers, immoral people, bogeymen one and all, that never were about to bring down the country. We get off on believing there is someone under the bed. We make money on it too.

Years ago I began arriving at national Ascendants—the nature or psyche of a country by their prison systems, which do not change. America's are Libran—vacillation, procrastination, justice, a conflict between rehabilitation and punishment, and high on the comfort scale.

Israel's prisons are much the same. We get along well with Israel which does not get along with its lunar (Moslem) Sagittarian neighbors. America does not get along with its solar (man on horseback) Sagittarian neighbors of South America.

Sagittarians have dungeons—Scorpio on the twelfth.

This all leads to finding an approach to the chart. America does not have an election chart like Baghdad and while there is consensus for the Independence Chart, July 4, 1776, there is no agreement on time or ascending sign.

As always I began with Fortuna. With the 8 Scorpio 23 Ascendant it falls at 20 Gemini 39 conjunct Mars in the eighth house. Not as bad as it looks for Mars is ruler of the Ascendant. The premise is now to see if the Parts fit the chart.

Fortuna conjunct Mars carries Mars energy and rulership to the Ascendant Sun and Moon. The nation is enhanced, exaggerated with its own ruler reaching Ascendant. Pluto, too, is the ruler of U.S. Pluto means big in mundane astrology.

Mars, ruling the first—the country itself has been dealt with. Mars also rules the sixth—big manufacturing, big military, big agriculture, big bureaucracy.

Venus/Uranus at 20 Gemini 57 conjunct Mars and Fortuna. Cancer Sun—America has always had large breasted sex symbols. We think about them en route to killing each other—with gunshot, of course—Mars/Uranus at 15 Gemini 13 conjunct Fortuna.

Sun at 13 Cancer conjunct Sudden Advancement and Sickness. Tiger Woods and Maalox.

The Midheaven is intriguing; Assassination at 18 Leo 56, Honor at 14 Leo 11, Peril or Dangerous Year at 17 Leo 50. The Midheaven is not empty. It is conjunct Sun/Neptune at 17 Leo 46. Some Mars action when available translates as attack on a leader. America's assassins are easy to understand. They just want to be stars (Leo on the tenth, Pisces ego extension on the fifth). This is deadly because Pisces is eight to Leo.

America invented Mother's Day. The Part of Mother at 0 Cancer 54 is conjunct Venus 2 Cancer.

The Part of Friends is at 24 Cancer 56 conjunct Mercury, as is the Part of Suicide at 24 Cancer 22. All too often, young people kill themselves in a family context at home.

The Moon in the fourth in Aquarius shows the various, eccentric, and extreme expressions of the family in America. It also shows why we move more often than other nationals. Conjunct Death at 21 Aquarius 19, domestic violence has always been with us. Ask Lizzie Borden. She was acquitted too. It is too much to expect social scientists and psychologists to know or deal with astrology but they would benefit from a few history books.

With Sun/Neptune in Leo conjunct the Midheaven, note originating signs. You see why any politician can and does talk successfully about the decay of the family. Like assassination, it is an ongoing matter.

To close this out on a light note, Commerce is at 19 Scorpio 26, Play (Sports) at 20 Scorpio 03, and Homosexuality at 20 Scorpio 46.

Sun/Mercury in the ninth is at 18 Cancer 44 and trine these positions. If you philosophize or pontificate on these subjects you can make it in America, or at least always have a listener. Note the recent passage of Pluto 13-27 Pluto regarding these subjects. Right now since these Parts must have a conjunction, they require synastry or fast planet transits. Listen to the radio. The Moon sets all Parts off once a month.

But also America says the business of the country is business. America started and continues to lead in gay rights, and sports franchises, leagues and player salaries are an American phenomena.

If we began with Fortuna, let's close with Spirit at 26 Pisces 8, without conjunction but in the fifth house of entertainment and stock market, both subject to booms and busts. Note also fads in entertainment. I have not done any work on them, but the midpoint activation points are 25 Taurus (Pluto) and 27 Aries (Moon).

Mundane astrology works on the interplay of the slow planets. The ancients made due with Jupiter and Saturn, but we have five.

In early 1996 the interplay of Saturn, Uranus, and Pluto continue. The picture is precise: Saturn/Pluto = Uranus by conjunction in Aquarius. This chart indicates change in and by the family and people. Tired of money and work problems, the government will be blamed (positions and synthesis of above).

V chips, soccer moms and medical marijuana are the tips of the iceberg. Government will answer with repression. Religion will remain intolerant as a whole. Pluto in Sagittarius is the kill for God position of the Conquistadors, who also wanted gold. The family is both victim and innovator.

Sources: U.S. Independence chart July 4, 1776 ; 2:20 p.m. LMT Philadelphia, Pennsylvania. Put forward by Marc Penfield, used by Michael O. Reilly in "Tomorrow's News" in *American Astrology*.

Baghdad the Survivor

James H. Holden, FAFA wrote an article on the founding of Baghdad for the September 12, 1996 issue of *Today's Astrologer*, the monthly publication of the American Federation of Astrologers. Holden does not use Fortuna in the article chart. I do not know if it was present in the chart as seen by him for a work source. The following matters may be assumed under the circumstances.

1. The chart was copied several times prior to two or three modern copyings.

2. Obviously the modern planets, Uranus, Neptune, Pluto were not there.

3. Zoller's listing of Al-Biruni's Parts would indicate the Moon's nodes were not present in the original chart as they belonged to the separate Vedic tradition.

4. From Al-Biruni's listing we know that the Persians retained the Midheaven, the Vedics using it only to calculate the all important Ascendant. Both saw it as a point, not as a house map. It appears that Alchabitius may be the earliest known person that we equal house practitioners can blame for the Midheaven-tenth house confusions, as well as other matters.

5. A daytime chart, the problems of deceit or error regarding nighttime Fortuna do not occur. We know Fortuna is at 25 Aquarius 45 whether the original astrologers published or hid the matter.

6. The chart consisted of seven planets, Sun through Saturn, the retrograde position of Jupiter noted. The Midheaven and Fortuna were probably noted as points.

7. We may assume that these Persian astrologers knew about Spirit in the eighth century, which brings us to the purpose of this chapter.

I had written a book and not mentioned elective astrology. I have not done much election and think of it as walking in sand which, when pushed down, rises elsewhere.

Noticing the position of Fortuna without conjunction I glanced up

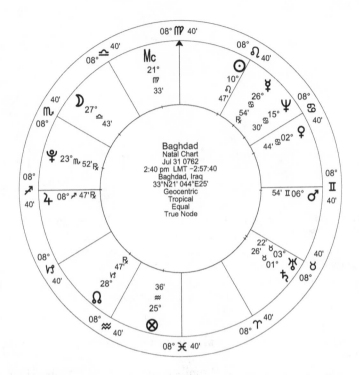

and saw the Midheaven. Immediately I calculated the Part of Spirit—21 Virgo 43. They had used the Parts.

Noting the rest of the chart, I believe that its originators had at this date retained a genuine understanding of the Parts. A true tradition existed for these astrologers.

Holden rightfully notes that the chart is part good and part bad—most elective charts are. From the perspective of the Parts and the mindset and realities of the day, a better chart is hard to imagine.

The next day I realized the obvious. The whole predictive system of Arabian parts was wedded to election. They did know the potential of the Parts beyond what I'd referred to as wrestler's names. By nature they looked for the best or the worst. What they called Fortuna was the coming of Jupiter to that point, bringing its blessings to the Ascendant Sun Moon.

The city must prevail—preservatory Sun trine Jupiter, Sun of leader in house of luck in own sign. Grand trines involving the Ascendant have incredible power. Here the Ascendant was as Jupiter itself—pure luck and plenty.

Each spring, the transiting Sun would trine Ascendant and Jupiter, aiding with the crops and the luck and power of the city and its ruler. Now, with the frozen nights behind and hot days ahead, was the time to mount expeditions. (Grand trine Ascendant-Jupiter trine Sun with transiting Sun trine Ascendant and outlet to Mars conjunct the Descendant). The reader may recall mention of Sun-Mars-Jupiter. Above all, keep the luck for yourself.

Recently someone noted that the U.S. Independence chart could not have a Scorpio Ascendant because it makes the Moon void-of-course and this in a great nation. Some horary principles do not function the same way in natal or mundane charts. That it is too late to find or save a cat is not the way it functions here. The void-of-course Moon may void a moment or a short term event, but not the life process. Void-of-course Moons, whether people or countries, are quarrelsome.

The chart would have been somewhat the same two or three or four days earlier. Not so. The whole purpose of the exercise was to put Spirit conjunct the Midheaven, not only energizing the Midheaven when transited by conjunction but bringing more solunar and Jupiter energy to the Ascendant: Spirit is ASC + Sun - Moon = Spirit (conjunct Midheaven—still nothing). Transiting Jupiter is conjunct Spirit when it is in full effect. ASC - Jup/Sun = Moon/Spirit MC transiting Jupiter. These fated people really knew how to work the odds.

Note the incredible power of each lunation bringing Fortuna and Spirit to Jupiter-Ascendant each month. Each year the fast planets would activate Fortuna and Spirit—Fortuna in mid-winter before spring planting and Spirit in late summer before the harvest.

Electional astrology is not easy. I'm sure the astrologers labored on this one. They narrowly averted the Moon-Saturn opposition. It appears that like the Vedics they may not have believed in out of sign aspects. They accepted separating aspects as retaining power (Sun trine Jupiter). The house position of a planet was more important than its aspects. The Caliph cared little that Saturn brought suffering and difficulty to his workers, servants, and soldiers. He was delighted to see it in his enemy's twelfth (twelfth of the seventh).

For his protection his astrologers gave him Moon/Jupiter in the twelfth at 18 Scorpio 18, in this chart the planets of life and death. To his enemies the astrologers gave Mars/Saturn in their twelfth to seventh but ninth to the ruler's tenth. Keep the luck for yourself. His soldiers would be brutal.

Holden implies that the astrologers erred insofar as the city has been sacked, burned, and overthrown by coup repeatedly over the centuries. The astrologers saw this as part of the natural order of things, as indeed it is. The issue was survival over time.

<%-2>They had amplified the Ascendant and Midheaven, brought it back to the king and his power, but they weren't through yet. The young apprentice noticed that while they were working the

193

Midheaven, with the Moon about to slip into Scorpio, that they also had a mutual reception from Venus' recent entrance into Cancer.

Four out of seven is not bad—Sun, Moon, Venus, Jupiter—especially the three benefics and power. At 27 Libra the Moon made a midpoint with the Sun at 19 Virgo 17 to the Midheaven. The apprentice was scratching his brick. He came up with Venus/Jupiter 20 Me 46. Spirit and MC were no longer empty.

The older astrologers knew they would be paid—Sun/Jupiter 9 Libra and Moon/mutual reception Venus 15 Libra in the eleventh, the king's revenues.

<%-2>Every astrologer has a blind spot. The old man did not know the three benefics together are the signature of massacre, in this chart in the sixth of the sixth, military massacre. The country would be rich. He never knew about the blood as he dreamed of gold.

In 1991, Saddam Hussein, one of the richest despots on earth, withstood an attack from the mightiest army on earth which inexplicably withdrew. Take your luck as it comes. Saddam Hussein committed massacres on the citizens of Kuwait. His army was in turn massacred. Presently he is confident of surviving the modern siege known as an embargo. He shrugs at the starving children and keeps his hand in massacring Kurds, whom everyone likes to massacre.

In Baghdad, luck and death have played at the same checkerboard for more than 1,200 years. Old Rawhlbaht and young Marsha Allah never knew how good they were.

I am indebted to James H. Holden and C. Edward Sachaw for the linguistic and calendar research necessary to make such a chart available, and to Al-Biruni for preserving it.

References: Chart from "A Mundane Chart for Baghdad," Today's Astrologer, September 12, 1996, pages 292 and 293. *A History of Horoscopic Astrology* by James H. Holden, pages 99-100. *The Chronology of Ancient Kingdoms: Al-Biruni*, translated by C. Edward Sachaw, pages 262-263.

Hurricane Marilyn

Hurricane Marilyn struck St. Thomas, Virgin Islands, where I was living at the time. All houses of my chart were disturbed, some destroyed, with damage even until 2006. Note Venus conjunct my Ascendant, Saturn conjunct my Fortuna, locking the Parts.

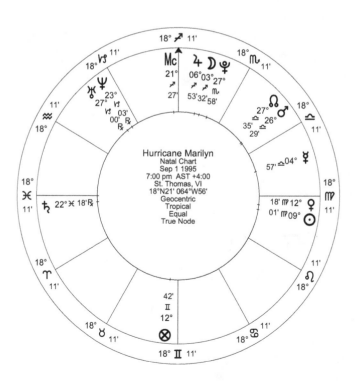

Hurricane Marilyn
Natal Chart
Sep 1 1995
7:00 pm AST +4:00
St. Thomas, VI
18°N21' 064°W56'
Geocentric
Tropical
Equal
True Node

Glossary

In writing about new matters or in viewing old matters from a new perspective, it is necessary to redefine terms or even create some new ones. The greatest obstacles to an understanding of the Parts were different names, supposedly for the same thing: Parts, Points, Lots, Fortunes. This was like saying tire, jack, brakes, steering are all the same thing. With the words misunderstood the idea could go nowhere. Earlier in the text I defined these at length in some context or another. What follows is for reference and may be an improvement to some text references.

Arabian Parts: Based on the Ascendant $A + B - C = D$ which is Ascendant + Planet B - Planet C = D which is Ascendant + Planet B - Planet C = Point (degree awaiting conjunction). Parts refer to $A + B - C$ or $A + B - C = D$, also to the name of D as in Part of Spirit, Part of Death.

Arabian Part Midpoint Complex: $A/B = C/D$. A/B is passive, here usually the ASC/B. C/D is dynamic. C is the Planet "in terms of" or acting on A/B as triggered by the conjunction to D, creating the dynamic midpoint. The algebraic formula is $A + B - C = D$.

Arabian Point or Point: This refers specifically to D in the equation $A + B - C = D$. This is the degree of the zodiac (D), here noted by name or symbol, that when transited by a conjunction locks and triggers the midpoint complex $A/B = C/D$ conjunct transit Planet.

Arabian System: A transit forecast system based on a conjunction to Point D in the equation $A + B - C = D$.

Balance Charts: Like derivative houses, but read from the position of a planet or Arabian Point (D). The balance house is integrated with the natal house in some fashion. The reading always involves the balance planet or Point.

Classic Parts: My term. The 63 parts involving the Sun, Moon and five planets of the ancients.

Cuspal Parts: These involve a cusp instead of two planets. The best known at the moment is the Part of Death, A + 8th - Moon = Death. I believe equal house charts should be used with cuspal parts. Cuspal Parts require two conjunctions. Note the ancient cuspal parts refer to significant events: seventh, marriage, divorce; eighth, death, etc.; ninth, a long trip; tenth, fate; twelfth, imprisonment or exile.

Defining Planet: Planet C, also referred to as "in terms of" and the adjective form of the planet as in, Venusian, also sometimes Venus Part, Mars Part etc. This is the planet to progress, direct or solar arc. It then moves conversely.

Degree Part: Occasionally there is a degree Part with the degree at B. These generally refer to fixed stars and the Moon. The same rule applies. They need two conjunctions as do the cuspal parts.

Fortuna: The most important degree in the chart when transited by conjunction. Here all three Ascendants, Sun, Moon Ascendant are activated in terms of the Sun when a transit conjunction contracts the degree of Fortuna. Only Spirit can also reach the three Ascendants.

Fortunes: The transits of Jupiter by conjunction and trines to the Point (D). Regarding the trines see intermittency. Transit Jupiter conjunct Fortuna or Spirit are the strongest Fortunes.

Framework: My term. The conjunctions of Jupiter and Saturn to Fortuna and Spirit, as well as their intermittencies, the trines of Jupiter and the squares, opposition of Saturn to same. Periods of fortune and misfortune may be projected well into the future.

Intermittency: My term widely treated in the text. It is an aspect other than a conjunction to a Part. It actually only functions when the Part in question is transitted by conjunction. The trines of Jupiter and the squares, opposition of Saturn to Fortuna and Spirit might well be termed the major intermittencies.

"In Terms of": My phrase coined to define the dynamic energy of C defining the nature of the Part. Sun at C is a solar Part, Moon at C a lunar part etc. It mixes with the Point conjunction to act on B which brings it all to the Ascendant.

Lots: The transit of Saturn by conjunction, squares and opposition to the Point (D). Regarding the squares and opposition see intermittency. Transit Saturn conjunct Fortuna or Spirit are the worst Lots.

Major Parts: My term though I feel some parallel name will be found. This refers to the solar and lunar Parts because each would involve two Ascendants (only Fortuna and Spirit can involve three): ASC + B - C = D; ASC + B - Sun = D (solar); A + B - Moon = D (lunar). Using the old planets there are 22 when the duplications of Fortuna and Spirit are taken out. These include the Lunar and Solar Reciprocals which also involves two Ascendants. These are the foundation Parts to which Jupiter and Saturn transits were noted.

Minor Fortunes: The intermittencies of Jupiter to Fortuna or Spirit, the conjunction of Jupiter to other Parts.

Minor Lots: The intermittencies of Saturn to Fortuna or Spirit, the conjunction of Saturn to other Parts.

Minor Parts, A: Planetary Parts other than solar or lunar, B Parts that are not based on the ASC, Both of these are sometimes called complexes and pictures in the text. C Proliferations.

Parts of the Ascendant: $A + B - C = D$; ASC + ASC - Planet = Part of the ASC. The transit by conjunction to D creates a midpoint directly to the Ascendant involving Planet C. This is treated in the text. I've come to believe there was no mystery about the Ascendant Parts. The ancient practitioners just knew about them. Bear in mind the many implications of the oral tradition in teaching. I use the conventional circle for the Solar Ascendant and the square for the Lunar Ascendant. Coming to the other planets it occurred to me to do this for their Part of the Ascendant, simply place the planet in a triangle which is much like the letter A. In Ebertin or any midpoint book you may read the Parts of the Ascendant as $C/D = ASC$. The extra stimulus of a second transiting planet and the rarity of lining up the two conjunctions is indicative of strong and rare events.

Part Using Part as Ascendent: These are Proliferations. The Part as Ascendant (A) is D. Without a conjunction to D, Part and Proliferation do not function. Without a conjunction to D' there is no Proliferation. The Part is noted because a planet is not always there and to give a precise degree. The transiting conjunctions are of course changing by degree.

Pictures: Here Arabic complexes where the Ascendant is not present but which are not attached to a Point D (see Proliferations). The algebraic equation may be used in any combination of planets: $A + B - C = D$. Sun + Uranus - Venus = Women or money upsets to men or lucky sudden moves with women or money. In the delineation of Charles, Prince of Wales, this falls conjunct his Ascendant. Note also Moon + Uranus - Sun. Volatility in terms of the Sun (around the king). Ibid. This is at 8 Sagittarius and will be contacted by transiting Pluto. Using a three degree orb, this occurs in December 1997. Remember the midpoint factor reduces this orb by half. The picture is thus Sun/Pluto = Uranus brought to the Moon. This will set the stage for transit Pluto conjunct the lunar Part of Saturn two years later in late 1999. Also Witte's term in Uranian Astrology for $A/B = C$.

Planetary Parts: The position C defines the planets ruling the Part. ASC + Moon - Sun = Fortuna. Fortuna is the Solar Part of the Moon. It's Reciprocal Spirit ASC + Sun - Moon is the Lunar Part of the Sun. ASC + Venus - Mars is the Martian Part of Venus and it's

Reciprocal, ASC + Mars - Venus is the Venus Part of Mars.

Point: In this text the degree of D, awaiting contact by conjunction to complete or trigger the equation A + B - C = D.

Points: Empty degrees in the zodiac thought to have importance. Arabian Parts, Nodes, Solstice Points, Critical Degrees and Fixed Star Degrees. I have come to believe that they do not function without conjunct planets—any of them. Note that every degree is activated by a monthly lunar conjunction. If you only use points with conjunctions you will have quantum improvement in your delineation. Conjunctions my be formed by: transits, progressions, solar arcs, natally or by synastry and by natal midpoints or transit midpoints

Proliferations: My term, with a bow to Robert Zoller and Robert Hand who must also like the ring of the word. These are Parts beginning from a Part. That is using the Point (D) as A' This might be natal (chart) or sought (transits). The proliferation intensifies or alters the Part through the original Point (D). When the conjunct planet is within orb, of D', D will receive the energy of the proliferation, exactly as the Ascendant of the original Part does, when D is contacted by conjunction. A + B - C = D; ASC + Moon - Sun = Fortuna conjunct transit Jupiter; Fortuna (Jupiter) + Mars - Sun = transiting Mercury; A' + B' - C' = D'. Such a proliferation would have arisen under some such condition. The king has transit Jupiter conjunct Fortuna and being personally and generally fortunate at this time wishes to know if he might wage war successfully. The proliferation reveals that the necessary Sun-Mars energy (Sun - Mars - Jupiter = War) is triggered by the position of Mercury. I'm convinced that here natal and transit planets would be mixed as the entire purpose would be to find some Sun Mars energy to put with Fortuna's Jupiter. Contrary to the misunderstanding of scholars these secondary Parts were of the utmost importance delineating the transit energy of the planet conjunct D, the Part.

Reciprocals: When B and C are transposed in the equation A + B - C = D, the reciprocal Part is equidistant from the original Part on the opposite side of the Ascendant Descendent axis. They are on same side East or West. A direct midpoint by Part and Reciprocal is formed to the Ascendant (conjunct ASC, opposition ASC). This is extremely powerful when both Parts are transited by conjunction. Reciprocals change the polarity as related to B and C. B is always negative and C is always positive. Note the running example in text; Red dress/Wallflower. Fortuna and Spirit are reciprocals.

Spirit: the second most important degree in the chart where the three Ascendants, Sun Moon Ascendant are activated in terms of the Moon when a transit conjunction contacts the degree of Spirit. Only Fortuna can also reach the three Ascendants.

Chart Sources

Al-Biruni (Abril - Rayhan Muhamman Ibn Ahmad Al-Biruni), *The Fortunes of Astrology*, Robert Hurzt Granite

Lind Weber (A), timed at birth EST correct, War Time a couple weeks later.

Lisa (Elizabeth) Steinberg (AA), Arlene Nimark quotes hospital records in *Astro Data V*

Department Store Collapses (A), news sources

Disappearance of Two Sisters (C), Daily News, USVI, various times appeared over several days

Yitzhak Rabin Assassination, news sources

Bill and Hillary Clinton, consensus charts; I believe in them; other times have appeared for both.

Charles Prince of Wales, AFA, April 1973 from Judith Gee of England, *Astro Data II*

Camilla Parker Bowles, Data News by Lois Rodden, Bio (B)

Alfred Witte, *Uranian Astrology Guide plus Ephemeris* ,Sylvia Sherman J Frank Manshe (A or B?)

Suzanne Valadon, Gauquelin 1092 vol 4, *Profiles of Women*

Romy Schneider, Jane Reynolds quotes Ebertin, *Profiles of Women*

Madame Du Barry (Marie Jean Bécu), date in *Americana*, time quoted by Penfield from an article by Fagan, *Profiles of Women*

Hedda Hopper, date from *Hedda and Louella* by Eeles. Time from SS 477 Penfield quotes SS at 4:00 AM (DD), *Profiles of Women*

Catherine the Great of Russia, Mark Johnson quotes Wemyss "*Wheel of Life*" Vol 4 "Born in the morning at half past two o'clock" Stettin was on Prussian time, *Profiles of Women*

Jeffrey Wolf Green, *The Mountain Astrologer*, April 1996 from himself

John Noxon Jr. and Lawrence Noxon, Carole McDonald quotes AFA for 7:00 AM, EST, rectified to 6:47 AM EST, *Astro Data V*

Male, Can't Get It Together, private (A)

Yasser Arafat, AFA, ``Future View'' by Judi Thomases

Church Blows Up, *Weekly World News*

Titanic's First Keel Plate Laid, news source

Titanic Sails, news Source

TWA Flight 800 Runway Mysteriously Breaks Up, CNN

TWA Flight 800 Mysteriously Breaks Up, CNN, FAA time (A)

ValuJet Crashes, Associated Press

Yitzhak Rabin, *The Mountain Astrologer*, January 1996, data from Rodden, time widely used in Israel (DD)

O.J. Simpson (AA), CSH Rodden II

David Ptasinski (Washing Dishes Saves His Life), *Weekly World News*

Benjamin Netanyahu, Selma Schepel quotes Micha Velner... personal information from Netanyahu 9:30 AM EEDT (-3hrs), Noel Tyl via Dalia Stupp gives 11:45 AM EEDT (DD), *Data News* #60, August 1996

Bibliography

The Fortunes of Astrology, Robert Hurzt Granite, Astro Computing Services 1980, San Diego, CA.

The Lost Key to Prediction: The Arabian Parts in Astrology, Robert Zoller, Inner Traditions International LTD. 1980 New York, New York.

Both contain full treatments and lists of the Parts by name and formula

Rules for Planetary Pictures: The Astrology of Tomorrow, Alfred Witte-Hermann Lefeldt, Witte-Verlag 1928, US Distributor Poseidon Books, Franksville, Wisconsin.

The Combination of Stellar Influences Reinhold Ebertin, Ebertin-Verlag, 1940; American Federation of Astrologers, Tempe, Arizona

Midpoints: Unleashing the Power of the Planets Michael Munkasey, ASC Publications, 1991, San Diego, California

Events and Nativities J. N. Bhasin Sagar Publications, 1974, New Delhi, India. To whom I am indebted for the concepts of Sudarshan and the influence of in sign planets on the ruler of the sign.

Ancient Hindu Astrology for the Modern Western Astrologer, James T. Braha Hermetician Press, 1986, North Miami, Florida

CPSIA information can be obtained
at www.ICGtesting.com
Printed in the USA
JSHW021726100622
26862JS00005B/97